Beginning Social Work Research

Morton L. Arkava
University of Montana, Missoula

Thomas A. Lane
Idaho State University, Pocatello

Allyn and Bacon, Inc.
BOSTON   LONDON   SYDNEY   TORONTO

Library of Congress Cataloging in Publication Data

Arkava, Morton L.
    Beginning social work research.

    Bibliography: p.
    Includes index.
    1. Social service—Research.   I. Lane, Thomas A.,
1937–   II. Title.
HV11.A67   1983   001.4'2'024362   82–11342
ISBN 0–205–07815–X

Printed in the United States of America.
10 9 8 7 6 5   91 90 89 88

Contents

Preface   *v*

PART I   Needs and Uses for Social Work Research

1. **Introduction to Social Work Research**   3
   The Need for Research 4;   Ethical Issues 5;   Organization of
   the Text 6;   Summary 6;   End Note 7

2. **The Scientific Approach**   8
   The Scientific Approach 10;   Purposes of Social Work
   Research 11;   Basic Research Versus Applied Research 12;
   Summary 13

3. **Research Procedures**   15
   The Language of Research 15;   Identifying Measurable and
   Nonmeasurable Objectives 17;   Variability 18;   Reliability 20;
   Validity 22;   Decision Steps in Research 24;   Summary 28;
   End Notes 30

4. **The Library and Social Work Research**   31
   Using the Library for Research 32;   Major Resources in the
   Library 32;   The Search Strategy 35;   Summary 36;   End
   Notes 38

PART II   Measuring the Results of Social Work Intervention

5. **Selecting Outcome Measures: The Dependent Variable**   41
   Social Work's Handicaps 41;   Historical Development of Out-
   come Measures in Social Work 44;   Client Self-Reports 49;
   Reliability of Self-Monitoring 52; Evaluation by the Practitioner
   53;   Measures of Family Functioning 55;   Behavioral and
   Cognitive Measures 58;   Individualized Outcome Measures 60;
   Negative Outcomes 63;   Program Evaluation 64;   Summary 68;
   End Notes 71

6. **Defining the Independent Variable**   75
   Prestructured Treatment Stimuli 79;   Treatment Typologies 83;
   Selected Practitioner Variables 86;   Operational Definitions of
   Treatment Methods 88;   Summary 90;   End Notes 92

7. **Experimental and Quasi-Experimental Research Designs**   95
   Experimental Designs 96;   Classic Experimental Control Group
   Designs 103;   Quasi-Experimental Designs 111;   Summary 115;
   End Notes 118

8. **Single-Subject Designs**   119
   The Baseline 121;   Design Structures 130;   Advantages and
   Disadvantages 147;   Summary 149;   End Notes 152

PART III   Adjunctive Aspects of Social Work Research

9. **Sampling Concepts and Techniques**   157
   Types of Samples 158;   Elements of Measurement 162;
   Summary 165;   End Note 166

10. **Survey Methods in Data Collection**   167
    The Questionnaire 167;   The Interview 171;   Summary 172;
    End Note 173

11. **Field Observation and Recording**   174
    Observational Roles 175;   Recording in the Field 176;
    Structured Observation 179;   Evaluation in the Natural Environ-
    ment 181;   Summary 184;   End Notes 185

12. **Other Methods of Research**   187
    The Case Study 187;   Secondary Sources of Data 188;
    Exploratory-Descriptive Studies 190;   Historical Research 191;
    Evaluation Research 192;   Summary 192;   End Notes 192

13. **Reporting, Writing, and Evaluating Research**   193
    The Report 193;   Interpreting the Results 193;   The Writing 196;
    Evaluating Research 197;   Summary 207

**APPENDIX — Sample Case Study: The Social and Economic Impacts of
Locating an Energy Center at Glasgow Air Force Base**   209
Introduction 209;   General Social and Economic Background
210;   General Economic Conditions and Population Characteristics 212;   Population Projection 214;   Projected Service Needs
218;   Economic Impact 225;   Summary and Conclusions 229;
End Notes 230

Bibliography   231

Index   239

Preface

Beginning Social Work Research is for undergraduate students taking a preliminary course in social work research. The book is intended primarily for upper-division social work students who have already completed introductory and intermediate classes in social work practice. A need exists for this book: few texts or courses have addressed the topic of research in social work, and many undergraduates have been dissatisfied with research courses in related disciplines because the content of such classes often is not relevant to social work.

This book addresses another problem—the complaint of many beginning-level social workers that a gulf separates the reality of everyday social work practice and the idealistic requirements of research. We have attempted to bridge this gulf by focusing on practical methods of research, methods that the beginning worker can incorporate into day-to-day practice. Because most new social workers are involved in direct client services, this book primarily discusses the most relevant research methods. (Graduate students usually receive additional advanced training in social work research.)

Other research methods are also examined, so that the social worker may be prepared to evaluate most types of research seen in the professional literature. Thus, *Beginning Social Work Research* prepares the social work student to assess research in the manner of an informed, intelligent, discriminating professional.

Because this book focuses on social work research, we have elected to provide only a few basic concepts in the area of quantitative analysis and statistics. We recommend that students supplement this text with a college course in statistical methods.

Beginning Social Work Research presents its information in three sections. Part I briefly describes the needs and uses for research in the social work profession and discusses the scientific approach to explorations of social phenomena. In some detail, it outlines the steps involved in conducting research projects. Chapter 4 familiarizes readers with ways to use the library in research.

Part II is the heart of the textbook. It instructs readers in the difficult tasks of choosing and defining the variables in treatment and research. It discusses methods of selecting worthwhile experimental conditions and of assessing the outcomes of research. Further, this segment describes extensively the investigative designs that are most used in social work research. It outlines the advantages and drawbacks of each plan. Chapter 8 is important in that it details the research designs that beginning practitioners will probably find most useful—the several varieties of single-subject strategies.

Part III introduces several important adjunctive aspects of social work research, including methods of compiling and evaluating research samples, procedures for observing research subjects, and systems for collecting and recording data. Chapter 12 outlines some secondary methods of performing research. The last chapter furnishes readers some basic information on the final step in the research process: writing and reporting the results of a scientific investigation.

This book's primary attribute is its simplicity—it assumes that the reader is a beginning social work student who knows little about the profession's research techniques or principles, and it proceeds from this "zero knowledge" base. In understandable language, it provides students a firm background in social work research—an area the importance of which, until now, too often has been ignored or downplayed by educators. The book is not oriented toward esoteric, specialized research considerations; rather, it addresses the everyday needs of the beginning practitioner in social work.

Beginning Social Work Research furnishes detailed, step-by-step instructions on practical research methods that social work students may use to evaluate common practice situations. It provides many examples of research designs in use, giving special emphasis to the highly useful single-subject designs.

Other features unique to this book include: (1) its explanation of treatment "outcome measures" (whose selection and description remain a continuing cause of controversy in social work), and (2) its thorough discussion of practical methods of examining and defining the variables (both dependent and independent) of treatment. In addition, at the end of each chapter a study aid, in the form of a summary of that chapter, is provided to help students gain a better grasp of the book's material. Finally, the book contains an extensive bibliography, which readers may draw on to explore further almost any specific research concern.

Special thanks are due to the reviewers of the manuscript who greatly improved the final product: Stanley Witkin, Anant Jain, Elizabeth Haddix, William Culp, Ann L. Overbeck, and Charles Horejsi. The authors also wish to acknowledge the contributions of John Russell, whose editing skill, patience, and sense of humor helped us to develop the completed manuscript, and Grace Sheldrick, Wordsworth Associates, for her editorial and production assistance.

M.L.A.
T.A.L.

Needs and Uses
for
Social Work Research

PART

I

Introduction to Social Work Research

1

How effective is social work intervention? Is one form of intervention, such as casework, more effective than another, such as group work? Is one theoretical approach to practice more effective than others? Can government agencies justify filling specialist positions with persons holding professional social work credentials? Are social workers with degrees more effective than those who lack degrees? How can a social service agency justify its budget and program of services?

Each of these questions represents areas of substantial concern for the social work profession. Each generates considerable emotion. Each stimulates debate. None can be satisfactorily resolved without research.

Research answers such questions through the application of tested procedures to social work problems. This scientific method has proved to be the most trustworthy known source of knowledge. Although its use cannot guarantee that a given scientific undertaking produces the best information, it is more likely to do so than any other procedures currently known.

Any research proceeds from wanting an answer to a question for which no acceptable solution exists. The importance of the scientific method of inquiry in social work has been increasingly recognized of late. The social work student, research worker, and practitioner must each possess skills in the scientific method.

The Need for Research

Social workers often are reluctant to conduct research. Initially, many social workers find connecting their everyday casework to seemingly lifeless research statistics a difficult chore. Yet most beginning social workers soon discover the importance of research to their work.

In social work practice, clients are rarely free to shop around for the most effective social worker. Because clients should receive the most appropriate treatment for their problems, social workers should possess research skills. Workers must (1) be able to assess the chances of improving the conditions that contribute to client problems, (2) know how to develop and evaluate programs to solve social problems, and (3) possess the skills to evaluate the effects of social work services on individuals, groups, and organizations. Research skills are especially important when social workers are attempting to evaluate the effects of their own practice.

Community organizers must know how to document social problems and must be able to determine whether existing programs are solving those problems. Unless they can document the extent of a problem and the way it affects people in the community, they will get little support for program development.

Agency administrators use research information not only to determine how effective their services are, but also to learn whether the program should be modified to provide other services. Again, this requirement means that they must know how to evaluate overall program effectiveness and must be able to conduct survey research and experimental research.

Social work research often is difficult to classify and categorize. The reason for this difficulty is that much research in the profession is directed toward solving specific problems related to some aspect of practice. The profession lacks a common body of social work theory; it draws instead from a variety of theories and disciplines for its research and practice methods. Just as the practice of medicine is based on a variety of sciences, such as chemistry and biology, the practice of social work is based on contributions from several other sciences. In the area of casework, for example, theoretical formulations and research results are derived from psychology, sociology, psychiatry, and counseling. Social work may borrow from these fields such practices as behavior modification, humanistic psychology, biofeedback, and the application of Freudian theory. Community organizers and agency administrators may draw their major theoretical orientation from the fields of sociology, economics, and management. However, because each of these theoretical perspectives has its own separate body of literature, often the theoretical concepts, propositions, and research findings of each are difficult to compare directly with precepts of the other fields.

Besides the different practice methods used (such as casework, group work, community organization, or agency administration), the profession also contains diverse specialized practice areas. Social workers function in a variety of specialized settings, each dealing with a unique population—for example, child welfare practice; school social work; medical social work (often divided into such subspecialties as psychiatric social work—both outpatient and inpatient); specialized areas in medicine (pediatrics or public health); practice in correctional settings, including probation and parole (adult and juvenile); institutional care (adult and juvenile); public welfare; practice with special minority populations (such as Native Americans); and practice in family service agencies.

This long list does not exhaust the settings in the practice of social work; it merely demonstrates that the interests and requirements of practitioners can be diverse. This diversity means that the profession cannot readily offer a comprehensive theoretical framework as a guide for all social work research.

Instead, social work practitioners or research workers employ a variety of theories from other professions, disciplines, and specialized problem areas. Although the diversity of social work practice may at first seem confusing to the student and new practitioner, it offers exciting possibilities involving a broad spectrum of problems, methods, and techniques to be explored. Despite the lack of a unified body of theory for social work, the theories developed from other disciplines are similar in that they all must meet the criteria common to scientific theory.

Theory functions as a tool of science in five ways: to (1) define the major orientation of a science by specifying the kinds of data that should be abstracted; (2) offer a conceptual scheme by which the relevant phenomena may be systematized, classified, and interrelated; (3) summarize facts into empirical generalizations and systems of generalization; (4) predict facts; and (5) point to gaps in a discipline's knowledge.

Ethical Issues

Because the subject matter of social work is human beings, ethical concerns often emerge during the conduct of scientific investigation. These concerns may be generated by the questions being asked in the research, the methods used to obtain the answers, the procedure used to select participants, what the participants are asked to do, or how the data are interpreted. Research should add to knowledge in the profession, but the research worker is also obliged to protect the rights and welfare of the participants in the research, the clients.

To ensure this protection, three elements are essential: (1) voluntary participation in research; (2) precautionary steps to ensure against physical or mental harm to subjects due to their participation; and (3) guarantee of confidentiality because research constitutes an intrusion into an individual's personal life.

When designing and conducting research, therefore, the social worker must seriously consider the ethical concerns. For an excellent discussion of the integration of social work ethics into practice, consult C. S. Levy, *Social Work Ethics.*[1]

Organization of the Text

This book acquaints the reader with the vocabulary, techniques, procedures, and values involved in the conduct of the scientific method of research. The major steps in the research process are elaborated on in chapter 3. The following list of the major steps in research is a general introductory guide only. (The reader should remember that, because this model is so general, what actually transpires in conducting a given research project may be more complicated.) The basic steps in research include:

1. Stating the problem.
2. Describing the design or identifying the research plan.
3. Determining the methods to be used to collect data.
4. Presenting the results.
5. Presenting the conclusions or interpretations.

Proper research addresses each of these steps. The remainder of this volume examines these steps in detail. It explores how each step is taken and how the result may be incorporated into a useful product.

Summary

Research is necessary to answer the many questions generated by social work practice. Any social work student or practitioner should possess some skills in the scientific research method. Workers must be able to assess their chances of helping clients, know how to develop and evaluate social programs, and be able to evaluate the effects of those programs. Community leaders and agency administrators require research skills for similar reasons.

Social work research is difficult to classify. Social work draws from a variety of other theories and disciplines. The profession itself embraces several diverse specialized areas, such as schools, hospitals, institutions, family service, and child welfare. This diversity presents problems, but it also offers an almost infinite realm of possibilities for exploration. Whatever the pursuit, the same broad scientific research process applies.

Scientific theory (1) specifies the kinds of data that a science should study, (2) offers a conceptual scheme for study programs, (3) summarizes facts, (4) predicts facts, and (5) suggests gaps in the knowledge of a discipline.

During scientific investigations, ethical concerns often emerge on several fronts. The research worker is obliged to protect the rights and welfare of research participants. Participation must be voluntary, research workers must provide every possible safeguard against harm, and participants must receive confidentiality.

Proper research follows five basic steps. The researcher (1) states the problem, (2) identifies the research plan, (3) determines methods of collecting data, (4) presents the results, and (5) offers conclusions.

End Note

1.   Levy, C.S. *Social Work Ethics*. New York: Human Sciences Press, 1976. Also see: Selltiz, Claire, Wrightsman, L.S., and Cook, S.W. *Research Methods in Social Relations*, 3rd ed. New York: Holt, Rinehart & Winston, 1976, chapter 7; and Bailey, Kenneth D. *Methods of Social Research*. New York: Free Press, 1978, chapters 17 and 18.

The Scientific Approach

2

The scientific researcher seeks answers to questions and solutions to problems in an attempt to understand, explain, predict, or control phenomena. To accomplish these tasks the scientific method is used, consisting of formally applying systematic and logical procedures to guide an investigation. All sciences, though they may differ in content or specialized techniques, employ similar procedures to advance knowledge. This chapter discusses the rationale, characteristics, goals, assumptions, and limitations of the scientific method as it applies to social work.

The sources of human understanding are diverse. Some knowledge is derived from scientific research, but much comes from such sources as parents, friends, acquaintances, authorities, reading, and casual observation—to name a few. Knowledge emerges from at least six sources: tradition, authority, experience, trial and error, logical reasoning, and the scientific method.

Tradition comprises the "truths" with which the members of an organized society grow up. Anthropologists and sociologists define such so-called truths as customs, which are handed down through generations until (through habit) people accept them as correct. One example is Americans' unquestioned acceptance of their form of government. Another is the belief in a supreme being that oversees human activities. This type of inherited or socially acquired knowledge becomes so ingrained that people rarely demand its verification. Social work, like other disciplines, has its own enduring body of uncontested information that is maintained by tradition. Seldom, however, does anyone question whether following such traditions is productive.

Tradition has some advantages as a source of knowledge. It unifies the group. It is efficient in that each individual does not have to begin anew trying to understand all aspects of the world. It facilitates communication by providing a common base for its subscribers. The major problem with tradition is that it remains unexamined. No one questions it; thus, its validity never has been evaluated.

Authority is knowledge that is believed correct because of its source. That is, someone like a lawyer, doctor, or priest affirms it. Thus, the basis of authoritative knowledge is a person who is expert in a well-defined or well-delineated area. In a complex society, knowledge by authority is unavoidable because of that society's technological changes and rapid accumulation of knowledge. Citizens must often make decisions about problems they know little about; therefore, they must trust the judgment of persons whose experience in a particular area makes them authoritative. A shortcoming is that authorities are not infallible, even though their knowledge (like tradition) often goes unchallenged. Although social work would encounter severe problems if every piece of information from social work educators were challenged, still it would stagnate without critical inquiries from social work students who ask such questions as: What evidence supports certain teachings? What is the authority's source of knowledge? How does the authority know that his or her claims are true?

Experience is a familiar and functional source of knowledge. The ability to generalize from one event to another is an important human capability. One limitation of experiential knowledge is that everyone has only a restricted set of experiences from which to draw. A second limitation is that two individuals may perceive the same experience quite differently.

Closely related to experience is trial and error. Users of this process try successive alternatives until they find one that answers their questions or solves the problem. Everyone uses the trial-and-error method at some time; it is a haphazard and unsystematic approach, however. Further, the knowledge obtained often goes unrecorded, and therefore remains inaccessible to others.

Logical reasoning employs logical thought processes. It combines experience, human intellectual faculties, and formal systems of thought into a problem-solving or knowledge-building system. There are two formal types of reasoning: inductive and deductive.

Inductive reasoning is the process of developing generalizations from specific observations. For example, a social worker observing the bewildered behavior of one group of hospitalized youngsters might conclude that all

9

children's medical separations from their parents will cause stress to all children. The opposite approach, deductive reasoning, is the process of developing specific predictions from general principles. For example, if the social worker assumes that separation anxiety does occur among hospitalized children in general, then he or she might predict that (unless their parents room there) the children in the hospital would exhibit symptoms of stress.

Inductive and deductive reasoning are useful means of organizing and understanding phenomena. Both play a part in scientific research.

The Scientific Approach

The scientific method is the most advanced means of acquiring human knowledge. It combines important features of induction and deduction with other characteristics to create an orderly system for obtaining knowledge. It uses programmed steps to minimize the possibility that the research worker's emotions or biases will affect the conclusions. Still, though the scientific method is more rigorous than any other strategy, it does not exclude researchers' experiencing the thrill of revelation and discovery; rather, it guides their explorations along the channels that most likely will produce positive results with the least expense and misdirected effort. This system, though not infallible, is generally more reliable than tradition, authority, experience, or trial and error. One other important feature that further distinguishes the scientific method from other approaches is its greater capacity for self-evaluation.

The scientific approach is predicated on three assumptions (basic principles that scholars accept as being true, without requiring proof or verification). The first concerns the nature of reality, the assumption in science that an objective reality exists independent of human discovery or observation. In other words, the world is assumed to be real and not a creation of the human mind.

The second assumption is a belief that nature is basically ordered and patterned. In a haphazard universe, knowledge would be very limited. Therefore, such a basic function as generalizing a finding from one subject to another, for example, would be impossible. The third assumption embraces determinism, which assumes that all phenomena have antecedents—that is, preceding causes. Assuming that nature is orderly, events must have causes. Science seeks to identify and delineate them.

The scientific method emphasizes using a systematic approach to problem-solving and to the expansion of knowledge. This approach requires the research worker to follow scientific procedures and to exercise control, objectivity, and empiricism. In a proper scientific inquiry, researchers should:

1. Identify and define the problem.
2. Predict anticipated outcomes.
3. Collect information bearing on the problem according to a plan.
4. Analyze the information.
5. Draw conclusions.

The key element in this process is control. To examine a problem, isolating relationships between the phenomena frequently is necessary: the scientist must attempt to control any factors not under direct study. The investigator who wants to study the effects of age on dietary habits, for example, must control for other factors that may appear in the environment.

Objectivity is attained when experienced judges agree on what they observe and record. Suppose one social worker observes an event and records the observation in numerical form. Four other workers of equal competence independently observe and record the same incident. When this happens, objectivity has been established: the researchers agree. Some fields of science, such as physics and chemistry, have developed instrumentation to facilitate their observations and thereby increase their objectivity.

Empiricism is the process of using evidence rooted in objective reality and gathered systematically as a basis for generating human knowledge. Empirical evidence consists of perceived facts—observations made known to people through the senses: the organs of sight, hearing, taste, touch, or smell.

Purposes of Social Work Research

Probably as many reasons for social work research exist as do research projects. Often these reasons, while legitimate, may be nonscientific or quasiscientific: research workers may be seeking ways to improve the delivery of human services, for instance, or may wish to authenticate social workers' claims to professional status. But any fully scientific endeavor in social work should have at least one of three primary objectives: to explore, to describe, or to explain.

Exploration
Suppose the researcher is curious about a situation and wishes to understand it better, or has a hunch to follow up. For example, there may be a question such as whether social workers of the same sex as the client establish rapport more effectively than do social workers of the opposite sex. To explore this question, the research worker might interview clients and practicing professionals doing same-sex or cross-sex counseling. The study might include in-

terviews of experienced workers. Exploratory research also might examine the feasibility of a more careful study, or might construct a new technique for getting better data.

Exploratory studies are valuable: they break new ground, and they often illuminate a problem. Their biggest drawback, although they may hint at answers or may increase confidence in a technique, is that they are seldom definitive.

Description

The social work student doing voluntary field work typifies this technique in use. In many undergraduate programs, the student must do volunteer work and keep a diary of observations. In other words, the student first observes and then describes a particular social situation.

Explanation

This technique asks for more than description of a problem. There must be an analysis. Rather than describing the cycle of poverty, for instance, the research worker would try to explain why the cycle of poverty is difficult to break. Explanation is the creative phase of research. Often a single explication cannot adequately show the manner in which complex social forces interact to produce a sequence of events. Thus, the research must include a probe much deeper than that involved in merely compiling descriptions. The goal of explanatory research is to allow the practitioner to predict specific outcomes with accuracy.

Basic Research Versus Applied Research

Another approach to classifying the functions of research lies in the degree of direct practical application inherent in the findings. Research may be labeled either basic or applied. Basic (or pure) research seeks empirical observations that can be used to formulate or refine theory. It is not concerned with solving the immediate problems of the discipline, but rather with extending the knowledge base of the discipline. (This aim does not preclude the practical application of the findings of basic research, but such is not the investigator's primary intent.) So far, little investigation of this nature has been conducted in social work.

The majority of social work research is applied; it addresses immediate problems facing the professional in practice. The goal of applied research most often is the scientific planning of induced change in a troublesome situation. Basic and applied research are complementary—the advancement of knowledge and the solution of problems are both scientific necessities.

Limitations of the Scientific Method

Although the scientific approach is considered the most advanced form of attaining knowledge, scientific research still cannot solve all puzzles, nor are scientists immune to making mistakes. Sometimes problems of morals, ethics, measurement, control, and human complexity simply cannot be resolved. Issues concerning values or ethics, for example, cannot be scientifically investigated because they raise questions that cannot be tested empirically. Researchers might be able to describe social workers' attitudes toward abortion or euthanasia. But no investigation could be expected to answer the question, "Should abortion (or euthanasia) be practiced?"

Another major stumbling block to the conduct of scientific inquiry in social work is the complexity of the subject—human beings. Each human being's personality, social environment, values, and life-style are unique. This individuality complicates objective study considerably.

Measurement problems are among the most difficult for social work. How can workers assess client change or measure attitudes? Social work's instruments are not as precise as those of the physical and natural sciences. Investigators can only remain aware of this condition and continue trying to develop and refine measurement techniques. The social work research setting must be controlled as much as possible. In field research especially, this requirement can pose problems.

Despite all these limitations and problems, however, social work research has made colossal strides. Increasing sophistication and dedication will allow the profession to continue its advances in the future.

Summary

The sources of human knowledge number at least six:

1. Tradition is composed of the "truths" that are handed down through generations of people. Traditions can contain useful information, but they rarely are examined for fallacies.

2. Authoritative knowledge is accepted as correct because it comes from some indisputable, expert source. Often, individuals must trust such expertise, yet (like tradition) the knowledge of authorities is not always flawless.

3.   Experience is a common source of knowledge. It allows people to generalize learning from one event to another. Any individual's experience is limited, however. Another limitation is that two persons may not perceive the same experience in identical fashion.

4.   Trial and error is a common problem-solving approach. Yet it is unsystematic, and because the findings often go unrecorded they may remain unknown to others.

5.   Logical reasoning applies the intellect to solving problems or building knowledge. Inductive reasoning develops generalizations from specific observations. Deductive reasoning develops specific predictions from general principles. Both forms are important in scientific research.

6.   The scientific method, a formal system of research procedures, is man's most advanced means of acquiring knowledge. It outshines such approaches as tradition, authority, experience, or trial and error. It allows for self-evaluation; it employs programmed steps. The scientific method is founded on three assumptions: objective reality, an ordered universe, and determinism.

Researchers using the scientific method must follow a specific procedure. They (1) define the problem, (2) predict the outcome, (3) collect information, (4) analyze it, and (5) draw conclusions. They also must control any factors external to the study, maintain objectivity, and exercise empiricism.

Social work research must have at least one of three objectives. It should aim to (1) explore a condition that arouses the curiosity of the research worker, (2) describe thoroughly an extant social situation, or (3) explain and analyze a phenomenon.

Research may be termed either basic or applied. Basic (or pure) research attempts to extend a discipline's base of knowledge. Applied research, which addresses the practical problems encountered by social workers, is more common in social work.

Despite the utility of the scientific method, however, some insoluble problems still face social work research: issues involving morals, ethics, measurement, and control, as well as the very complexity of human beings themselves.

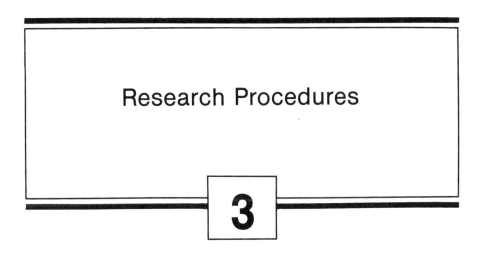

Research Procedures

3

Scientific research involves both independent and interdependent decisions and actions. The research process is a complex yet orderly procedure for solving problems or creating new knowledge. This chapter introduces the language of scientific research and the steps in the research process at which major decisions must be made.

The Language of Research

Scientific Concepts

Concepts are the basic terms used by members of a specific professional or occupational group. Conceptualization is the process of refining general or abstract ideas. There are numerous definitions of concepts, but all are complicated because the term *concept* itself represents a concept. For social work purposes, a concept may be thought of as an abstract generalization that allows social workers to summarize and order some important aspects of society.

Any discipline must carefully define its concepts because good research requires observable, measurable phenomena. If research concepts are ambiguous or not clear, the outcome or quality of the research will be directly affected because it will be difficult to develop objective and reliable methods of measurement. The careful explication of concepts in clear, precise language facilitates the research process and is essential for the building of scientific knowledge.

To specify, refine, or limit the meanings of concepts, scientists give them verbal labels or terms. Take the term *client*, for example. Social workers use the concept to refer to a person receiving direct services from a member of the profession. Yet a client may be an individual, or it may be a group, an organization, or a community. Moreover, social work's concept of client may not necessarily resemble the perception of other professions toward their clients.

Operational Definitions

An operational definition defines a concept by specifying the activities or operations necessary to measure it. In other words, an operational definition is a blueprint with which the investigator conducts certain activities in a specific way.

The use of operational definitions is fairly common in social science research. The practice raises basic research questions, however. Can the concept of depression, for example, be defined in such a way that it can be measured? To define depression, could investigators just study specific indicators, such as attempted suicides? Does depression encompass a common set of behaviors that share some common feature and that therefore can be treated by using a common set of techniques? When selecting any research project, the researcher needs to consider questions such as these.

The ease with which concepts can be operationalized varies. Such concepts as weight, height, and sex are relatively straightforward; but the concepts in many potential areas of social research are far less easy to define.

Consider the helper working with a depressed client. The objective is the reduction of depression. But because a variety of indicators may be used, the helper first must define how any reduction of depression will be measured.

An operational definition of the reduction of depression might be expressed in terms of such activities as the number of the subject's daily contacts, how often the subject leaves the house, job-seeking activity, or the frequency of suicide attempts. When used to represent the overall condition of depression, however, the indicator becomes an operational definition of that concept.

The following list demonstrates the potential difficulty of operationalizing a concept.

Identifying Measurable and
Nonmeasurable Objectives

The research worker must be able to develop research objectives that are measurable. The following exercise tests readers' ability to distinguish between measurable and nonmeasurable objectives. Classify each stated objective as either measurable or nonmeasurable in its present form.

Objectives	Measurable	Nonmeasurable
1. Understand the principles of social work.	____	____
2. Write two examples of a successful social work principle.	____	____
3. Name the bones of the hand.	____	____
4. Know the needs of child care associated with abandoned children.	____	____
5. Develop a positive attitude.	____	____
6. Appreciate the value of sports.	____	____
7. Write an essay on task-centered casework.	____	____
8. Demonstrate a knowledge of the principles of task-centered casework.	____	____
9. Be able to understand well the principles of Freudian psychology.	____	____
10. Really understand how to conduct research.	____	____
11. Write a description of each of the steps involved in conducting evaluation research.	____	____
12. Foster a sense of self-respect in a client.	____	____
13. Reduce the school dropout rate of a group of children.	____	____
14. Develop a nonjudgmental attitude.	____	____
15. Foster respect for the law.	____	____

The correct answers:

1. Nonmeasurable   3. Measurable   5. Nonmeasurable
2. Measurable   4. Nonmeasurable   6. Measurable

7.	Measurable	10.	Nonmeasurable	13.	Measurable
8.	Measurable	11.	Measurable	14.	Nonmeasurable
9.	Nonmeasurable	12.	Nonmeasurable	15.	Nonmeasurable

After learning to distinguish between measurable and nonmeasurable objectives, the student's next step is to learn to write objectives so that they are measurable. An easy way to start is to rewrite nonmeasurable objectives into measurable forms. Consider two examples:

Objective 1, Understand the principles of social work, might be restated: Write two examples of a social work principle.

Objective 4, Know the needs of child care associated with abandoned children, could be rewritten: List at least eight requirements for the adequate care of abandoned children.

The social worker who cannot identify objectives such as the foregoing with 100 percent accuracy will probably find identifying measurable objectives a difficult task. The two steps clearly are interrelated. The ability to identify measurable objectives correctly is crucial in evaluating the effectiveness of social work practice.

One other point regarding operational definitions: not all people will agree with the way a specific investigator conceptualizes and defines a phenomenon. Yet if a researcher performs these tasks clearly and concisely, the "consumers" of the research (such as other scholars and the public) will know exactly what the researcher means and how to measure similar phenomena.

Critics charge that research workers often dilute a concept in the process of operationally defining it. Nevertheless, definition is a necessary step in quality research. Research workers who do not perform thorough work will find that accurate evaluation of their research is nearly impossible.

Variability

A key word in scientific literature is *variable.* A variable is simply something that varies, that acquires different values in different situations. For the research worker, a variable is a symbol (X, Y, stress, or poverty, for example) to which numbers are assigned. A variable might take on a set of numerical values. The research worker might differentiate degrees of poverty, for instance, by separating them in various income levels:

Poverty—	$	0–6,000
Level 1—		0–2,000

Level 2—   2,000–4,000
Level 3—   4,000–6,000

An underlying assumption is that the levels selected are useful. The investigator also must be sure to explain them in the research report. The complexity of assignment may range from two to any number of variables. An example of the use of two variables would be to differentiate the sexes in a study by assigning them the numerals 0 and 1.

The types of variables with which the student of research should be most familiar are *independent variables* and *dependent variables*—the presumed cause and the presumed effect of a phenomenon. The independent variable is what researchers presume causes the behavior or phenomenon under investigation; the dependent variable is the presumed effect. The research worker usually is most interested in understanding, explaining, or predicting the dependent variable.

The classification of variables as dependent or independent is not sacrosanct. That is, in one study, a variable may be a dependent variable; in a subsequent study, the same variable may be independent. For example, in one study, cigarette smoking may be selected as the independent variable if smoking is thought to contribute to lung cancer. In another study, smoking might be the dependent variable—perhaps if the study is examining the effects of advertising on the number of cigarettes smoked in a certain region. In the first project, smoking is the presumed cause of the phenomenon (lung cancer). In the second, it is the presumed effect (of advertising efforts). In short, the designation of a variable as dependent or independent is a function of the role it plays in a particular investigation.

Social work researchers most often perceive the dependent variable as the "outcome" of social work practice. Because social work occurs in a variety of settings—adult prisons, mental hospitals, treatment centers, schools, communities, families—the dependent variable often is the effect that a specific intervention or treatment produces. An example of an analogous dependent variable in medicine might be *the reduction of pain or illness or the modification of a physical disability.* For the social work practitioner and research worker, the problem is to identify clearly outcomes or dependent variables that are specific enough for measurement. This feature is essential in scientific research.

The problem of selecting outcome measures for the profession is not at all new. In the 1931 National Conference on Social Work, the president of that organization, Richard C. Cabot, urged the profession to evaluate the outcome of its efforts.[1] Over the years, diverse outcome measures have evolved within the profession. But many have been used without sufficient concern for their fundamental characteristics. The two major characteristics of any measurement—reliability and validity—must be considered when selecting outcome measures.

Reliability

Before a measurement is selected for use, its reliability must be appraised. A measure's reliability is its capacity to gauge consistently the phenomenon being measured. In other words, a reliable measure reveals actual differences in what is being measured—rather than differences inherent in the measurement process itself. Differences that result from the measurement process may cause erroneous data to be produced. Reliability tests focus on the measuring instrument rather than on what is measured.

Sources of Error

A variety of possible sources of error exists in any measurement process. One source of error lies in the ambiguous definitions of outcome variables. For example, some of the early social-work research attempted to evaluate social work practice by asking practitioners to judge how much improvement occurred for a specific client. But different practitioners, lacking specifications of just what constituted improvement, were likely to judge client improvement differently. Therefore, such judgments, due to a lack of precise definition, automatically were subject to some variation. Such vague measures reflected practitioners' disagreement over definitions as much as they actually measured anything—client improvement, for example.

Another common source of error lies in the methods of observing and recording data. Some social-work outcome research is based on studies of agency case records, for example. Yet, case records often represent the selective recording practices of the professional. When conducting interviews, the practitioner rarely writes a full description of the interview itself; often, the professional omits many details and confines the case recording to "relevant details." Thus, because of professionals' selective recording practices, any attempt to evaluate a case from such records is subject to some problems of reliability.

To compound the same example, interviews often are verbal accounts of day-to-day living experiences. As such, they are subject to errors in recall, to possible distortion, and to selective reporting. Clients, like professionals, have neither the time nor the inclination to describe every detail of their experience unless carefully prodded. Consequently, client reports may contain inaccurate information—and therefore may constitute a further source of error.

Other errors can develop from variations in conditions for collecting the information. An interview conducted in a client's home may yield results that differ from those obtained in an office setting. Variable information also may result when different persons conduct the interview; a female interviewer may obtain different results from a man. Differences in the interview situation may cause further disparities: The room could be too hot, too cold, or have major distractions.

To complicate matters further, the instrument itself might constitute a source of error. For example, an open-ended questionnaire may require that responses be classified and coded. But the classifying and coding process may yield different judgments unless each rater receives the same clear, precise instructions. This risk can be reduced by using objective questions. Even then, however, the process of scoring remains a possible source of error.

This discussion is not a comprehensive outline of the problems of achieving reliability. But it should help the research worker to identify some of the more common problems inherent in selecting a reliable instrument.

Improving Reliability

Fortunately, some standard techniques can help researchers determine and improve the reliability of research instruments. One of the most common procedures employs several independent raters, who observe and independently code the same materials or events. The extent of their agreement or disagreement is then compared by statistical techniques, generally in the form of a correlation coefficient. (Raters' accuracy, incidentally, often can be upgraded by proper training.) If agreement is sufficiently high and consistent, the instrument is considered reliable. The level that constitutes "sufficiently high" depends in part on the number and nature of the analysts, on the method of computation, and on the statistical confidence level selected by the researcher. Procedures like these were used to establish reliability for the Community Service Scale, an instrument developed to assess the outcomes of social casework. (The CSS is discussed in detail in chapter 5.)

Another approach to assessing and improving reliability lies in the events or behavior being studied. Many evaluative studies devote great effort to establishing the reliability of a system for scoring case records (such as in the CSS instrument), but they tend to skip the important step of establishing the reliability of the case records themselves. Because of selective reporting by both clients and social workers, case records and other reports are subject to recording errors. The case record may not reflect accurately either the interview or the actual state of events in the client's life.

Several techniques can help reduce these kinds of errors. For the analysis of interviews and other therapeutic encounters, such as meetings with groups, reliability can be increased by using several observers, then comparing the extent of consensus among their independent accounts of the event. Another technique is to record the event on audiotape or videotape. To determine if client accounts of adjustment are indeed accurate, it may be desirable or even necessary to establish other sources of information about a client. This practice is common among child welfare workers who, to corroborate information provided them by a child, for example, will check with other sources (family members or school personnel).

Reliability in evaluation studies depends in part on the completeness and accuracy of data, in part on how explicit the definitions are, and in part on the training and accuracy of the coders. Care in each step of the research process can help investigators achieve a high degree of reliability. The task is by no means impossible, but it does require hard work and attention to details. Moreover, as well as establishing reliability for the instrument and for the raters, social scientists need to ensure that reliability among different raters remains uniform at all times. Achieving reliability requires periodic checks throughout the study period. Reliability cannot be assumed; it must be established by verifiable means.

The use of standardized measures, such as some of the established psychological tests, at least partially solves the problem of reliability. Standardized psychological tests normally provide the information about reliability: how it was established, on what norm group, and statistical measures of different forms of reliability. These all are reported in data provided by the test publisher. Standard references also provide more comprehensive evaluations of test data. Such evaluations are reported in the *Mental Measurements Yearbook*, by Oscar Burros,[2] as well as in the reference *Tests in Print*.[3]

Validity

The validity of a measure is the extent to which it measures or assesses what it is supposed to. Whereas reliability pertains to how the measures are taken, validity concerns what is measured and the meaning of the results. Satisfactory reliability ensures that the findings do not result from inconsistent measurements. Satisfactory validity, on the other hand, ensures that the findings mean what they appear to mean. In its broad sense, validity denotes the extent to which a test measures or predicts that for which it was designed. In other words, validity is the most basic and perhaps the most important single attribute of a measure. In contrast, reliability says nothing of the worth of a measure. A measure can be perfectly reliable, but unless it also is valid, it may be worthless. Take, for example, a specific test designed to predict potential occupational success. How well it performs may be said to be a measure of the validity of that test. However, a measure may have a high degree of validity for one purpose but almost none for other purposes.

Various definitions apply to different kinds of validity. These definitions include content validity, predictive validity, and construct validity. Although volumes have been written about these various forms, for practical purposes most beginning social work practitioners will concern themselves primarily with predictive validity.

Predictive validity, also called empirical or criterion validity, is established by determining how well a measure predicts subjects' performance against a specific criterion. A measure's predictive validity is determined by operationally defining what outcomes the measure can predict. The measure's success in predicting an outcome determines the extent to which it may be considered valid. For example, a social worker may wish to use an instrument designed to predict postinstitutional adjustment for juvenile offenders discharged from a correctional facility. If the worker uses that instrument to screen people for discharge, then its validity may be determined by comparing its predictions for individuals against various criteria for postinstitutional adjustment. A reasonable criterion in this case might be that the parolee commit no further offenses in a given time period. Thus, the validity of the test is determined by how accurately it predicts the recidivism rate for this population.

Validity is ascertained by a specific definition of what the test or measure is designed to do. A test might, for instance, successfully predict parolee postinstitutional adjustment and be valid for that purpose. Yet it might prove ineffective—and therefore invalid—in identifying potential marital problems for a released individual.

Another example lies in the way schools establish predictive validity for achievement and intelligence tests. From such tests, administrators predict students' likely academic performance. They compare student scores on specific intelligence exams—the instruments—with the grades students earn in school—the criteria.

Several factors affect the possible predictive validity of a measure. One factor is the selection of criteria used to establish validity. These may vary from study to study, with different scores being obtained from each set of criteria. Therefore, research scientists must carefully choose criteria that are most relevant to the purpose of their research.

A second factor concerns the specificity of the criteria and of the measure itself. In terms of what they are intended to do, some tests are defined more specifically than others. For example, easily identified criteria such as school grades can be used to validate a scholastic aptitude test. But establishing acceptable standards for validating an attitude scale or a value scale is much more difficult, because individual attitudes and values are less tangible traits.

Social workers should keep in mind a rule of thumb that will help them select relevant measures for research. For a measure to have any utility, it must provide accurate information that can help others predict future events and behaviors. That is, the less specific the measure, the less useful it will be in predicting events and behaviors.

Predictive validity generally is reported as a numerical figure called a validity coefficient. This is a measure of predictive validity found by calculating the coefficient of correlation between the measure and a specific criterion. For most of the standardized psychological tests, reports of validity are available.[2,3]

23

Decision Steps in Research

Chapter 1 declared that the purpose of this text is to provide the professional or student social worker with the tools, detailed procedures, and methods used to conduct and evaluate research. This book is intended to help readers learn how to develop new knowledge, evaluate prior research, and apply their knowledge to social work practice.

This section of the book outlines the complete research process, especially the decision steps that confront the investigator.

Some research textbooks list as few as five or six major decision steps in the conduct of research. Others show as many as fifteen steps. The difference usually is only that some authors place certain steps within others; the sequence and logic system of all remain similar, however. This text proposes nine steps as distinct and separate activities:

1. Identifying the problem.
2. Searching the literature.
3. Defining the variables.
4. Stating the hypothesis.
5. Selecting the design.
6. Choosing the universe, population, or sample.
7. Collecting data.
8. Analyzing data.
9. Interpreting and presenting the findings.

1. Identifying the Problem

This step is obvious but difficult. Areas of study may be easy to identify, but planning the subsequent investigation properly can be considerably more difficult. There is no set pattern for identifying problems for investigation, and the sources of inspiration for research topics are varied. Two common stimuli to research are the scientist's concern about a social issue and his or her experience. Perhaps the most important attribute a prospective researcher can possess is intellectual curiosity.

One topic of considerable research interest in social work today is the physical and mental abuse of children. Sources of information on this topic include books, social work courses, the news media, and the personal experiences of abused persons.

The investigator, once having identified a general area or topic of interest, should begin to consider the boundaries of the investigation. The researcher must take care to limit the scope so that it remains manageable. A good method is to pose a series of specific, answerable questions about the topic. So that the researcher may proceed properly, questions must be skillfully phrased. Whatever the effort required, it must be expended at this point: good research depends on the researcher's framing good initial questions about the project.

Some typical questions regarding the sample topic of physical or mental abuse of children:

- What are the characteristics of the abuser?
- What are the characteristics of the abused?
- Under what conditions does abuse occur?
- Where does the abuse occur?
- How does the abuse occur?

The first-time research worker should not be discouraged by a failure to select a good research topic on the first attempt. Even the most experienced investigator may need considerable time and effort to delineate a research problem.

2. Searching the Literature

The literature search enables the investigator to examine previous research and scholarly inquiry into the selected subject. The search has at least three functions. It may disclose that someone else already has performed essentially the same research. In such a case, the investigator may choose another problem and start over or may choose to replicate the study (duplicate or repeat the same research in a new setting). Replication, for the beginning research worker, is an excellent activity because it eases the many decisions required during the conduct of inquiry. Many disciplines fail to give replication its due as a legitimate and worthwhile research function.

A second function of the literature search is to provide a substantially better insight into the dimensions and complexity of the problem. Because research is a source for building a knowledge base, learning about previous thinking on the topic is an essential step. It may clarify what the investigator was groping with while choosing the problem in Step 1. A thorough search lays the foundation for good research.

A third function of the literature search is that it equips the investigator with a complete and thorough justification of the subsequent steps, as well as with a sense of importance of the undertaking.

The literature search focuses on three types of information. The search may: (1) uncover findings from previous studies on the general problem, (2) reveal some theoretical issues that bear on the topic, and (3) acquaint the research worker with methodological issues and procedures.

A word on the role of theory or theoretical frameworks in research: A theory is a generalized, abstract explanation of interrelationships among phenomena. Its principal purpose is explaining and predicting those phenomena. Theories perform two roles in a research project. Research may aim either to develop a theory or to test a theory. Social work research is more often concerned with the latter function.

3.   Defining the Variables

The process of defining the major variables of the research study is both important and demanding. The importance of this step lies in the social work profession's need to build its cumulative knowledge on a solid foundation of interrelated research findings. Much of the available social work research unfortunately is not closely interrelated. Most studies cannot readily be replicated because the major research variables, the independent variable and the dependent variable, have not always been carefully and accurately defined. Hence, subsequent researchers cannot do further study and evaluate the same variables. This deficiency has been largely responsible for the proliferation of so many different research projects in social work—many of which apparently are studying similar variables but whose efforts produce little cumulative knowledge.

This step—defining the major variable—demands both imagination and precision. The researcher faces the difficult task of carefully describing each of the variables in such a way that others, by using the same variables for other independent research, can duplicate his efforts. Imagination is required to devise variables that can be adequately and carefully described and that will provide answers to the research question.

The process of defining the independent and dependent variables is a major step in the conduct of research. Chapters 5 and 6 are devoted to that process.

4.   Stating the Hypothesis

The hypothesis states the researcher's conception of the relationship between the variables being studied. It is a prediction of what is expected. A hypothesis is typically expressed either as a statement of a relationship or as a statement of no relationship. The latter form is referred to as a null hypothesis, shown symbolically as Ho. Whatever the form, a hypothesis must be stated in such a way that it is capable of being tested.

A hypothesis for a study of child abuse might be stated thus: "Parents who abuse their children tend to be younger, on the average, than non-child-abusing parents. In other words, the incidence of parental child abuse decreases as parents' age rises." The study would then attempt to prove or disprove that hypothesis.

5.   Selecting the Design

Selecting the research design is a decision that confronts every investigator in the early stages of a project. The most fundamental design choice is whether the study will be experimental or nonexperimental. In experimental research, the degree of active control exercised by the investigator is significantly greater and the assignment of subjects to study groups is carefully controlled. The experimental research worker does something to the subjects by manipulating the dependent variable, then observes the consequences. In contrast, the nonexperimental research worker merely collects data without introducing changes: he or she simply observes or measures existing conditions.

One important kind of research design is the single-subject design (discussed in chapter 8), which tests clinical practice knowledge in individual cases.

6. Choosing the Universe, Population, or Sample

The concepts of universe, population, and sample refer to the individuals or groups that will be included in the study. The term *universe* refers to all potential subjects who possess the attributes in which the researcher is interested. *Population* is a term that sets boundaries on the study units. It refers to individuals in the universe who possess specific characteristics. For instance, "All social workers who were licensed in Idaho on January 1 through 10, 1982" constitute a population. In the example of child abusers, the population of the study might include all individuals referred to a community's child-protection services. A *sample* is the element of the population considered for actual inclusion in the study.

These concepts are used to describe exactly who may or may not be included in a study and to describe the group from which results were taken. Most studies attempt to generalize from a sample to a larger population. Chapter 9 discusses these concepts in detail.

7. Collecting Data

The success of a study often depends on correct data collection. However, the collection of the data is a difficult and time-consuming phase of any research project. Research investigators must decide how to collect the data and what techniques to use. Considerable administrative and clerical work is involved in this phase. Research assistants must be trained; often the quality of the research depends heavily on the performance of assistants. Data collection techniques are discussed more thoroughly in chapters 10 and 11.

To collect information from abusing parents, questionnaires or personal interviews might be used.

8. Analyzing Data

After collecting the data, the researcher must organize and analyze the information. This step may involve several procedures—evaluating the usability of the information, getting it into a form for analysis, or perhaps performing a statistical manipulation called coding. Seldom are the data in an original form that allows easy analysis. The research worker typically must either transcribe or transform the data (as the case may be) into a format that allows statistical manipulation. Although some researchers perform such coding by hand, most are now processing research data with computers.

The forms of statistical analysis range from simple to complex. The inexperienced research worker typically will begin by using descriptive statistics, including such mathematical operations as means, medians, modes, frequencies, and percentages. To best communicate descriptive statistics, the investigator may present the data in charts, tables, or graphs. A more advanced use of statistics is the inferential method, which is used to test hypotheses. The application of both types to social work research is discussed in chapter 9.

9. Interpreting and Presenting the Findings

The results have been compiled. Do they confirm the hypothesis? Or should they cause the research worker to reject the hypothesis? If the findings confirm the hypothesis, writing an explanation will be a fairly straightforward task since the findings fit the initially posed framework. If the data do not confirm the hypothesis, however, the investigator must revise the earlier thinking.

The results of any investigation are of limited value if they are not communicated to others. The research worker's final responsibility, then, is to share findings with colleagues and the public. Of several forums for this final step, the two most common are professional meetings and professional journals. The format of this procedure is fairly standardized within the profession and is discussed in chapter 13.

This chapter has covered the essential steps and decisions that beginning research workers can anticipate using in the typical investigation. The amount of time each step requires varies; usually the greatest amount of time must be invested in the data-collection phase. Different researchers naturally find different stages of an investigation most to their liking. Each step, though, is guaranteed to offer the scholar some degree of challenge, inspiration, and reward.

Summary

Scientific research attempts to solve problems or to create new knowledge by explaining or clarifying concepts. A concept is an abstract generalization that allows social workers to summarize and order important aspects of society. Research concepts must be as clear and unambiguous as possible, even though defining practice terms sometimes is a difficult undertaking.

Social science research often uses operational definitions, which define a concept by specifying the operations necessary to measure it. Yet the measurement process in social work sometimes can become difficult. Regardless, the objectives of research must be measurable: Investigators must know how to specify objectives and must be able to write them in terms that are measurable.

Scientific research involves variables—factors that may vary, that may possess different values in different situations. Two significant types of variables are independent and dependent—the presumed cause and the presumed effect of a phenomenon.

The designation of a variable as dependent or independent may vary between studies. Furthermore, a given aspect of research may be the dependent variable one time, the independent variable the next, depending on the focus of the particular study. The social work researcher usually is most interested in the dependent variable. In social work, the dependent variable often is the effect or outcome of a specific treatment.

Measuring outcomes is difficult. Over the years, the profession has used many outcome measures. The two most important characteristics of any measure are its reliability and validity. Reliability refers to how consistently a measure gauges the phenomena it is designed to delimit. The reliability of a measure must be determined because in any measurement process a variety of possible sources of error exist. These range from imprecise standards for client improvement to improprieties in the instrument itself.

To improve reliability, one of the best approaches is to use several independent observers and then compare the extent of their agreement. The more consistent the observers' agreement, the greater is the instrument's reliability. Research workers must be aware, too, that case records from which they glean information may contain inaccuracies and ambiguities. Using tested measures such as standardized psychological tests can help solve problems of unreliability.

A measure's validity is its most important attribute. Validity refers to how well a measure assesses what it is supposed to. There are various kinds of validity, including content validity, construct validity, and predictive validity. The last is most important to beginning social work practitioners. It is established by determining how well a measure predicts a subject's performance against a specific criterion. To ascertain validity, the users of a test or measure must define specifically what it is designed to do. A test might be highly valid for one purpose yet invalid for another. As with reliability, several factors can affect a measure's predictive validity. The difficulty of establishing standards for various kinds of scales can vary widely.

There are nine major steps in conducting research.

1.   Identifying the problem to be investigated. When choosing a research topic, the investigator must try to limit the problem and keep it within manageable boundaries. The best approach is to pose a few specific questions about the topic.

2.   Searching the literature. A search acquaints the worker with previous inquiries into the subject. It improves insight into the topic and supplies a sense of the importance of the endeavor. It improves the research worker's understanding of how to conduct the subsequent study steps.

3.   Defining the variables. This step demands both imagination and precision. Well-explicated research variables are necessary, if other examiners are to be able to replicate a study.

4.   Stating the hypothesis. The hypothesis predicts what the research worker expects to learn or prove. It usually is expressed as either a statement of relationship or no relationship.

5.   Selecting the research design. The major choice here is deciding whether the research will be experimental or nonexperimental—whether some experimental condition will be introduced into the study or whether existing conditions will simply be observed or measured.

6.   Choosing the universe, population, or sample. Typically, the sample to be studied is isolated, and then an attempt is made to generalize the sample findings to a larger population.

7.   Collecting data. This is a difficult and time-consuming phase. It can involve completing questionnaires and checklists, conducting personal interviews, and expending long hours in observation.

8.   Analyzing data. The research data must be transcribed or transformed so that they may be statistically manipulated. Beginning research typically uses descriptive statistics—mathematical operations such as means, medians, modes, frequencies, and percentages. A more advanced approach is the use of inferential statistics.

9.   Interpreting and presenting the findings. To have any value, the results of a study must be interpreted and communicated to colleagues and the public. The two most common forums are professional meetings and professional journals.

End Notes

1.   Cabot, Richard C. "Treatment in Social Casework in the Need of Criteria and of Tests of Its Success or Failure." *Proceedings of the National Conference of Social Work* 58 (1931): 3–24.
2.   Burros, Oscar, ed. *Mental Measurement Yearbook*. 7th ed. 2 vols. Highland Park, N.J.: Gryphon Press, 1972.
3.   Burros, Oscar K. *Tests in Print*. Highland Park, N.J.: Gryphon Press, 1969.

The Library and Social Work Research

4

The best place to initiate research is the library. Unfortunately, many students do not understand the workings of the school library, and most cannot use it effectively. Typical student complaints range from, "I couldn't find it in the library" to "Nothing has been written on my topic" to "It's a waste of time to go there."

In spite of such reactions, the library remains the richest source of information available for research. University libraries contain virtually all the knowledge that social work professionals and students might seek. Too frequently, however, investigators fail to consider the library an integral component of the research process.

For social work students and professionals, the library is the primary place to develop conceptual frameworks for such endeavors as term papers, theses, dissertations, and research reports. In addition, social workers may use the library to update their knowledge of recent research, new therapeutic techniques, practice philosophies, and contemporary issues.

Knowing how to use library information effectively is essential for producing good research. Yet, most students and faculty members do not know how to use the library properly. Many believe that, when a real need arises, they can learn their way around the library; they assume that using the library is an easy skill to acquire, requiring little knowledge or experience. Thus, many people remain uninformed about how to use the library, and many are unaware of the wide range of services offered by a school library. This chapter introduces some fundamental library-use concepts and procedures.

Using the Library for Research

A comprehensive library search is necessary at three specific points in the research process: during formulation of the problem, when reviewing the literature, and when explaining the research results. The library search is essential in establishing the theoretical bases for planning and conducting research.

For ideal use of the library, the beginning investigator should recognize the basic differences among sources of information.

Primary literature is the best source available to the researcher. It typically contains the most current and detailed information published about a particular subject. Examples of primary literature include technical reports, research reports, theses, dissertations, documents, and autobiographies. Primary sources deserve high regard because they provide the direct results of previous research—not an interpretation of that research from some other perspective.

Secondary literature is a reevaluated and summarized version of one or several pieces of primary literature by someone other than the original authors. The most common example of such works is the textbook. The value of secondary literature is that it provides both a synthesis of information on a subject and references to the original sources.

Tertiary literature is the information in encyclopedic works. An example is the *Encyclopedia of Social Work*.

Major Resources in the Library

The Card Catalog
The card catalog is the index to all the books in the library. It is the best source for assessing secondary and tertiary literature, but it may not list some primary sources, such as journal literature or government documents, that might be needed for the research.

Card catalog information for each book includes the complete citation, the book's location in the library, and cross-references to oversize books, specialty collections, reference books, and some documents. Some card catalogs contain periodical titles, but none cite periodical articles.

The size, arrangement, and location of card catalogs vary. The librarian should be consulted on the use of a particular library's card catalog. Figure 4–1 shows how information is depicted on a typical card.

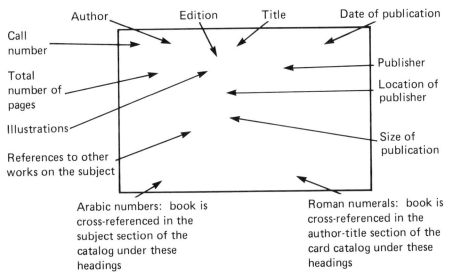

FIGURE 4–1. Locations of information typically found on a card in the subject section or author–title section of a library's card catalog.

For best use of a card catalog, the following steps are helpful:

1. Identify a list of major subject headings associated with the research topic.
2. Identify authors who publish in the topic area. (Professors and text-books are good sources of suggestions for relevant authors.)
3. Search the card catalog for the headings and authors identified.
4. Record each pertinent reference and its call number.
5. Note and locate any cross-references.
6. Locate each book in the stacks using the call numbers indicated by card catalog. Refer to the library directory, if necessary, to obtain the location in the building of particular categories of books.

Many libraries have converted their card catalogs to computer catalogs (on-line), or to a microfilm or microfiche catalog generated by a computer called a COM catalog. Within a few years, these innovations will revolutionize library cataloging, a trend that should be extremely helpful to research. A librarian should be consulted about any questions concerning the card catalog.

Periodicals, Indexes, and Abstracts

The periodical, a regularly published type of primary literature, is a major source of information. Periodicals include journals, magazines, and newspapers. Many professional journals are available to the social worker. Some are specialized; others are more general. Some examples of journals in several practice areas:

School Social Work:
Social Work in Education
School Social Work Quarterly

Health and Medical Social Work:
Social Work in Health Care
Health and Social Work

Family and Children's Services:
Social Casework
Child Welfare
Smith College Studies in Social Work
Clinical Social Work Journal

General Social Work:
Social Work
Social Service Review
Practice Digest
Journal of Social Welfare
Human Services in the Rural Environment

Social Work Research:
Social Work Research and Abstracts
Journal of Social Service Research

Social Group Work:
Social Work with Groups

International Social Welfare and Journals from Other Countries:
British Journal of Social Work
Canadian Welfare
International Social Work
Social Work Today
Social Worker-Travailleur Social
International Child Welfare
Indian Journal of Social Work

Public Social Services:
Public Welfare

Social Work in Sectarian Agencies:
Journal of Jewish Communal Service
Catholic Charities Review

Aging Services:
Journal of Gerontological Social Work

Social Work Education:
Canadian Journal of Social Work Education
Journal of Education for Social Work

Administration:
Administration in Social Work

Additional information on relevant journals is available.[1]

Specific citations to articles in periodicals are given in periodical indexes and abstracts. Indexes constitute the primary means of locating references for research. They can be used to locate books, periodical articles, pamphlets, and other types of literature about a research problem.

Abstracts provide a brief summary of an entire article and give citations. They allow the reader to ascertain quickly whether an article pertains to the subject of inquiry. Abstracts the social work student ought to be familiar with are *Sociological Abstracts, Social Work Research and Abstracts*, and *Psychological Abstracts*. Other good references to periodicals are the *Social Science Citation Index* and *Current Contents/Social and Behavioral Sciences*.

Documents are another major type of primary literature. They include all publications of municipal and state governments and of the federal government. The United States Government, in fact, is the largest publisher of printed material in our country and is a particularly valuable source of information in social work.[2]

Another important source of bibliographic information is computer data bases. Most major libraries have computer terminals that connect to such systems as Education Resources Information Center (ERIC) and the *Sociological Abstracts*. A computer search costs from $5 to $25—a small price for the speed and thoroughness of the results. A data-base search quickly provides specific bibliographic source information. An individual might need days to accumulate the same facts.

The Search Strategy

When initiating a literature search, the investigator must first define the topic of research. It is important to narrow the topic, then to focus on the precise subject to be investigated. Usually several research paths may be followed; the student must choose one and remain on it. For example, a student interested in the problem of child abuse might approach the problem from any of several perspectives: historical, statistical, sociological, or psychological. To proceed efficiently, the student must specify a course of study. Otherwise he or she easily could waste time collecting resources that pertain only indirectly to the subject.

At the start of a search, students can save considerable time and effort by consulting a reference librarian about sources, strategies, and services. Research workers need to learn at the outset which sources are available at the library they are working in. While constructing a bibliography, research workers should examine any secondary literature, periodicals, documents, and special bibliographies that are relevant to the subject area.

The reference department of the library should be able to provide basic facts from pertinent bibliographies, dictionaries, encyclopedias, yearbooks, atlases, and statistical handbooks. Some common social science reference tools include *Encyclopedia of Social Work, Statistical Abstract of the U.S.*, and *A Dictionary of the Social Sciences.* In addition to these specialized bibliographies, two general works—the *London Bibliography of Social Sciences* and the *International Bibliography of Sociology*—are useful references. Again, the reference librarian can greatly facilitate the student's use of these references.

After assembling a general bibliography, the student should scan it for inapplicable materials and discard them. Next the student can examine carefully the bibliographies in the selected books and journals to expand the working source list. While doing this, the student should note any books or articles that seem to relate most to the research topic, then should read them, taking notes. Students may return to reference sources as necessary for definitions of terms, statistical data, and other information.

If sources crucial to the proposed research are not in the library, the student should consult the librarian about obtaining them through the interlibrary loan system. Interlibrary loan allows one library to borrow publications from another for individual use. Through this system, the research worker also may obtain photocopies of journal articles not in the local library. The potential user should realize two things about interlibrary loan, however. Acquiring the needed materials takes a certain amount of time, and fees usually are charged for the service.

Table 4–1 summarizes the literature search strategy.

Summary

The library is the best source of research information for the student or professional. Too many investigators, however, do not know how to use the

TABLE 4-1.   Literature Search Strategy

1.   State the topic, limit the range, and list all relevant synonyms.
2.   Locate a good general introductory text on the topic, one that includes a selected bibliography of the basic books and studies.
3.   Try to locate a literature review about the specific topic and the general research area.
4.   Locate all relevant books; be sure to use the Library of Congress *Subject Headings* book to locate relevant subject terms, and use them while searching the card catalog.
5.   Using indexes and abstracts, locate relevant journal articles and other research reports; make a list of the indexes and abstracts that seem pertinent to the area of study.
6.   Locate other relevant material, published and unpublished, such as government documents, theses, and dissertations.
7.   If any statistics or other pieces of discrete information are needed in the research, ask the reference librarian how to use the library to obtain such data.
8.   If a computer search of such abstracting services and indexes as *Psychological Abstracts*, *Index Medicus*, *Sociological Abstracts*, or ERIC might be worth the time and money, consult a reference librarian for search sources and search profile methodology. Start early; these searches take three to five weeks.
9.   Know the procedures for interlibrary loan and begin the literature search immediately; interlibrary loan takes time.
10. Ask a reference librarian for suggestions about other indexes, abstracts, or research tools—either in the local library or in other libraries.

library effectively, and too many are unaware of the wide range of available library services.

A library search must be performed at three points in the research process: during formulation of the problem, when reviewing the literature, and when explaining the results. There are three basic types of library information. Primary literature (technical reports, dissertations, and autobiographies) contains the most current and detailed information on a given topic. Secondary literature (textbooks) synthesizes available information on a subject and provides references to original sources. Tertiary data is the information contained in such volumes as encyclopedias.

The card catalog is the index to all the books in a library. It provides references to all a library's volumes except some journals and documents. Cards in the catalog supply the complete citation for a given work, the book's location in the library, and certain cross-references. Card catalog sizes and styles vary. Some are being replaced by computerized reference files.

To use a card catalog, the research worker should (1) identify major research subject headings, (2) identify authors in those fields, (3) search the catalog for selected headings and authors, (4) record each pertinent reference and its call number, (5) note any cross-references, and then (6) locate each work chosen.

A variety of professional periodicals valuable to the social work researcher can be found in libraries. Periodical indexes are primary means of locating such references for research. Abstracts give citations and provide brief summaries of articles. Documents, which can be another useful source of social work information, include all government publications.

For a nominal fee, researchers can locate bibliographical source data through computer searches via such systems as ERIC, which can provide, in short order, information that the individual working unaided might need days to acquire.

The student beginning a literature search must be careful to define specifically the research topic and the precise course of study. Otherwise considerable time might be wasted chasing resources that are only marginally useful. Researchers also should try to learn at the outset which sources are available at the local library. A check of the library's reference department might uncover some important bibliographical data.

Important missing works often may be obtained through the interlibrary loan system. However, gaining materials in this way usually requires time and payment of a fee.

End Notes

1. Markle, Allen, and Rinn, Roger. *Author's Guide to Journals in Psychology, Psychiatry and Social Work*. New York: Haworth Press, 1977.
2. The best references to sources for U. S. Government documents are: *U. S. Superintendent of Documents Catalog of Public Documents*, 1893–1940, Washington, D. C.: U. S. Government Printing Office. Monthly. (Provides bibliographies of the publications of all branches, departments, and agencies of the federal government.) *U. S. Superintendent of Documents Monthly Catalog of United States Government Publications*, 1895–present, Washington, D. C.: U. S. Government Printing Office. Monthly. (Similar to above.) *Government Publications and Their Uses*, L. F. Schmeckebier and R. B. Eastin, eds., Washington, D. C.: 1969, Brookings Institute. (A useful introduction to the research use of documents.)

Measuring the Results
of Social Work
Intervention

PART

II

Selecting Outcome Measures:
The Dependent Variable

5

Social Work's Handicaps

A revolution of tremendous proportions has transformed the physical and biological sciences during the past century. Scientists in these fields have achieved innumerable successes; their discoveries, in turn, have produced great advances in medicine and engineering.

The social scientists, however, have been less successful. Their quest for scientific knowledge—for data that would allow the formulation of basic laws of behavior to guide the practice of social work and other human service professions—has lagged. Of course, many differences exist between the physical and social sciences and between the research methods each uses to acquire and develop knowledge. Perhaps the most significant difference lies in the stability of their objects of study.

Take, for example, the physical scientist who wishes to study, under different conditions, the behavior of an element such as lead. Such research can readily be understood and replicated. The findings can serve as a foundation for others to build on, both because of the stability of the element and because the physical scientist may make precise descriptions of the experimental conditions. Procedures for the identification of substances such as basic elements or compounds are well established. They can be described in terms of mass, temperature, and atomic structure; another scientist can readily understand those descriptions. Further, conditions for treating the substance are similarly well standardized. Scientists can heat it, cool it, or subject it to specific pressures. They then can measure its reactions and can report all the results in a standardized format that others easily can understand and replicate.

Analogous elements are absent in the social and behavioral sciences, however. Often it is impossible to replicate even the most fundamental social science research because precise definitions and descriptions of major research variables are lacking. Yet without replication, the social work professional cannot readily build on the work of others to expand the profession's knowledge base.

The ability of members of the physical sciences to develop stable measures has been the primary means allowing the rapid expansion of knowledge in those fields during recent decades. For example, scientists first had to establish standard measures of temperature, pressure, and volume before they could formulate a general law of the interrelationship of pressure and temperature. Once these steps were achieved, however, others could build on those concepts to develop the steam engine and the internal combustion engine. The areas of atomic physics and chemistry evolved similarly. First, pioneers developed an understanding of the structure and function of the atom. Next, others developed and tested further explanations of the relationship between mass and energy. Ultimately, scientists were able to develop methods of controlling and harnessing atomic power.

In the social sciences, developing a base of knowledge to facilitate a cumulative approach to solving practical problems remains a highly desirable goal. Achieving a modest measure of cumulative knowledge in social work is difficult, but should not be impossible.

Establishing Measures

First, the profession must perform some fundamental work to establish precise measurements for the major variables in social work research. Once the profession has achieved some agreement on how to measure its major variables, research workers and practitioners can standardize and measure those variables in identical ways. With standardization, social scientists will find it possible to replicate research and to build on the work of others—and ultimately to construct a knowledge base that is more than one experiment deep.

The Dependent Variable

Defining the dependent variable—also commonly referred to as the *outcome measure*—creates enormous confusion and disagreement in social work and in related professions. In social work, part of the lack of agreement on standard outcome measures relates to the broad nature of the profession. Social work takes place in an immense variety of settings. Its practitioners work with a wide range of people and problems—from gifted school children and their families to adult prisoners, alcoholics, and patients in mental hospitals. Consequently, because of these diverse areas of concern, identifying a simple standard outcome measure for the entire profession is difficult. In medicine, a broad common outcome measure might be "the reduction of pain, illness, and physical disability." For social work, however, no common framework exists by which the profession might select a standard outcome measure that could serve as a guide for judging and evaluating all social work practice. A beginning might be made by considering Atherton's formulation:[1]

> Social work is the technology whose central idea is delivery of social services designed to control dependency. The term dependency is used here to mean a state of being in which one is not able to carry on with the business of living in his culture by use of his own resources, skills, abilities, and knowledge. The dependent then is one who needs resources that enable him to perform legitimate social roles that he is not now performing satisfactorily either in his judgment or in the judgment of society. The resources needed may be his own, of which he's unaware, or those that have been or could be socially provided. The role of social work is to create or restore a state of being which allows the dependent person to become an interdependent unit of social interaction.

Atherton's definition offers a useful common framework from which social workers, regardless of the practice setting, can attempt to assess their performance. In this framework, practitioners can view the results of practice as attempts to reduce certain forms of dependency and to increase clients' independent behavior in such a way that they gain maximum human freedom.

For the practitioner and research worker, the problem is to identify clearly outcome measures that (1) reflect the goals of the profession, and (2) are specific enough that others can measure them in the same way. This latter feature is essential for the production of basic knowledge that can be replicated.

Selecting Outcome Measures

The selection of worthwhile outcome measures for social work practice depends in part on their reliability and validity (discussed in chapter 3). However, the selection process also is influenced by the practical question of what is being evaluated. The beginning social work practitioner will encounter several kinds of evaluation research. The most basic kind of evaluation concerns the research evaluation of direct professional social work services provided to specific clients by a specific practitioner. This form of evaluation may focus on a specific problem group, such as juvenile delinquents or child-abusing parents, or it may examine a special practice technique, such as behavior shaping. All social work practitioners are concerned with this type of evaluation research; the selection of appropriate outcome measures reflecting objectives of the practitioner is extremely important. Specifically, evaluating direct social work services supplies evidence the profession needs to justify its continued existence.

A second type of research confronting many practitioners may be broadly termed "program evaluation," involving the assessment of an entire program of services. Such programs may or may not involve professional social work services. For example, in many programs, such as Big Brothers or Big Sisters, direct services to clients are provided by volunteers rather than by social work professionals. The social work staff often serves in an administrative capacity—screening and matching applicants, raising money to operate the program, and providing program direction, supervision, and general administrative services. Even though programs such as these are required to employ valid and reliable outcome measures, their outcome measures may differ from those used for direct services. The measures selected for each will depend on the objectives of each. One type of program may establish broad objectives—the reduction of juvenile delinquency, for instance. To evaluate this kind of program, specific outcome measures—criteria that paint a valid picture of how well an objective is achieved—are necessary. In contrast, the practitioner providing direct services may prescribe a much more limited objective for a given client. If the particular goal is to improve a child's school attendance, for example, the outcome measure will be unique to that case.

A third category of outcome measures concerns the services provided to families and groups. Many social workers are committed to the professional goal of maintaining and enhancing family life, a goal consistent with the professed sentiments of the United States Government and of many religious organizations. Many social service agencies are committed to providing family solidarity and enhancing the quality of family life. Evaluating services in these cases requires outcome measures that are reliable and valid for assessing certain characteristics of families, rather than the traits of individuals.

Historical Development of Outcome Measures in Social Work

Because an existing outcome measure may fill a research worker's requirements, practitioners familiar with extant measures often can save themselves the time and expense of developing a new measure. The following review of social work research efforts (1) familiarizes the beginning social work student with some of the past research programs in the profession, and (2) reviews some of the outcome measures currently employed in social work practice and research.

The Community Service Scale

The staff of the New York Community Service Society worked a number of years to develop its Community Service Scale—a standardized method for assessing the results of social casework. The CSS requires the caseworker to write a detailed case summary describing four client characteristics: adaptive efficiency, disabling habits and conditions, verbalized attitudes and understanding, and environmental circumstances. The worker is required to assess client change or "movement" in terms of these four general categories. Hunt and Kogan operationally define movement as "the change that occurs in an individual client and/or in his environmental circumstance between the opening and closing of his case as judged by a trained caseworker."[2] The worker is required to judge the amount of movement in each category on a scale ranging from $+4$ through 0 to -2. A $+4$ signifies great improvement; a -2 indicates considerable client deterioration (despite treatment) in a particular category. The CSS approach attempts to standardize caseworker judgment so it can be used as a reliable measure of change in clients.

Research studies on this important instrument have established a pattern that has influenced the subsequent development of outcome measures in social work. This pattern exhibits several common features that have persisted in other instruments. First, the CSS Movement Scale uses the caseworker's judgments as an outcome measure. The CSS research has established that, given the proper instruments, such as the anchored judgment scales, caseworkers can indeed make reliable judgments. Further, they established that reliability coefficients can be increased by providing special training to the raters.[3] The extent to which these judgments provide a valid measure of change is open to considerable question, however. Briar concluded that the CSS studies were not successful in their attempt to validate the movement measures as predictors of client functioning.[4]

A second characteristic of the CSS research, a feature that also has been employed in other outcome measures, is its use of case records as the basis for judgment measures. The reliability of this procedure remains open to criticism.

The St. Paul Scale

The CSS research has been followed by several other research projects that have developed other similar instruments. Among those was the St. Paul Scale of Family Functioning, developed by the St. Paul Family Centered

Project.[5] This scale, and others that followed, assessed family functioning rather than individual functioning. Like the CSS Scale, the St. Paul instrument uses social worker judgments to assess outcome.

The Geismar Scale

Ludwig Geismar, the principal author of the St. Paul scale, later developed his own version of a scale to measure family functioning.[6] His approach requires that the family be regarded as a social system. Geismar developed a scheme that contains descriptions of family functions, described in the form of scales. These scales include nine general categories:

- Family relationships and family unity
- Individual behavior and adjustment
- Care and training of children
- Social activities
- Economic practices
- Home and household practices
- Health conditions and practices
- Relationship to social workers
- Use of community resources

Briefly, social workers using the Geismar Family Functioning Scale collect information, write a case study, and make scaled judgments about how well the family functions. Geismar reports that his scale's degree of reliability is high. He studied inter-rater reliability using two or more independent raters: agreement on their scores was in excess of 85 percent.

Geismar also asserts that the Family Functioning Scale's validity is high, and that it compares favorably with CSS Scale results for the same cases. Performing such comparisons is a standard procedure for determining validity: results obtained with a new instrument (in this case the Family Functioning Scale) are compared with the results of another standardized instrument (CSS Scale).

The impact of the CSS instrument, the St. Paul Scale, and the Geismar Family Functioning Scale can be documented by examining the major evaluation research reported in social work literature. In a series of now classic evaluation studies, conducted mostly in the 1960s and early 1970s, these scales were used extensively. They also were supplemented with a variety of other outcome measures.

The Vocational High Study

One of the evaluation studies using the CSS Movement Scale received considerable notoriety within the social work profession. It is described in a book entitled *Girls at Vocational High.*[7] In this comparative study, research workers provided casework and groupwork services to 189 adolescent girls who had demonstrated school problems and delinquent behavior. The experimental group of 189 was compared to a control group of 192 similar girls. In other words, this study employed a classic experimental design involving an experimental group and a control group, both selected randomly. Differences between girls in the two groups were studied by means of before-and-after evaluations based on a variety of outcome measures.

Outcome measures used in this study included the CSS Movement Scale, academic grades in school, and conduct at school. Investigators used sixteen measures of school performance and behavior, including such factors as whether a girl dropped out or finished school, whether she advanced with her class or fell behind, and whether or not she was truant. Health records and the number of out-of-wedlock pregnancies were also compared. Several psychological tests were used, including two personality tests: the Cattell Junior Personality Quiz, and a sentence-completion test designed by the staff. Attitude tests and some sociometric devices also were used.

Yet, despite the impressive range of outcome measures, the results of this study revealed few statistically significant differences between the experimental group and the control group.

Although this study often is cited as an indictment of social work, nonetheless it provides a useful example of the difficulty of selecting appropriate outcome measures. In a thorough critique of the research conducted in this project, Macdonald pointed out: "The authors gave little attention to the validity and reliability of the instruments for this assessment."[8]

The Chemung County Case

Another instructive inquiry was one known as the Chemung County Study.[9] In it, the major research question asked was whether professional social workers are more effective than untrained workers in the rehabilitation of multiproblem families. Since this study focused on the family rather than on individuals, the outcome measures selected for its use included the St. Paul Scale of Family Functioning and the CSS Movement Scale. The study's design involved before-and-after measurements, an experimental group and a control group, and a second control group that was assessed only after the experiment (an "after only" group).

The research did not demonstrate any statistically significant differences between the experimental and control groups on the outcome measures used. The authors did comment, however, on the high degree of agreement between the two instruments. They reported that a case-by-case comparison was made of the scores on each of the two measures. They found: "In more than 40 percent of the cases the ratings were the same, while in another 40 percent the differences were no greater than one degree."[10]

The Area Development Project
A third study also involved the provision of services to multiproblem families. Workers on the Area Development Project[11] provided a special program of extensive casework, groupwork, and community organization services to an experimental group of ninety-two multiproblem families. Outcome measures of these families were compared with those of a group of 122 control families who were provided the "ordinary" community services; assignment to the two groups was by random selection. The outcome measure used was the St. Paul Scale of Family Functioning. Research results showed that the group receiving the special program of services (the experimental group) improved significantly over the control group.

The New Haven Neighborhood Improvement Project
This project also involved services to multiproblem families. This study[12] provided a program of diverse services to an experimental group of thirty families. These families were evaluated by comparing them with a control group with similar characteristics. Before-and-after measures were taken of the experimental group and of the comparison group. Again, since the focus of this research was on family functioning, the outcome measures reflect that purpose. The St. Paul Scale of Family Functioning was selected as one of the outcome measures. Several other outcome measures also were used, however; these included delinquency rates and the economic dependency of residents. On the St. Paul Scale of Family Functioning, results of this study showed significant improvements for the experimental group. The other outcome measures, however, showed no statistically significant differences.

Serving the Aging
This is the title of another experiment that used some of the outcome measures considered here. This project[13] provided a series of health and social services to a population of aging New York City residents. The study employed a design that compared three different types of service. One group of 142 clients received the regular ongoing services provided through one of the district offices of the Community Services Society. A second group of 139 clients received special services for the aging, limited to four interviews in a two-month period. A third group of 42 clients received a combined service consisting of collaborative services between a caseworker and a public health nurse. There was no limit on the number of interviews for the latter group.

In this study the short-term service and the combined services constituted the experimental programs, which were compared to the regular service group. Evaluations were based on a variety of outcome measures, including the CSS Movement Scale, physical and mental health records, mortality, morale, and similar variables. The results of the study do not indicate that either of the experimental programs of service to the elderly were convincingly superior to the agency's normal service program.

Other Elements of Measurement

This review of research is not intended to be a comprehensive overview of social work evaluation research. But it gives the reader a sample of some of the outcome measures used in social work. Other aspects of research use a variety of other outcome measures; they are difficult to classify, however, because of their diversity. A partial list of commonly used outcome measures includes client self-reports, evaluation by the practitioner, evaluation by a trained observer, evaluation by others in the natural environment, behavioral measures, measures of cognitive factors, social indicators, individualized treatment outcome measures, and measures of family functioning. These can be classified according to two major dimensions—content and source.

Content refers to the exact focus of the measure. By example, behavioral measures, cognitive measures, family functioning scales, and social indicators each focus on different content.

The *source* of a measure may greatly affect its quality. Measures consisting of client self-reports differ from those obtained through practitioner evaluation; evaluations by trained observers differ from reports by clients' family members.

In all cases, the evaluation incorporates at least these two dimensions: source and content. In some cases, the outcome measure may involve more than one area of content and also may have more than one data source.

Client Self-Reports

Self-reports are among the oldest outcome measures in social work and related human services. Depending on the theoretical orientation of the practitioner, such procedures may be labeled self-monitoring, self-recording, or self-observation. Clients using self-reports may be asked to record episodes of a specified behavior as well as events that surround the behavior. They may also be asked to report feelings, thoughts, dreams, or discomfort.

Thoresen and Mahoney suggest that self-observation may be divided into phases.[14] The first phase is discrimination, in which the person must decide whether or not the behavior or feeling has occurred. Accurate discrimination must be guided by a clear operational definition. The second phase consists of recording the feeling or behavior. To ensure accuracy, the person must record the incident at the time of occurrence, rather than later rely on memory alone.

Self-monitoring and reporting procedures are widely used to collect information about cognitive or covert outcomes. For the self-recording of behavioral outcomes, a variety of methods exists. Frequency counts are perhaps the most commonly used self-reports. Subjects record each occurrence of a response and the time it occurred. This procedure is useful where the target behavior, such as nail biting, is discrete and relatively low in frequency.

Frequency Counts

Some target behaviors—such as watching television or talking on the telephone—are not discrete but continue over a period of time. In these cases, it may be more practical to record the amount of time the individual performs the behavior, rather than the frequency alone, thus gaining a measure of both frequency and duration.

Thoresen and Mahoney note that frequency counts are often impossible to obtain for certain covert behaviors, such as thoughts or urges, because these may run together with no clear onset and clear end. Also impractical to record are the occurrences of behaviors that have high rates of frequency. A practical solution to these and similar problems is the use of time sampling methods. These methods involve measuring the behavior for specific time intervals—for fifteen minutes every four hours, for example.

Research workers have developed different devices to help them gather and record self-report data. The most popular is the paper-and-pencil technique, using five by eight inch cards to list the behavior, days of the week, and the time in one-hour increments. The client then has only to check the appropriate time and day for each instance (Figure 5–1).

Cards of this type could be used to collect frequency counts of almost any single behavior. The data can then be summarized and used as an outcome measure.

Another paper-and-pencil device is a behavioral diary, in which the client keeps a more detailed record of the behavior and the events surrounding it.

Electronic devices and mechanical counters, such as golf-stroke counters, also have proved useful. Many people concerned with exercise and weight control use some form of pedometer, which fastens to the clothing and automatically counts the number of steps taken daily. Other devices include stopwatches and alarm clocks, and electronic equipment such as audio or videotape recordings. The use of these and other devices may be somewhat limited, however, by such factors as time, cost, and convenience.

Reactivity

The very act of self-monitoring may produce changes in the client. These changes are called the reactive effects of self-recording. They sometimes are produced by the client's self-measuring the outcome variables.

	Sunday	Monday	Tuesday	Wednesday	Thursday	Friday	Saturday
6 AM							
7 AM							
8 AM							
9 AM							
10 AM							
11 AM							
12 N							
1 PM							
2 PM							
3 PM							
4 PM							
5 PM							
6 PM							
7 PM							
8 PM							
9 PM							
10 PM							

For the week of _____

FIGURE 5-1. Self-Recording Device

51

There is some evidence that the process of self-monitoring actually can affect the behavior itself. However, different research findings concerning reactivity are not entirely consistent. Thomas, Abrams, and Johnson studied the effects of self-monitoring on the frequency of multiple tics and concluded that self-recording resulted in a reduction in frequency.[15] In another experiment, McKenzie and Ruskall demonstrated that self-monitoring could help reduce absenteeism and tardiness among school children participating in an athletic program.[16]

Many practitioners deliberately use the reactivity of self-monitoring as therapy. They find that one who remains constantly aware of a problem may try harder to help oneself. For example, some practitioners report that the self-monitoring of tardiness for high school students results in a decrease in tardiness. Others use self-monitoring to help people treat undesirable behaviors ranging from nail biting to excessive drinking.

On the other hand, research workers have demonstrated that under some conditions self-monitoring is not reactive. For example, Mahoney, Maura, and Wade reported that self-recording of weight and eating habits failed to influence subjects' weight loss and eating habits.[17] And Kantorowitz, Walters, and Pezdek explored the effects of self-monitoring on cigarette smoking; they reported that self-monitoring techniques did not significantly affect their subjects' smoking rates.[18]

It appears that self-monitoring is sometimes but not always reactive. Reactivity seems to depend on the nature of the behavior, on the timing of self-monitoring, and on its duration—among other variables. To better assess the possible reactivity of self-report data, investigators may wish to use a control group.

Reliability of Self-Monitoring

The reliability of self-monitoring data is important in evaluating those data as outcome variables. Of course, some information simply cannot be obtained except by self-report; thus, its reliability must remain unverified. Reports on such covert behaviors as thoughts, urges, and feelings are available only from the client. And there is no way to determine objectively the accuracy of such reports because covert behaviors cannot be observed by others.

To verify the reliability of self-reports on overt behaviors, researchers can compare client reports with data collected by other observers. Here again, the research reports on reliability are not consistent. Some studies show relatively high reliability for self-recording.[16,17] Others, however, indicate fairly low reliability. Various research workers who found poor reliability indicate that the degree of correspondence between self-report data and observer-collected data ranges from approximately 35 percent to approximately 75 percent.[19]

Proper training and reinforcement may increase the reliability of self-report data.[20] Reliability can also be increased by teaching clients to report their covert behaviors at times when doing so does not conflict with other activities.

Self-reports of covert behaviors can provide important sources of data that can be obtained in no other way. And self-monitoring may be a worthwhile technique. But research evidence indicates that self-report data may not be reliable unless the subject is carefully taught self-reporting techniques and strategies.

Howe has developed some guidelines for evaluating client self-reports in social work research.[21] He recommends that research workers:

1. Make intensive efforts to check the reliability of self-reports, including using trained observers to spot-check the accuracy of observation and recording techniques.
2. Use public classifications of behavior, not private schemes.
3. Make efforts to ensure that the client's problem is consistent with the behavior under observation.
4. Ensure that client recording is not done before or during the time the problem behaviors occur.
5. Construct behavioral codes and instruments that are simple, concise, and easy to use.
6. Emphasize the observation of positive conduct instead of negative behaviors, when possible.
7. Stress the accuracy and completeness of observations and recording, regardless of the outcome.
8. Use personal follow-up methods, such as phone calls and home visits, to determine if the client data are valid.
9. Provide clients training in observation and recording.

Evaluation by the Practitioner

Practitioner evaluation constitutes one of the most widely used outcome measures in social work research. It is basic to the CSS Movement Scale and the Geismar Family Functioning Scale. For analysis, the technique can be divided into three phases: data collection, recording, and data analysis.

For all the instruments already described, the social worker performs data collection through a variety of techniques—including office interviews, home visits, meetings with other members of the family, meetings with other social agency staff, and client self-reports.

In the recording phase for each of these instruments, the social worker employs a standardized recording format to ensure appropriate coverage. For example, in the CSS Movement Scale, the social worker records data that fit the four categories described as types of evidence of client movement. These are adaptive efficiency, disabling habits and conditions, verbalized attitudes, and understanding and environmental circumstances.[2] The recording is generally accomplished through written case records.

Finally, in the analysis phase the worker evaluates the case record to determine if any client change or movement has occurred. This analysis is accomplished in the CSS Movement Scale and in the Family Functioning Scale by use of an anchored numerical scale. With this measure, the professional estimates the extent of change in each category of behavior included in the case record. Descriptive case illustrations are provided as a frame of reference to anchor judgments about movement.

The use of professional judgments as outcome data may suffer from several limitations. In the data collecting phase, for example, observations may take place in office interviews or in home visits—but conditions for either of these methods are not standardized. This is an important consideration, because there may be a difference in the reactivity of data collected under different conditions. Some researchers have reported reactive effects, for example, from data collected in a home visit in a family setting.[22] But others report that information collected in applied settings, such as in a professional office, hospital ward, or school classroom, is less subject to reactivity.[23]

These findings suggest that data obtained under different conditions may not be comparable. Consequently, when using practitioner judgments for outcome measures, the research worker needs to specify the conditions under which data are collected.

The recording phase presents a second consideration in the use of practitioner judgments. Many social workers are reluctant to take extensive notes during an interview. They often write case records afterwards, relying on brief outline notes and memory to help reconstruct interview data. Postinterview recording can cause errors in the data; the practitioner is likely to forget certain elements in an interview. Another possibility for error arises when the practitioner selectively records only those elements he or she considers important.

These recording practices may produce incomplete and unreliable data. The problem can be reduced by workers' using mechanical or electronic recording devices, such as tape recorders, or special recording aids, such as checklists, during the interview.

The data analysis phase offers another chance for error. Both the CSS Movement Scale and the Geismar Family Functioning Scale may be analyzed and scored by someone other than the practitioner. This feature is necessary to produce objective outcome measures. It allows the research worker to determine the reliability of the data analysis procedure by comparing the extent of agreement among different raters. For both these instruments, the inter-rater reliability scores are reasonably high, but are based on comparisons of independent ratings for the analysis phase only.

Hunt and Kogan reported that inter-rater reliability for the CSS Movement Scale increased by providing training for the raters. The technique of separating the data analysis from the previous two steps of observation and recording is an excellent safeguard against possible practitioner bias. The objectivity of the professional comes into question because in effect he or she also is the subject of evaluation. To lessen the chance of bias, therefore, separating the data collection and recording steps from the data analysis phase should be standard practice in outcome evaluation. When this distinction is not made, less reliable results are produced.

Measures of Family Functioning

Many social service programs aim to improve family functioning. Consequently, a great many efforts to devise measures of changes in family functioning have been made. The Geismar Family Functioning Scale reviewed earlier in this chapter stands out as an example of this campaign. Other standardized assessment techniques and instruments also exist.

Instruments for assessing family functioning can be divided into three major groups, each concerning a different aspect of family life: measures of marital adjustment, measures of parent–child interaction, and measures of overall family functioning.

Marital Adjustment

The assessment of couples' compatibility is important to social work practitioners whose concern is marital problems and their consequences, such as separation, divorce, broken families, unhappiness, and depression. A variety of marital adjustment and marital prediction instruments is in widespread use. One such measure, developed by Locke and Wallace, has been widely used in social work research. The Locke-Wallace Marital Adjustment Test consists of a structured self-report inventory of thirty-five items. The authors have reported high reliability and validity figures both for the test's marital adjustment and the marital prediction components.[24]

Other authors (both before and after development of the Locke-Wallace Test) have designed a number of other marital adjustment inventories. In 1976, Spanier reported the development of a new scale to assess the quality of marriages.[25] In many respects, Spanier's Dyadic Adjustment Scale is an updated revision of the Locke-Wallace instrument. The thirty-two-item self-report measure is designed for use by married or unmarried couples.

Spanier's scale focuses entirely on adjustment; it does not deal with marital prediction, as does the Locke-Wallace instrument. Spanier provides an impressive array of sophisticated information on the scale's reliability and validity.

In addition to these two scales, which provide standardized outcome measures for assessing marital relationships, other instruments may help individual practitioners to evaluate and guide a marital counseling practice. One such instrument is the Marital Pre-Counseling Inventory developed by Stuart and Stuart.[26] This inventory consists of a self-evaluation form that each marital partner can complete separately. It is contained in an eleven-page booklet, divided into thirteen areas, and accompanied by detailed instructions for its use. The Stuart inventory is a behavior-oriented device that helps the practitioner examine specific problem areas in the marital relationship. No data are available on its reliability and validity; nonetheless, it may serve as a useful device for the practitioner who wants to standardize marriage assessments. It also may be a worthwhile outcome measure for marriage counselors.

Parent–Child Interaction

One of the most comprehensive systems for assessing parent–child interaction is the Behavioral Coding System developed by Patterson and his associates.[27,28] This approach assesses and treats behaviorally deviant children in the home. Using Behavioral Coding System procedures, trained observers audit parent–child interactions in the home. These measures are supplemented by parental telephone report data and by observation in other natural settings, such as school classrooms.

The Behavioral Coding System for observing and coding family interaction is complex, involving twenty-nine behavioral code definitions. Each is behaviorally specific. The manual for home observation contains descriptions of behaviors, of the observation system, and of how family interactions are coded.[28] Detailed information also is provided about the training of observers.

The Behavioral Coding System was developed over a period of approximately eight years; Patterson cites a considerable amount of research indicating high levels of reliability and validity.

The Behavioral Coding System is a sophisticated and complex assessment procedure that offers great promise as a means of standardizing naturalistic data collection for family research. It offers a comprehensive assessment system that can be employed both in natural settings and in clinical settings. The extensive research on reliability and validity of the BCS eclipses what has been done on most other measures of family interaction.

Measures of General Family Functioning

The measures of parent–child interaction were developed to analyze specialized aspects of family functioning. However, many practitioners are concerned primarily with methods of assessing overall family functioning, such as are provided by the Geismar Scale of Family Functioning. In addition to the Geismar instrument, many other measures with similar capabilities have been developed. Most of the measures of family functioning are based on two data sources: self-report retrospective data from interviews and questionnaires, and direct observations of behavior in a treatment setting or a limited home visit. Very few of the available measures of family functioning are based on systematic in-home observations. Patterson's Behavioral Coding System represents a significant departure from tradition in this area of family research. Building on this approach, Steinglass developed a new method for observing families in their homes.[29]

Steinglass's method is the Home Observation Assessment Method. The HOAM is a system for conducting in-home observations of family interaction over extended time periods. It is based on the use of a behavioral coding system similar to Patterson's. HOAM coding is performed by two highly trained behavioral observers; each follows one adult in the subject family, observing and recording behavior. A time-sampling recording system is used, and recorders may spend as much as four hours for each in-home coding session. Steinglass reported evidence of satisfactorily high levels of reliability and validity.

Hudson, Acklen, and Bartosh have developed an excellent scale to measure intrafamily stress.[30] Their Index of Family Relations is a twenty-five-item self-report measure that is unique because it was developed specifically for use in social work practice. Hudson and associates characterize the IFR as a short-form instrument designed to measure problems in family relationships. It measures intrafamily stress without regard for any specific dyadic component of the family. In other words, it measures problems in family relationships as seen by a specific member of the family. For comparison purposes, social workers may use the scale individually with each family member.

According to its developers, the IFR "can be used by social workers who are not behaviorally oriented to monitor and evaluate clients' progress in treatment on a case-by-case basis."[31] It is a useful measurement device for social work practitioners who regularly conduct family treatment. The IFR can be administered at selected intervals during treatment to determine whether the problem in the family relationship is improving. Then, if necessary, workers may redirect intervention efforts.

Of all the instruments for measuring family relationships, the IFR is the most appealing because it is based on convincing research for both reliability and validity. Hudson and associates reported high levels for both characteristics.

In summary, the measures of family functioning may be specialized or general. Two of the specialized measures are measures of marital adjustment and measures of parent-child interaction. More global measures of family functioning also are available. When conducting research on the family, the research worker should attempt to specify as precisely as possible the area of family functioning to be studied, to allow the most appropriate measures to be selected.

Behavioral and Cognitive Measures

The content of diverse outcome measures may differ according to the kind of data sought. Data may be classified according to two major distinctions—presence or absence of external sources of verification. That is, the kinds of measures that may be applied to a behavior depend on whether it is observable (overt) or may only be speculated about (covert).

Behavioral measures evaluate the overt characteristics of a subject's behavior. Behavior consists of three dimensions—frequency, duration, and quality, which can be consistently assessed by independent observers. Frequency refers to how often the behavior occurs. Duration refers to how long it lasts. Quality is the accuracy or precision of the behavior. Measuring the quality of a behavior is more difficult than measuring frequency or duration. To measure quality, the social worker must discriminate between behaviors that meet a specific criterion and those that do not. In other words, the worker must distinguish between acceptable behaviors and unacceptable behaviors.

These three dimensions provide objective criteria by which independent observers can readily measure a behavior. Behaviors can be measured in these terms, and the measurements may be verified by independent observers. Consequently, properly defined behavioral measures should possess the quality of reliability.

Cognitive measures assess private, covert events, such as thoughts, feelings, urges, or fantasies known only to the individual who experiences them. Cognitive events, though more difficult to measure and assess, are equal in importance to behavioral events, because often they involve the private thoughts that may be linked to behaviors. The separation of behavioral and cognitive measures may be convenient to the researcher, but it is not an accurate reflection of the human condition. The measurement of cognitive events is limited to self-report methods only; there are no direct methods to validate measures of cognitive events.

Nisbett and Wilson note that cognitive events are the subject of increasing attention in the area of behavioral research. After reviewing some of the problems of assessing cognitive events, they reported that these events are best amenable to assessment through the use of self-monitoring techniques, questionnaires, and interviews.[32]

In contrast to cognitive events, which are private, overt behaviors are available for observation by independent observers and can be objectively defined. Because behaviors are easier to measure and because highly reliable measuring systems are available for them, behavioral measures have become a popular outcome measure among many practitioners and researchers. Behavioral data may be gathered by self-reports or by direct behavioral observers.

Self-report methods allow clients to monitor and report specific behaviors occurring in their normal living experiences. Self-reports are researchers' only means of monitoring cognitive events and some other tangible but private events. Many practitioners use self-reports for dual purposes—to collect information about the effects of treatment, and to harness the reactive, therapeutic power of some self-monitoring procedures. The major limitations of self-monitoring processes are related to problems of poor reliability, and sometimes to the reactivity of the measure.

Kanfer and Saslow have developed an excellent guide for conducting a behavioral interview.[33] Their behavioral interview guidelines could help in the collection of research outcome data and provide the information necessary for developing a treatment plan.

Behavioral surveys, questionnaires, and inventories offer reasonable alternative methods for collecting behavioral data. Good inventories can provide a quick, inexpensive, and reliable measure of selected behaviors. Critical factors in their use are the proper selection of an instrument and paying careful attention to reliability and validity.

Numerous behavioral self-report inventories, questionnaires, and checklists—many developed for specialized purposes—have become available. The Marital Pre-Counseling Inventory developed by Stuart and Stuart is one example.[26] Literally hundreds of other specialized behavioral self-report measures are available; for example:

- The Dating Frequency Questionnaire is a self-report checklist focused on dating frequency and problems.[34]
- The Marital Activities Inventory deals with marital adjustment and leisure time activities.[35]
- The Eating Patterns Questionnaire is a self-report measure designed to gather information about specific patterns of eating; results are used to help therapists design changes in eating behaviors.[36]
- The Behavioral Fear Questionnaire, based on self-reports, helps analyze fears of snakes, rats, beetles, and spiders.[37]
- The Fear Survey Schedule contains a list of fifty common fears that the client rates in order of personal importance.[38]

These examples are only a few of many available specialized behavioral self-report measures. Haynes gives a comprehensive review of available instruments.[39]

The behavioral self-report measures offer several benefits to research workers and practitioners. They are relatively inexpensive, easy to administer, and may save time. Most important, they offer a standardized method of collecting data. The value of this advantage lies in the potential ease of replication. If the data collection method is standardized, it can be repeated with some precision. As with other outcome measures, however, the behavioral self-report measure is subject to reliability and validity requirements.

Observation is the second major method of collecting behavioral data. Direct monitoring of an individual's behavior by an independent observer is probably the most important form of behavioral measurement. The major advantage of observation is that investigators can assess reliability by comparing the reports of several observers. Further, behavioral observations may be conducted in a variety of locations by a variety of people. Behavior can be observed in natural settings, such as at home and in school, or in simulated settings at a clinic or laboratory. Observations can be conducted by professional practitioners or by other specially trained observers, including parents and family members.

Individualized Outcome Measures

Because much of social work practice is oriented to providing casework services to individuals with specialized problems, many social workers find the idea of developing individualized outcome measures for each case very appealing. If a person seeks help for a problem in marital adjustment, for example, practitioners would attempt to develop an outcome measure that reflects the unique characteristics of that person's situation. This idea is not new or unusual; Mary Richmond and other early social work writers emphasized the need to individualize both treatment and evaluation.[40]

The individualized approach has two major limitations: the variability of the evaluation procedures, and the lack of specification of outcome measures. Recent developments in assessment techniques offer possible solutions to these problems. Simply stated, the criteria for the acceptable use of individualized outcome measures are the extent to which a given measure can be replicated and the validity of the measure. Replication requires both an adequate description of the data collection method and a detailed description of what is being measured.

The problem of specification of individual outcome has been examined by a number of mental health researchers. Bergin conducted an extensive review of research dealing with psychotherapy outcomes. His recommendation: "Outcome research should be directed toward answering *what* treatment, by *whom*, is most effective for *this* individual with *that* specific problem, and under *which* set of circumstances"[41] (authors' italics). Bergin also suggested that outcome research should shift its emphasis from general to more specific outcomes.

Evaluation Procedures

A procedure that was developed by mental health professionals and offers promise for use in social work is *Goal Attainment Scaling.*[42] Compton and Galaway have incorporated Goal Attainment Scaling into a social work practice framework. They describe the procedure as a useful method of developing measurable, concrete goals for social work practice. According to these writers, "Goal Attainment Scaling is particularly useful to the social work practitioner because it permits the individualization of goals."[43]

Goal Attainment Scaling employs four steps. Workers first collect information about the individual or organization involved. Next, they list the major areas in which change would be feasible and is needed. They then develop specific outcome predictions for each of these major areas. Finally, in a follow-up interview, workers score the outcomes.

A similar procedure created by Weed was designated the Problem Oriented Record.[44] The POR was developed for medical use; however, Klonoff and Cox adapted the system to evaluate and measure treatment outcomes in psychiatry.[45]

Within the social work profession, several writers also have developed specific procedures for establishing individualized treatment goals. Kane demonstrated that the POR can facilitate evaluation in social work practice. Her approach requires that "practitioners would need to define problems at the outset and these would not disappear until solved or consciously reformulated."[46] She views the POR as a technique to help social workers determine if their goals have been met.

Reid and Epstein devised a system for identification and specification of individualized treatment goals. Their approach involves the following series of steps: The practitioner and the client jointly explore problems of concern to the client; they define the problems in explicit behavioral terms; they rank them in order of priority; they select a particular "target problem" and further clarify it by joint exploration. Finally, "An explicit agreement between the caseworker and client is called for. Usually the caseworker states the substance of what he and the client have apparently agreed upon."[47]

The system allows for working on more than one problem; however, Reid and Epstein call for specification of priorities when several problems are to be treated. They also have a system, called the Task Achievement Scale, for evaluating the outcome of practice. Their scale measures the "extent to which a given task is accomplished."[48] It consists of four different definitions of task achievement levels. The authors report high reliability for this scale in tests comparing ratings by independent judges. They also have attempted to establish validity for the procedure by using, as a criterion, the client's own assessment of change, then comparing it with the results obtained on the Task Achievement Scale.

The Reid and Epstein approach offers some unique advantages as an outcome measure for social work practice. Its principal advantage is that it is already thoroughly integrated into a theory and method of social work practice. It is easy to understand and to use. The resulting outcome measures are specified in a manner that allows for replication, which makes this a valuable tool for social work research.

Wodarski and Bagarozzi also provide for the collection of individualized outcome data. Applying some principles of behavior modification to social work practice, they recommend that outcome assessment should involve three essential operations. (1) Social workers should analyze, in terms of observable events, the behaviors chosen for modification. (2) Workers should define the behaviors in such a way that two observers can agree consistently that the target behavior has occurred. (3) Workers should systematically collect data to determine whether any antecedent or consequent events (that is, behaviors that immediately precede or follow the target behavior) are influencing the problem behavior.[49]

Wodarski and Bagarozzi list five techniques that can be used to help collect assessment data. These techniques are: self-inventories, behavior interviews, behavior samples, behavioral diaries, and baseline measures. They recommend that a contract between client and worker be used as a record of treatment objectives.

The methods advocated by Wodarski and Bagarozzi are consistent with behavioral practice in other helping professions; they also can be successfully integrated into social work practice.

Single-Subject Methodology

One approach to the problem of designing reliable and valid individualized outcome measures offers both flexibility and scientific rigor. It is contained in the single-subject design methodology (described fully in chapter 8).

The single-subject design offers an unusual degree of flexibility. It can be used to study a broad range of individual client problems. It can also be used in a variety of theoretical frameworks. Further, it gives practitioners a powerful set of tools for evaluating and assessing outcome in social work practice. This approach to evaluation has been incorporated into social work practice by a number of practice researchers.

Bloom presents an extremely useful approach to the use of single-subject designs in practice.[50] His system is the Problem-Oriented Evaluation Procedure. The PEP system involves four steps. Practitioners first identify the precise nature of the client's problems. Next, they monitor the target events during the intervention period. Then, they compare the number of events during intervention with the number of preintervention occurrences. Last, practitioners evaluate how well any changes in client behavior have fulfilled the intervention plans.

Bloom's measurement system is guided by the requirements for scientific investigation and works well within a social work context. Bloom claims good reliability and validity for the PEP system. The use of independent observers ensures reliability. Bloom addresses validity by discussing content validity, predictive validity, and construct validity within the context of a single case.

Some of the other authors incorporating the elements of single subject design into social work practice models include Hudson,[51] Jayaratne and Levy,[52] Howe,[53] and Fischer.[54]

The single-subject design strategy offers both the flexibility and the rigor required to design individualized outcome measures for use in social work. The method has been tested and adapted for social work practice and has been used by a variety of practitioners. Incorporated into practice theory and methods by practice theorists, it offers an excellent solution to a recurring problem in the profession.

Negative Outcomes

Research reports express increasing concern with the possible negative outcomes of all forms of human service interventions, including those resulting from social work practice. Bergin and Lambert conducted a comprehensive review of research concerning evaluation of therapeutic outcomes. Their position was that "treatments which are capable of producing beneficial effects are capable of also producing harmful effects."[55] Bergin used the term *deterioration effect* to describe the condition of clients who were worse after treatment.

Fischer conducted a review of outcome studies in social work.[56] He expressed concern over finding that approximately half of those clients who were the subjects of outcome research either deteriorated to a greater degree, or improved at a slower rate, than did control subjects. The clients in these studies were for the most part either multiproblem families or juvenile delinquents, and the criteria for improvement ranged from mortality to ratings of client and family functioning.

Hartley and colleagues discovered evidence of a deterioration effect in clients involved in encounter groups as a form of treatment.[57] Lieberman and his colleagues also revealed similar findings of deterioration associated with some forms of group treatment.[58] Guttman reported deterioration among some clients receiving conjoint family therapy.[59] Richard Stuart, in

63

studying the problem, concluded that "the patient who enters psychotherapy does so not without a distinct risk of deterioration or of simply wasting his time and money."[60]

Bergin and Lambert reached a similar conclusion after reviewing therapeutic outcome research for a variety of human services. Their summary of the deterioration problem states that "the 'deterioration effect' is a significant problem . . . that is not limited to individual psychotherapy."[55]

Although some practitioners have found fault with the deterioration findings of some research work, the consistency of the findings across methods, professions, and theoretical orientations suggests that there really is a cause for concern. However difficult the idea is to accept, the responsible practitioner must be prepared to collect negative outcome data as well as positive data. It is not easy to anticipate all the negative effects treatment may engender. For example, the practitioner working with a married couple may find that a decision to treat either partner as an individual may improve that partner—but may further damage the marriage. Other, more subtle, negative outcomes include factors such as sustained and unrealistic dependency on the practitioner. Even though this result may be gratifying to the practitioner, it may have negative consequences for the client.

Social workers have no standardized deterioration measures to apply in practice. However, any outcome measure selected should reflect both positive and negative effects. When collecting data, it is important to plan to collect the full range of data available, including the negative outcomes.

Program Evaluation

The evaluation of social service programs, like the evaluation of social work practice, involves the selection and use of outcome measures. However, although the methods are essentially the same, and the same research designs may be used, sometimes different outcome measures are needed.

Outcome measures for programs are derived from an analysis of the goals and objectives of the program itself. Clearly identifying a program's specific objectives often is difficult because many program directors have described their objectives in terms that are too vague. It is hard to imagine, for example, an outcome measure that would reflect such broad statements as "improving the lot of mankind," or "alleviating human suffering." To confuse the potential program evaluator further, many programs describe their objectives in terms of the frequency and types of their services, rather than in terms of the possible outcomes of those services. An agency might, for example, announce that its objective is to provide counseling services for one thousand unmarried mothers in a given year. Fine, but how may the evaluator appraise the quality and value of that counseling?

Program evaluators can ease their task by examining separately the two major aspects of program objectives: efficiency and effectiveness.

Program efficiency concerns primarily the units of service. A unit of service may be defined in several ways. It could refer to the number of persons served by the program. It could also refer to the number of client contacts made by the professional staff, for example, by counting the number of in-office interviews the staff conducts. Other examples might be the number of persons processed at intake, or the number of hospital beds in use. These examples are simply workload measures. The program administrator may find it useful to examine such statistics to decide how efficiently the program is functioning, but such data say little about the impact of the program on the community.

Still, measuring efficiency is not unimportant. Measures of efficiency may be important administrative tools for improving the service delivery system.

Another popular measure of efficiency is cost. A variety of methods abounds for conducting a cost analysis; the principles of cost analysis are easily understood, however. Cost analyses relate the overall expense of operating a program to the more specific cost of providing a unit of service. For example, cost analyses may specify the exact cost of conducting an interview, of making a home visit, or of processing an intake application.

Gruber has explained the use of cost accounting methods as they apply to social service programs. He defines cost accounting as a method "to determine how much it costs an organization to produce, market and deliver a product."[61] He views a specific unit of service in a social service agency as synonymous with a product; therefore, the use of an accounting system makes sense in that context. The unit of service may be defined in whatever way the program staff chooses. Gruber suggests that day-care service, for example, may be defined as "(1) a full day of day care for a child, (2) two half-days of day care," et cetera.[61] The costs of providing a unit of staff time (one hour or one day) may be calculated as another unit of service.

Gruber indicates that cost accounting and service accounting procedures can improve the efficiency of an agency's services.

The assessment of program efficiency can serve a useful function, especially for program administrators. However, outcome measures reflecting efficiency do not provide answers concerning the value of a program; they do not deal with the program's intended impact. Measures of efficiency may allow the program to develop a streamlined approach to service. They may increase the speed of services. But if those are the only measures available, questions about the worth of the program remain unanswered.

Evaluating program effectiveness involves selecting outcome measures that reflect the program's goals and objectives. The program with clearly defined and described objectives is rare. More often, the research worker needs to extract the objectives from a variety of sources. Such sources include the following:

The program's charter or articles of incorporation; the legislation that created the program (if the program is provided by a government agency); public laws, including budgets, which often contain explicit statements about a program's intended aims; the program staff, who may identify both intended and perhaps unintended objectives; government officials, legislators, and others who may possess information about program objectives (for private agencies, boards of directors may serve the same function); and the client groups served by the program, who may constitute an important source of information about program goals.

Program objectives must describe the intended result of services, rather than the process of providing those services. Again, a great many programs mistakenly list as their objectives the services they offer, instead of the intended outcome of those services. For example, a program of services for delinquent children listed one of its objectives as "the provision of counseling services for delinquent children." This statement exemplifies the classic error of confusion of the method with the objective. The counseling services may indeed be important, but counseling is not an end in itself. The objectives of counseling services offered to delinquent children should include an intended result, such as reduced recidivism rates for those delinquents.

The program objectives should specify the conditions and the population that the program is intended to affect. Once program objectives are selected, the evaluator needs to select outcome measures or indicators that accurately reflect those objectives. The problems of selecting program outcome measures are identical to those of selecting practice outcome measures. Many of the outcome measures used to evaluate practice also can be used for program evaluation. However, it may be necessary either to select more general outcome measures or to develop outcome measures specifically for the program.

Examples of some general outcome measures include delinquency rates, crime rates, divorce rates, recidivism rates, mortality, morbidity, unemployment rates, and income levels. This list is far from comprehensive, yet it demonstrates that data for many general outcome measures may be found in current public records. Probably all of the measures listed are available in public records and reports.

A second category of program outcome measures is the program-specific measure designed to reflect some unique program quality. Several different kinds of measures can be used to evaluate unique program features; these include measures of client satisfaction, ratings by professionals, and more specialized approaches such as goal attainment scaling.

Many programs are rightly concerned with client satisfaction, because programs are set up to serve people. Methods for systematically measuring client satisfaction include interviews, questionnaires, and public meetings. To avoid biased evaluations, careful attention should be given data collection methods. Proper sampling procedures may be especially critical for evaluating large programs.

Professional judgments, obtained by systematic methods, may be appropriate for evaluating some program effects. Research workers may need to request that special medical personnel evaluate certain health factors (for example, the presence of disease in clients who were provided services to help reduce that disease). Several types of nutritional or health programs might require such specialized evaluation efforts. Again, sample selection and data collection methods must be carefully controlled, and the professionals making the required judgments must be competent. Some research problems may require the specialized training of professionals.

Specific program measures may involve both client judgments and professional judgments. Or they may require other methods and indicators that reflect the unique quality of the program. Wherever possible, a systematic approach to the development of outcome measures should be sought. The general methods necessary to achieve this are exemplified by the Goal Attainment Scaling system developed by Kiresuk.[42] This system offers a useful frame of reference for the development of specialized program outcome measures.

Unfortunately, the selection of unique program outcome measures may yield an evaluation effort that is of little use to anyone outside the program. As with other types of research, program evaluation also suffers from the problem of replication. If the outcome measure selected for the program is unique, replicating that measure may be impossible. If replication is impossible or unlikely, research workers may be unable logically to apply the findings of a specific research project to other programs. The tendency for programs to select unique outcome measures has contributed to the problem of poor "generalizability." Investigators can lessen this problem and strengthen the knowledge base for program evaluation by conscientiously selecting program outcome measures that are applicable to more than one program (Table 5–1).

TABLE 5-1. Guidelines for Selecting Outcome Measures

1. When possible, use standardized outcome measures, such as existing tests with established reliability and validity.
2. When individualized outcome measures are selected, refine the measure with a standardized procedure, such as the Goal Attainment Scaling procedures or the procedure recommended for single subject designs.
3. Employ more than one method of collecting the same data. For example, if client self-observation is selected, supplement it with independent observations made by others. When observers are used, obtain information from more than one observer.
4. For program evaluation, do not use only outcome measures that are unique to the program. Instead, select measures that allow the generalization of results to other programs.

Summary

Measuring the outcome of social work practice has always been difficult. In the social sciences, the characteristics of the subjects—human beings—are infinitely more varied and unstable than the phenomena examined by physical and biological scientists. This fact complicates the replication of research in the social sciences and the comparison of results among different studies.

One cause of the difficulty of defining the dependent variable, or outcome measure, in social work stems from the profession's variety of practice settings. For the profession at large, perhaps the most specific common outcome measure possible is reflected in this statement: Practice should attempt to reduce certain forms of dependency and to increase clients' independent behavior so that clients may gain maximum human freedom.

Types of social work evaluation research—each requiring specific outcome measures—include assessing the value of professional services made to individual clients, assessing an entire program of services, and assessing services to families and groups. Both practitioners and research workers should endeavor to select outcome measures that reflect the goals of the profession and that are specific enough to allow replication.

Evolution of Outcome Measures

An important standardized instrument for assessing the results of social casework is the CSS Movement Scale, developed in the early 1950s, which instructs the caseworker to examine four primary client characteristics and to rate changes in each on a scale. The CSS Scale attempts to enhance reliability by standardizing caseworkers' judgments of client movement. The St. Paul Scale of Family Functioning, which assesses families rather than individuals, followed the CSS Scale. Later still, Ludwig Geismar developed a scale that assessed family functioning by examining nine categories of family behavior and relationships.

Numerous other outcome measures are used in social work. They include client self-reports, evaluation by observers, social indicators, and practitioner evaluations. All may be classified according to two major dimensions: area of content and source of data. All evaluations incorporate these two facets; some may have more than one data source and more than one content area.

Types of Outcome Measures

1. *Self-reports.* Clients use self-reports both to record episodes of a problem behavior and to document events that surround the behavior. Self-

reports are especially important in one regard: They are the practitioner's only means of recording clients' private thoughts and covert behaviors. For self-recording overt behavioral outcomes, a variety of methods exists, including using cards, logs, diaries, and mechanical counters.

Frequently, the act of self-monitoring affects the target behavior. However, this effect—reactivity—can be difficult to document; its strength depends on such variables as the setting, the type of behavior, and the duration of the behavior, among others. In any event, many practitioners deliberately use the reactivity of self-monitoring as a therapeutic tool.

The reliability of some self-reports—those recording covert behaviors such as thoughts and emotions—cannot be verified. Self-reports of overt physical conduct can be checked for reliability by observers. But even then the kind of observer (professional, paraprofessional, untrained family member) has considerable bearing on reliability. Important in obtaining reliable self-reports is carefully teaching clients some strategies for self-monitoring.

2. *Practitioner Evaluation.* One of the most widely used outcome measures, practitioner evaluation comprises three phases: (a) collecting data (in office interviews, home visits, or meetings with other professionals and family members), (b) recording the data, usually into written case records, and (c) analyzing the data to learn the degree and direction of client change.

The use of practitioner evaluations presents several potential limitations: a lack of standardization for recording data (and concurrent differences in reactivity); the reluctance of some social workers to make comprehensive notes during an interview (resulting in blank spots in the case record, written later); and the chance for bias when practitioners themselves analyze the client data obtained (instead of an unbiased rater's doing so).

3. *Family Functioning.* Instruments for assessing family functioning are designed to examine one of three areas of family life: marital adjustment, parent-child interaction, or overall family functioning. The first two areas require specialized measures; the third employs general instruments. Research workers should select the measure most appropriate for their area of study.

a. Of the many scales that are in use for assessing marital adjustment, three important measures are the Locke-Wallace Marital Adjustment Test, the Spanier Dyadic Adjustment Scale, and the Stuart Marital Pre-Counseling Inventory.

b. One of the most comprehensive systems for assessing parent-child relations is the Behavioral Coding System, which assesses and treats behaviorally deviant children. Trained observers follow BCS procedures to audit parent-child interactions in the home.

c. Most of the measures of overall family functioning are based on two data sources: direct observations of behavior, and self-report data from interviews and questionnaires. The Home Observation Assessment Method uses two trained observers to record the behavior of a family's adults. Another excellent scale is the Index of Family Relations, a self-report measure developed specifically for use in social work.

4. *Individualized Measures.* Social workers often need outcome measures for individual cases. The two major limitations of the individual- ized approach are the variability of evaluation procedures and the lack of specification of outcome measures. To cure or minimize the latter problem, practitioners can use one of several procedures such as Goal Attainment Scaling, the Problem Oriented Record, the Reid-Epstein Task Achievement Scale, or the three-step Wodarski-Bagarozzi design. Five techniques that practitioners can use to collect individual assessment data are self- inventories, behavior interviews, behavior samples, behavioral diaries, and baseline measures.

Single subject methodology can be used in a wide variety of theoretical frameworks to study a broad range of individual client problems. It offers practice research workers considerable flexibility as well as the re- quired scientific rigor. One good single subject design is Bloom's Problem- Oriented Evaluation Procedure. Its four basic steps are identification of the problem, monitoring target behavior, comparing behavior during interven- tion with baseline measurements, and evaluation of change.

Behavior and Cognitive Measures

Research information may be classified according to whether it may be in- dependently verified. Behavioral measures evaluate subjects' overt or observable conduct, the three aspects of which are frequency, duration, and quality. Cognitive measures assess covert events such as private thoughts and urges. Both types of events are important to the practitioner and the research worker.

Overt behaviors can be monitored by independent observers or by self-reports and can be objectively defined. Cognitive events are best assessed through the use of self-reports, questionnaires, and interviews. For assessing both types of behavior, a wide variety of self-report measures—inventories, questionnaires, and checklists—is available. They cover some very special- ized topics. They are easy to administer, and most important, they offer a standardized method of collecting data, making replication simpler. Behavioral observation, the direct monitoring of an individual's behavior by one or more observers, can be a highly reliable technique for collecting data about overt conduct.

Program Evaluation

Like the evaluation of social work practice itself, program evaluation in- volves the selection and use of outcome measures. The factor that often makes analyzing program outcomes difficult is vaguely defined program objectives. Too many program directors describe their objectives in terms of the frequency and types of their services, rather than the quality, the actual benefit, to people in need of that service.

Program evaluators should examine separately the two major aspects of a program's objectives—efficiency and effectiveness. Efficiency refers to units of service and can be defined in several ways: numbers of persons serviced, contacts with clients, and so on. Efficiency also could be defined through cost analyses. However, though they are worthwhile, efficiency measures say little about the effectiveness of a program. It is the measuring of effectiveness that requires specifically stated program objectives. To be measurable, the objectives must describe the intended result of services rather than the process of providing services. Objectives must specify the population and the human conditions the program intends to affect.

Often, measures used to evaluate practice also can be used to evaluate programs. But sometimes new measures are needed. One source of program outcome data is public records such as crime rates, unemployment rates, and income levels. Another is the program-specific measure, which reflects some unique program quality such as client satisfaction. Such information may be learned through processes like administering questionnaires or conducting interviews or public meetings. In some cases, professional judgments may be a good means of evaluating programs. In any event, in program evaluation, as in practice evaluation, research workers should attempt as much as possible to allow for replication of their procedures.

Negative Outcomes

Research workers must be aware that intervention may produce no change in a client. Worse, at times it actually may have a deterioration effect; that is, intervention might cause a client's condition to decline. Some investigators have found either deterioration or inadequate improvement in as many as half the cases studied. Thus, the responsible practitioner must be prepared to collect negative outcome data as well as positive data—despite a present lack of deterioration measures in the profession.

End Notes

1. Atherton, Charles R. "The Social Assignment of Social Work." *Social Service Review* 43 (1969): 422.
2. Hunt, J. McV., and Kogan, Leonard S. *Measuring Results in Social Casework: A Manual on Judging Movement.* New York: Family Service Association of America, 1952, p. 25.
3. *Ibid.,* p. 83.

4. Briar, Scott. "Family Services." In *Five Fields of Social Service*, edited by Henry S. Maas. pp. 18–19. New York: National Association of Social Workers, 1966, Also see: Borgatta, Edgar F., Fanshel, David, and Meyer, Henry J. *Social Workers' Perceptions of Clients*. New York: Russell Sage Foundation, 1960.

5. Geismar, Ludwig L., and Ayres, Beverly. *Measuring Family Functioning*. St. Paul: Greater St. Paul United Fund and Council, 1960.

6. Geismar, Ludwig L. *Family and Community Functioning*. Metuchen, N.J.: The Scarecrow Press, 1971.

7. Meyer, Henry J., Borgatta, Edgar F., and Jones, W.C. *Girls at Vocational High: An Experiment in Social Work Intervention*. New York: Russell Sage Foundation, 1965.

8. Macdonald, Mary E. "Reunion at Vocational High." *Social Service Review* 40 (June 1966): 175–189.

9. Wallace, David. "The Chemung County Evaluation of Casework Service to Dependent Multi-Problem Families: Another Problem Outcome." *Social Service Review* 41, no. 4 (December 1967): 379–389.

10. *Ibid.*, p. 387.

11. United Community Service of the Greater Vancouver Area. *The Development Project Monographs I, II and III*, 1968–1969.

12. Geismar, L.L., and Krisberg, J. *The Forgotten Neighborhood: Site of an Early Skirmish in the War on Poverty*. Metuchen, N.J.: Scarecrow Press, 1967.

13. Blenkner, M., Jahn, J., and Wasser, E., *Serving the Aging: An Experiment in Social Work and Public Health Nursing*. New York: Community Service Society of New York, 1964.

14. Thoresen, C. E., and Mahoney, M. J. *Behavioral Self-Control*. New York: Holt, Rinehart & Winston, 1974.

15. Thomas, E. J., Abrams, K. S., and Johnson, J. B. "Self-Monitoring and Reciprocal Inhibition in the Modification of Multiple Tics of Gilles de la Tourette's Syndrome." *Journal of Behavior Therapy and Experimental Psychiatry* 2 (1971): 159–171.

16. McKenzie, T. L., and Ruskall, B. S. "Effects of Self-Recording on Attendance and Performance in a Competitive Swimming Training Environment." *Journal of Applied Behavior Analysis* 7 (1974): 199–206.

17. Mahoney, M. J., Maura, W. G., and Wade, T. C. "The Relative Efficacy of Self-Reward, Self-Punishment and Self-Monitoring Techniques for Weight Loss." *Journal of Consulting and Clinical Psychology* 40 (1973): 404–407.

18. Kantorowitz, D. A., Walters, J., and Pezdek, K. "Positive Versus Negative Self-Monitoring in the Self-Control of Smoking." *Journal of Consulting and Clinical Psychology* 46 (5): 1148–1150.

19. Fixsen, D. L., Phillips, E. L., and Wolf, M. M. "Achievement Place: The Reliability of Self-Reporting and Peer Reporting and Their Effects on Behavior." *Journal of Applied Behavior Analysis* 5 (1972): pp. 19–30. Also see: Risley, T. R., and Hart, B. "Developing Correspondence Between Non-Verbal and Verbal Behavior of Preschool Children." *Journal of Applied Behavior Analysis* 1 (1968): 267–281.

20. Fixsen, Phillips, and Wolf, "Achievement Place."

21. Howe, M. W. "Using Clients' Observations in Research." *Social Work* 21 (1976): 28–33.

22. Johnson, S. M., and Bolstad, O. D. "Reactivity to Home Observations." *Journal of Applied Behavior Analysis* 8 (1975): 181–185.
23. Werry, J. S., and Quay, H. C. "Observing the Classroom Behavior of Elementary School Children." *Exceptional Children* 35 (1969): 461–476. Also see: Wright, H. F. *Recording and Analyzing Child Behavior: With Ecological Data from an American Town.* New York: Harper & Row, 1967.
24. Locke, H. J., and Wallace, Karl M. "Short Mental-Adjustment and Prediction Tests: Their Reliability and Validity." *Marriage and Family Living* 21 (1959): 251–255.
25. Spanier, G. B. "Measuring Dyadic Adjustment: New Scales for Assessing the Quality of Marriage and Similar Dyads." *Journal of Marriage and the Family* 38 (February 1976): 15–28.
26. Stuart, R. B., and Stuart, F. *Marital Pre-Counseling Inventory.* Champaign, Ill.: Research Press, 1973.
27. Patterson, G. R. "Naturalistic Observation in Clinical Assessment," *Journal of Applied Child Psychology* 5 (1977): 309–322. Also see: Patterson, G. R., et al, *A Social Learning Approach to Family Intervention,* vol. 1. Eugene, Ore.: Castalia Publishing Company, 1975.
28. Reid, J. B. *A Social Learning Approach to Family Intervention,* vol. 2. Eugene, Ore.: Castalia Publishing Company, 1978.
29. Steinglass, P. "The Home Observation Assessment Method (HOAM): Real Time Naturalistic Observation of Families in Their Homes." *Family Process* 18 (September 1979): 337–354.
30. Hudson, W. W., Acklen, J. D., and Bartosh, J. C. "Assessing Discord in Family Relationships." *Social Work Research and Abstracts* 16 (Fall 1980): 21–29. This article contains the complete IFR, including scoring instructions.
31. *Ibid.,* p. 22.
32. Nisbett, R. E., and Wilson, T. D., "Telling More than We Can Know: Verbal Reports on Mental Processes." *Psychological Review* 84 (1977): 231–259.
33. Kanfer, F. H., and Saslow, G. "Behavioral Diagnosis." In *Behavior Therapy: Appraisal and Status,* edited by C. M. Franks. New York: McGraw-Hill, 1969.
34. Klaus, D., Hersen, M., and Bellach, A. S. "Survey of Dating Habits of Male and Female Students: A Necessary Precursor to Measurement and Modification." *Journal of Clinical Psychology* 33 (1977): 369–375.
35. Birchler, G. R., and Webb, F. L. J. "Discriminating Interaction Behaviors in Happy and Unhappy Marriages." *Journal of Consulting and Clinical Psychology* 45 (1977): 494–495.
36. Wollersheim, J. P. "Effectiveness of Group Therapy Based upon Learning Principles in the Treatment of Overweight Women." *Journal of Abnormal Psychology* 76 (1970): 462–479.
37. Efran, J. S., et al. "Should Fearful Individuals Be Instructed to Proceed Quickly or Cautiously." *Journal of Clinical Psychology* 33 (1977): 535–539.
38. Long, P. J., and Lazovek, A. P. "Experimental Desensitization of a Phobia." *Journal of Abnormal and Social Psychology* 66 (1963): 519–525.
39. Haynes, S. N. *Principles of Behavioral Assessment.* New York: Halstead Press, 1978.
40. Richmond, Mary. *Social Diagnosis.* New York: Russell Sage Foundation, 1917.
41. Bergin, A. E. "The Evaluation of Therapeutic Outcomes." In *Handbook of*

Psychotherapy and Behavior Change, edited by A. E. Bergin and S. L. Garfield, p. 253. New York: John Wiley and Sons, 1971.

42. Kiresuk, T. S., and Sherman, R. E. "Goal Attainment Scaling: A General Method for Evaluating Comprehensive Community Mental Health Programs." *Community Mental Health Journal* 4 (1968): 443–453.

43. Compton, Beulah R., and Galaway, Burt. *Social Work Process.* Homewood, Ill.: Dorsey Press, 1975, p. 384.

44. Weed, L. I. "Medical Records that Guide and Teach." *New England Journal of Medicine* 278 (1968): 593–657.

45. Klonoff, H., and Cox, B. "A Problem Oriented System Approach to Analysis of Treatment Outcome." *American Journal of Psychiatry* 132 (1975): 836–841.

46. Kane, R. A. "Look to the Record." *Social Work* 19 (1974), p. 417.

47. Reid, William J., and Epstein, Laura. *Task-Centered Casework.* New York: Columbia University Press, 1972, p. 72.

48. *Ibid.*, p. 238.

49. Wodarski, J., and Bagarozzi, D. A. *Behavioral Social Work.* New York: Human Services Press, 1979.

50. Bloom, Martin. *The Paradox of Helping.* New York: John Wiley and Sons, 1975.

51. Hudson, W. W. "Elementary Techniques for Assessing Single Client/Single Worker Interactions." *Social Service Review* 51 (1977): 311–326.

52. Jayaratne, S., and Levy, R. L. *Empirical Clinical Practice.* New York: Columbia University Press, 1979.

53. Howe, M. "Casework Self-Evaluation: A Single Subject Approach." *Social Service Review* 48 (1974): 1–23.

54. Fischer, Joel. *Effective Casework Practice.* New York: McGraw-Hill, 1978.

55. Bergin, A. E., and Lambert, M. J. "The Evaluation of Therapeutic Outcomes." In *Handbook of Psychotherapy and Behavior Change*, edited by S. L. Garfield and A. E. Bergin, p. 152, 2d ed. New York: John Wiley and Sons, 1978.

56. Fischer, Joel. "Is Casework Effective: A Review." *Social Work* 1 (1973): 5–20.

57. Hartley, D., Roback, H. B., and Abramowitz, S. I. "Deterioration Effects in Encounter Groups. *American Psychologist* 31 (1976): 247–255.

58. Lieberman, M. A., Yalom, I. E., and Miles, M. B. *Encounter Groups: First Facts.* New York: Basic Books, 1973.

59. Guttman, H. A. "A Contraindication for Family Therapy." *Archives of General Psychiatry* 29 (1973): 352–355.

60. Stuart, Richard B. *Trick or Treatment.* Champaign, Ill.: Research Press, 1970, p. 58.

61. Gruber, A. R. "The High Cost of Delivering Services." *Social Work* 18 (1973): p. 35.

Defining the Independent
Variable

6

The foundation of experimental research is its systematic use of an independent variable, often called the treatment or the experimental condition. For social work research to be useful, investigators must control the independent variable and must define it as specifically as possible. The task is not always easy.

In social work research, the aim of experimentation usually is to evaluate, for use in practice, the potential worth of treatment methods. The typical experiment uses one of three approaches: (1) providing the independent variable to one group and withholding it from another, (2) providing assorted degrees of the independent variable to different groups, or (3) presenting entirely different conditions to separate groups. For example, an investigator may seek to examine the effects of providing a program of casework services to a group of child-abusing clients. The aim is to determine whether supplying such treatment (the independent variable) reduces the incidence of child abuse (the dependent variable).

Similar conditions may be applied to single-subject designs and to other forms of within-subject research (these designs are discussed in chapter 8). Investigators first take baseline measures of the problem behavior (the dependent variable). Next, they expose the client to the treatment (the independent variable). Then, to determine the treatment's effectiveness, they compare client reactions to varying amounts and degrees of treatment.

Whether the investigator uses between-group experimental designs or single-subject designs, the experimental conditions remain essentially the same. Investigators compare research subjects according to their response to the independent variable. In either case, the central idea in experimental research is that some subjects, under certain controlled conditions, are exposed to the independent variable. Campbell and Stanley refer to this process as manipulating the independent variable.[1] In other words, the research worker must be assured that the independent variable is applied to the right subjects at the right time and place. This requisite necessitates that the research worker control the independent variable and manipulate it at will.

Unfortunately, many social work investigators do not achieve the required degree of control over the independent variable. Hence, they cannot deliberately manipulate it. Often, the reason for poor control is that the independent variable is inadequately defined and described.

Social work practitioners use a variety of methods and techniques. Some therapists practice group work methods, some practice casework methods. Yet even within the framework of a specific practice method, such as casework, a wide range of techniques and personal practice styles exists; therefore, casework itself does not constitute a unitary method of practice. Furthermore, even when caseworkers share similar training and a common theoretical orientation, what they do in practice often seems less related to their background than to a specific client's needs.[2]

Because such diversity in practice exists, experimental research designed to assess the effectiveness of global concepts (such as "social work practice" or "casework practice") is confronted with an enormous practical question: How can the investigator define and describe the independent variable? The question arises because what one practitioner does in practice may not be identical to the performance of another, even when both use the same approach and are treating the same problem.

The problem for the research worker attempting to evaluate practice, then, is this: Because the behavior of the two practitioners may differ, all clients or subjects will not be exposed to identical experimental conditions (independent variables). Unless the research worker can be sure that the treatments of different practitioners are identical, the use of between-group experimental research methods becomes almost pointless.

This limitation afflicts many of the large-scale evaluation studies designed to test the effectiveness of "social work" methods or of "casework" techniques.

The 1965 book, *Girls at Vocational High* (discussed more thoroughly in chapters 5 and 7) illustrates one such inconclusive experiment.[3] This project was flawed because the various kinds of unstructured treatment given the girls in the experimental group simply were not equivalent. For one thing, the four-year experiment started by providing casework services and later changed to group treatment methods. The research report supplies no evidence of standardized treatment methods or of explicit treatment goals. Apparently, the treatment focused on the girls themselves rather than on their families. The research merely concluded that there were few significant differences between the experimental group and the control group.

In a later review of this case, Macdonald commented on the "treatment" condition: "Data on the treatment program are most unsatisfactory to the close reader. Neither the length of time that the girl was in contact with the agency nor the number of interviews or group sessions is given."[4] Further, "No attempt was made to analyze the treatment group even to the extent permitted by the available data on service. . . . The profession wants to know what works with what cases and why."[4]

Briar also discussed the problem of describing the experimental condition for the *Vocational High* project. He primarily examined the casework services provided in this research. Briar's analysis was, "Since casework is not a unitary method, but is actually many things, it cannot be tested without further specification and differentiation—one can only test *a* casework method, not *the* casework method, since the latter does not exist."[5]

Both of these reviewers criticize the lack of description of the independent variable in this experiment. Their comments are representative of the remarks of others who also have noted the difficulty of conducting "global" assessments of such broad concepts as social work or casework without adequately describing each.

Other classical experiments conducted in the same era suffer from similar limitations. One of the most notable was the Cambridge-Somerville Youth Study, reported in 1951.[6] In this classic study, a group of boys was provided social work services aimed at preventing juvenile delinquency. Boys in the experimental group were compared with an equal number of youths who had been randomly assigned to a control group. The experimental and control subjects were matched on the basis of a number of characteristics. Comparisons of final delinquency rates for the two groups established no significant differences.

In this experiment, as in the *Vocational High* project, the same lack of specificity about the independent variable exists. Descriptions of both experiments lack enough detail to reconstruct exactly what treatment the practitioners provided. Further, there is no way now to establish whether the treatments furnished each client were identical.

The lack of specificity of the independent variable gives rise to a second problem in social work research, that of replication. To permit replication, the research worker must clearly define the experiment's variables. Unless research can be replicated, it is impossible for other researchers to verify results or to compare methods and techniques. Even more important, investigators cannot build on previous research. Where the possibility of replication is lacking, future researchers are precluded from using earlier research to refine and improve techniques and concepts.

When they are barred from replicating research, practitioners cannot learn what specific techniques work in solving specific problems simply because for a technique to be replicable it must be adequately described.

Research investigators can improve descriptions of treatment methods in several ways to help others understand clearly what approaches work best. The social work profession requires more precise definitions of its treatment procedures than its research currently produces.

Briar has discerned a trend toward greater specificity in practitioner descriptions of treatment methods. The Chemung County Study, a more recent research project,[7] was reviewed by Briar, who noted that "An important feature of the design was that two experts rated the quality of casework service provided to the demonstration cases."[8] Briar also observed that Reid and Shyne, in a review of research on brief and extended casework methods, exhibited even greater specificity in describing the independent variable.[9] Reid and Shyne's research compared the relative effectiveness of brief casework to that of extended casework. Their clients were randomly assigned to the different treatment conditions. Briar wrote:[10]

> The Reid-Shyne study goes a step beyond the question of effectiveness to ask which of two methods is more effective. Consequently, their results point a direction for casework practitioners to follow in order to maximize their effectiveness. More generally, effectiveness studies could be made more attractive to practitioners if researchers put their questions in a form that would yield more useful information to the practitioner.

These research investigators and others have recognized one of the problems basic to social work research. The logic of evaluation research in social work requires that the research worker design a study that can demonstrate the extent to which a particular form of social work intervention affects the problems of a client or group. This logic normally requires that the research include a control group, an experimental treatment, and reliable and valid outcome measures for comparing persons who receive the treatment with those in the control group.

Many social work researchers have accepted the logic of establishing an experimental research design for evaluating practice. Some also have addressed the problem of developing outcome measures. Few, however, have described the experimental treatment in sufficient detail. Many practitioners and research workers have neglected this important detail because of one common assumption about the nature of social work practice: the notion that all social work interventions are similar and are essentially equivalent. This assumption has led to the profession's numerous attempts to assess global practice elements.

Yet the assumption of equivalency of treatments is not consistent with experimental research. The very nature of experimental research requires that the details and characteristics of treatment be approached as empirical questions and not be assumed. The extent to which research can be verified by replication depends on how well the treatment variables can be replicated. Furthermore, if the results are to help extend and generalize practice to new situations, then treatment methods must be described in sufficient detail. The task for the research worker, then, is to develop means of describing treatment techniques that will allow others readily to understand and replicate those techniques.

Achieving this objective—adequate description of treatment tactics—is difficult. The research worker must select from among several methods for defining and describing treatment practices. These methods range from highly structured treatment programs to very unstructured approaches. The more highly structured the treatment, the easier it is to describe and replicate; the less structured it is, the more difficult its adequate description becomes. Some of the specific techniques to isolate and describe various dimensions of treatment include the use of prestructured treatment stimuli, treatment typologies, selected practitioner variables, and operationally defined treatment methods.

Prestructured Treatment Stimuli

One way to achieve a highly reliable description of the independent variable is to standardize the specific treatment stimulus to which the client is exposed. Many practitioners argue that it is impossible to standardize any treatment completely because each client is different and, therefore, each treatment episode is different. However, varying degrees of standardization can be achieved by using prestructured treatment stimuli.

Of these there are two types: the totally prestructured stimulus, which does not require the active involvement of the practitioner, and the partially prestructured treatment stimulus, which requires some practitioner involvement.

Totally prestructured treatment stimuli are found primarily in the forms of audiotapes and videotapes, movies, and self-help books. An enormous variety of prestructured treatment materials is available commercially and is widely prescribed by human service practitioners.

One of the most common problems for which self-help prestructured treatments are used is general stress. Many practitioners believe strongly that stress is responsible for many kinds of problems, including tension headaches, irritability, tiredness, and depression. In treating these afflictions, therapists usually try to teach the client various methods of relaxing, which in turn reduce stress. The theory is that once the client learns to relax, problems that are considered symptoms of the stress will disappear.

To teach people to relax, a number of techniques may be used. Some practitioners prescribe teaching the client progressive relaxation techniques by means of prerecorded audio tapes. Tapes on relaxation training may be purchased commercially from at least two sources. Some practitioners produce their own tapes as well.

Another form of relaxation training incorporates a prestructured format involving various biofeedback devices, some of which are accompanied by recorded audio cassette instructions. These devices also are available from commercial sources.

In addition to stress management, audiotapes are commonly used for treating such problems as weight control and habit control, and for self-hypnosis training and assertiveness training.

Self-help manuals are another common form of prestructured treatment stimuli. Manuals are available for treating a wide range of problems. Some of the more common self-help handbooks describe methods of controlling habits like smoking, overeating, and excessive drinking. There are manuals on managing problem children, relaxing, assertiveness training, improving marriages, training the mentally retarded in self-care skills, and on general methods of self-help and self-change.

Other forms of packaged (or "canned") materials include videotapes and motion picture films. Because of the specialized equipment required, these are less available to most people than audiotapes and manuals. But with the increasing availability of home video cassette equipment, they are growing in popularity. Videotapes and films have been used in assertiveness training and relaxation training. They are becoming increasingly popular for teaching people how to be better parents and how to manage problem children.

Users may learn from these standardized prestructured treatments with no assistance from the practitioner. Many such materials also may be used as adjuncts to structured treatment that involves the practitioner. For example, some of the motion pictures marketed by the American Personnel and Guidance Association for teaching skills to parents are designed for use with practitioner involvement.

Another example is a set of audio tapes for assertiveness training.[11] These tapes include a so-called practitioner manual that gives the therapist specific instructions for conducting and enhancing self-directed assertiveness training.

Many other self-help devices, such as handbooks on weight control, habit control, and self-change, also are accompanied by practitioner manuals. These forms of prestructured treatment are less rigid than the entirely canned methods. They may be thought of as partly structured treatment stimuli. They are not so completely ordered as the entirely canned materials, but they retain a high degree of structure when used with a practitioner manual.

The practitioner manual itself lies near the less structured end of the continuum of prestructured treatment stimuli. This set of directions for practitioners to use during certain treatment procedures does not provide as much structure as do the canned materials, such as tapes.

The manual allows the practitioner to incorporate specialized techniques into practice. It offers a reasonable alternative to the inflexible canned programs, but retains enough treatment structure to allow for comparisons and replication.

Practitioner manuals are available to treat a wide variety of problems. Some of the more common manuals describe training for relaxation, developing assertiveness, quitting smoking, weight control, learning social skills, systematic desensitization, interpersonal skills for retarded persons, and treatment for alcohol abuse.[12]

Treatment manuals may be highly structured or only moderately structured. The degree of structure among the practitioner manuals also varies widely. Furthermore, the canned materials, such as audio cassette tapes, may be combined with practitioner manuals to produce a semistructured form of treatment. The following example is a brief section of a highly structured practitioner manual developed by Miller for progressive relaxation.[13]

Okay, we are ready to begin. Get comfortable in the chair, sit back completely, close your eyes and keep them closed until instructed to open them again. (Begin music.) (1) We are going to tense the muscles of the right hand and forearm and I want you to tense these muscles by making a tight fist with your right hand . . . feel the muscles pull across your fingers and the lower part of your forearm. Focus on the tension; feel how tight the muscles are; feel the tension. (Tension is maintained for seven seconds.) Okay, relax!

Contrast Miller's detailed rules with these less structured instructions for social skills training used by Mungas:[14]

I would now like each of you to think of a situation that you find particularly difficult. (Allow some time to think about it.) Let's go around the room and share some of these situations. (The therapist can mention a personal situation if he feels comfortable with it.) . . .
1. Have the subject describe the situation.
2. With the help of the group members, clarify the situation so that it can be concisely and concretely stated.
3. Have the subject role-play it with either you or another group member.

In comparing the two manuals, it is apparent that Mungas leaves the practitioner several optional ways to apply treatment. The practitioner is free to use a personal style and methods in the suggested role-play procedure. Obviously, the more highly structured manual by Miller is easier to replicate, but it regulates somewhat the practitioner's responses to the client; thus, it leaves the practitioner less freedom in selecting and using treatment methods.

Advantages

The prestructured treatment approach offers both research workers and practitioners some distinct advantages. For the research worker, the more highly structured the treatment, the easier is its replication. Naturally, the research worker would prefer the advantage of greater specificity of the independent variable; the prestructured treatment offers that advantage.

In addition to the gains to research, prestructuring also benefits the client. The self-help materials may be much less expensive to use and more convenient than relying on the practitioner. Also, the client using canned self-help materials retains more control of his or her life and problem. This condition is desirable from the perspective of the social work profession. It is consistent with one of the profession's major objectives, that of enhancing the person's capacity to function in an independent manner.

The manuals can be advantageous to the practitioner, also. They provide a source of training, an inexpensive and convenient mode of learning new methods and techniques. Some self-help materials can help to ease the demands of a heavy caseload.

Disadvantages

The use of prestructured treatment suffers some disadvantages, however. One of the main drawbacks of any prestructured treatment is its apparent unattractiveness to some practitioners. Many social work professionals avoid prestructured treatment packages, feeling that they are inflexible and do not fulfill their client's needs. Others insist that, to motivate the client to participate in the treatment, the involvement of the practitioner is necessary. Still others point to the expense, noting the costly equipment that some forms of prestructured treatment, such as videotape players, require.

All these arguments have some validity. Indeed, the relative effectiveness of many prestructured treatments remains unproved. However, all the arguments applying to prestructured treatment also may apply to normal social work practice.

Research Concerns

From a research perspective as well, prestructured treatments suffer some limitations. For example, when less structured forms of practitioner manuals are used, a great deal of practitioner variation may occur in treatments of different cases. This fluctuation is undesirable because it leaves the research worker with no clear indications of the causes for any changes in client behavior.

For the research worker, a second concern is assuring that the practitioner follows the directions in the manual. Unless the treatment session is recorded, there is no control over how closely the practitioner adheres to the instructions in the practitioner manual.

No easy solution is apparent. Yet prestructured treatments offer the social work profession some important options, the potential of which merits careful consideration.

Treatment Typologies

The treatment typology describes the essential attributes of a particular treatment package and the ways in which it differs from other treatments. A treatment typlogy should provide details on how treatment is to be conducted. A good typology should help the practitioner select the best intervention available for treating a particular client's specific problems.

The treatment typology approach is based on the idea that treatments may be classified and described according to certain characteristics. Classifications can be made on the basis of the practitioner's theoretical orientation (such as client-centered therapy or behavior therapy), or on the basis of observations of what transpires in the treatment session itself, or on some other basis (such as the intent of the practitioner).

Practice can be classified in a variety of ways. Some of the more common categories include the method used in practice (such as individual versus group treatment); theoretical orientation or "school" of treatment (such as analytic, client-centered, behavioral, Gestalt, rational-emotive); and practice style and techniques.

Germain conducted a comprehensive review of the development of treatment typologies in social work. She observed that during the 1930s and 1940s, several attempts were made to systematize treatment techniques. "Some classifications," she found, "were based on the dynamics of the procedures and others were based on the goals and methods."[15] Germain examined classification efforts made by Hollis, Austin, Ripple, Perlman, and others.

One of the more notable attempts to develop a treatment typology in social work was the research of Florence Hollis. Hollis was a strong advocate of the development of a treatment typology. "The task is worth the effort," she asserted, "for one essential approach to understanding any system of treatment is to study the details of treatment—analyzing what actually goes on. For this task, an appropriate typology of treatment procedures is essential."[16]

Hollis also recognized the potential value to research of describing treatment more specifically: "To accomplish this end we must develop tools of content analysis that can be used by different researchers with some degree of reliability so that results can be compared and findings can become, in some measure, additive."[16]

Hollis attempted to classify casework treatment by analyzing casework interviews. She used written case records (process recordings) and transcriptions of tape recordings. Her typology was based on the assumption that "treatment consists of a blend of relatively few procedures. The extent to which each type of procedure is used varies from interview to interview in the same case and in different treatment periods of the same case."[17]

Her classification of treatment procedures actually is a typology of communications that occur in casework. She proposed that all exchanges between the practitioner and client could be classified along five dimensions.

Reid further developed Hollis's typology. In their 1969 book, Reid and Shyne presented a typology of casework treatment that included ten techniques, three of which were reassurance, advice, and confrontation.[9]

This classification scheme was used to study differences in two casework service patterns, brief service and extended service. Research workers, using extensive descriptions of the two techniques, were able to study and compare the actions of caseworkers providing each form of service. The caseworkers' efforts were classified according to the standard descriptions of casework techniques contained in the Reid and Shyne typology. Reid confirmed the value of this procedure for studying the differential use of casework techniques.[18] Turner reported using a similar typology for casework research based on Hollis's work.[19]

The casework typology developed by Hollis and later modified by Reid was subject to certain limitations. Briar specifically noted that the Hollis typology should be recognized as an important first step in the development of a useful typology. But he pointed out that, for several reasons, the typology has limited usefulness for social work research.[20]

> The typology is defined in psychological terms and therefore, does not adequately subsume more socially directed procedures. And it is predicated on an insight theory of individual change, the validity of which is questionable. The research conducted thus far on the typology has focused on the correlates of variations in the use of these procedures by practitioners.

Apparently, Reid also recognized the limitations of the original Hollis typology, for he later developed a separate typology for studying social work practice.

In 1972, Reid and Epstein published *Task-Centered Casework*. Their task-centered approach offers much greater specificity in describing the exact nature of the intervention than previous typologies allowed. In 1975, Reid took a major step toward placing task-centered casework on firm empirical grounds. In a five-step plan called the Task Implementation Sequence (TIS), he operationally defined the treatment variable of task performance. TIS is a progressive treatment sequence. Its components are "enhancing commitment, planning task implementation, analyzing obstacles, modeling, rehearsal, guided practice and summarizing."[21]

The introduction of these specific tasks was part of an initial effort to specify the treatment variables contained in the task-centered approach. This endeavor resulted in greater specificity of the treatment variable. Rossi reported using the task-centered approach in practice research to help a mute child.[22] Tolson reported using the task-centered approach with marital problems.[23] Although the task-centered design has not solved all of the problems related to developing a usable typology, it does represent progress in this area.

In addition to the work on casework typologies in social work, similar efforts to develop methods to analyze and specify the critical elements of treatment have proceeded in related helping professions. In general, the research in psychology and allied fields has focused on identifying the essential elements of interpersonal helping treatments or therapies.

The most widely known research of this type examines the "therapeutic relationship." This line of study began when Carl Rogers reported that he had isolated some of the essential ingredients of successful therapy.[24] His research was extended by Carkhuff and associates.[25] In a series of studies, the Carkhuff team developed a typology for describing the therapeutic relationship and identified what they felt were the essential components of all interpersonal helping processes.

Rogers originally proposed that, for effective interpersonal helping to take place, the therapist–practitioner must demonstrate three essential qualities or "core conditions": empathy, warmth, and genuineness.[26] To these three core components, Carkhuff, Truax, and others added the therapist attributes of concreteness, confrontation, self-disclosure, and immediacy of relationship.[27] They also developed scales and measurement procedures to gauge the extent to which practitioners express the helping characteristics in treatment.[25]

Carkhuff and his associates have influenced many social workers; however, not all agree with their approach. A useful perspective is provided by Strupp, who has conducted research on the essential components of therapy. Strupp suggested that two important principles could be used to guide research on treatment techniques. Strupp argues that the conditions (warmth, genuineness, and empathy) recognized by Carkhuff and associates as necessary for a therapeutic relationship actually are *general* conditions for human rapport. He points out that a good human relationship, "while important, is generally viewed as a *precondition* for the therapist's technical interventions."[28] He suggests that it is important for research to determine when the therapist has made a contribution "over and beyond the provision of a good human relationship."[28] For this reason, therapists must specify in detail what occurs in treatment.

Reviews of social work research indicate that treatment typologies have been popular for describing practice methods and techniques. Unfortunately, it seems the treatment typology approach has not been useful for social work research. Reviewing research on casework effectiveness, Briar

85

and Conte commented that "in nearly all studies of effectiveness, including one of the few reported in recent years, casework has been defined as whatever trained caseworkers do that is not otherwise identified."[29]

The treatment typology approach depends on the ability of the research worker to provide a scheme that can accommodate and classify all that transpires during treatment. It also assumes that the research worker has an accurate description of what transpires during the treatment.

The latter requirement represents a major weakness in the treatment typology approach. Research workers seldom directly observe social work treatment. They often rely on tape recordings of treatment sessions or on case records. Records are subject to errors in observation, recording, and recall. Tape recordings and videotapes are less prone to error but are expensive and time-consuming to analyze, and taping sometimes produces unfavorable client responses.

A second weakness is that treatment typologies do not always provide for classification of all aspects of the treatment. If a step is omitted, the research worker will be unsure whether the missing item was responsible for any changes observed in the client.

A further limitation is that many treatment typologies are based on abstract concepts, such as the intent of the practitioner in asking the client a specific question, that cannot be observed in the treatment situation. Such typologies can hardly produce reliable classifications of treatment.

Reid and Epstein have made some use of an alternative method, the Task Centered Approach, which is based on analysis of the practitioner tasks in treatment.

To date, treatment typologies have not been widely used in social work research, indicating that they are either too difficult for practical research use or that many research workers find them unacceptable.

Selected Practitioner Variables

In distinguishing which treatments are most effective, one important factor may be the personal characteristics of individual practitioners. Many investigators have sought to define practitioner contributions to the success of any treatment procedure. Some believe that the professional's techniques, skills, and methods are the only important variables; but others feel that certain practitioner idiosyncracies make a difference in treating some clients.

Because social work research is concerned with identifying all of the variables that may contribute to the success or failure of treatment, research workers must consider every element in treatment—including the characteristics of practitioners. The practitioner variables indicated by social workers as important include experience, sex, race, and socioeconomic status. Many practitioners argue that one or more of these attributes might be major factors in the outcome of social work treatment. If these components indeed are contributing or causal factors, then careful research should be able to document clearly the impact of each on the results of practice.

Extensive reviews of research on therapist variables have been conducted by Fiske,[30] Garfield,[31] Auerbach and Johnson,[32] and Parloff, Waskow, and Wolfe.[33] All tend to arrive at similar conclusions. According to Parloff, Waskow, and Wolfe's description,[34]

> The therapist variables most frequently selected by the researcher for study are, unfortunately, such simplistic, global concepts as to cause this field to suffer from possible terminal vagueness. Therapist variables categorized as personality, mental health, experience, sex, race, socioeconomic status and so on, can be usefully related to specific treatment goals only at a gross probabilistic level.

Research workers have drawn a few specific conclusions about practitioner variables. One of the more popular topics in social work literature of the 1970s is the issue of matching practitioner and client according to race, sex, or social class. Parloff, Waskow, and Wolfe stated that their review of writings on this question allowed them "to draw no firm conclusions about the influence of such matching."[35] They noted, however, that obtaining evidence about practitioners' attitudes and biases is becoming increasingly difficult—because of the desire of most to depict themselves as free of biases. The authors also suggested that practitioners' experience with a particular population might significantly affect their treatment effectiveness.

The race or sex of the practitioner may not be so important as other attributes, such as competence, sensitivity, warmth, understanding, and several other interpersonal skills. Sattler's insightful comment on the matching of practitioner and clients summarizes the problem.[36]

> The contention that only Black therapists can adequately treat Black clients is as much a racist notion as the contention that Black therapists cannot treat White clients. . . . Setting special standards for a person because he is Black and insisting that only another Black can understand him is to make him less than equal, to deprive him of his humanity.

Parloff, Waskow, and Wolfe reported several general conclusions regarding the effects of selected practitioner characteristics on the outcome of treatment. Their studies of research evidence did not confirm the popular belief that the practitioner's sex is a major factor in determining the outcome of treatment. They also found that any evidence suggesting that practitioner experience is important to the outcome of treatment is "surprisingly weak and not adequately tested."[37] They further concluded that the evidence does not support the notion that having undergone personal psychotherapy is requisite to practitioner effectiveness. They decided that the interaction of race, sex, and social class as client–practitioner variables has not been adequately tested. They also came to believe that therapist attitudes, and demographic variables such as sex, race, and social class may "play a lesser role in brief crisis-oriented therapies and in behaviorally-oriented therapies than in long-term psychodynamically oriented therapies."[37]

The idea of matching practitioners and clients on the basis of selected characteristics has some support in the practice literature. Many social workers argue that the matching of practitioner and client according to variables like sex and race will influence the outcome of treatment. However, no convincing evidence of any positive effects of matching has yet appeared. Not that these variables are unimportant. But research has not clearly demonstrated the connection between selected practitioner variables and specific treatment outcomes. To establish firm conclusions, particular studies must be carried out to explore these relationships.

A difficulty arises in drawing conclusions about therapist variables from the available research: Many inquiries to date have been designed to test *other* independent variables, such as therapeutic techniques. Investigators often make after-the-fact inferences about the effects of extraneous practitioner variables. But it is usually impossible to separate the confounding effects of other treatment variables from the practitioner characteristic selected for study. Research work in this field of exploration may want to provide more systematic control of selected practitioner variables than examiners have done in the past.

Operational Definitions of Treatment Methods

Research in social work is not exempt from the requirements of experimental rigor. As in any form of scientific research, the treatment procedures tested in social work research should be reproducible. One research worker should be able to repeat another's procedures at a later time and obtain similar findings.

Chapter 3 reviews methods for developing reliable, objective, and valid dependent variables (outcome measures). But much social work research provides inadequate descriptions of the independent variable. The preceding three sections of this chapter discuss some specific methods of overcoming this deficiency. Another way to address the lack of fully described independent variables lies in the use of operational definitions of treatment methods.

Webster defines operationalism as "the view that concepts or terms of purportedly factual statements must be definable in terms of identifiable and repeatable activities." Thus, in social work research, the activities that constitute the independent variable must be described accurately, so that others may repeat them. This requirement has not always been met with equal fidelity in social work studies involving between-group designs. However, a few research workers have begun to achieve this condition with consistency. Briar and Conte recognized the single-subject design's potential for improving the quality of social work research. They recognized that social work research has suffered from problems of adequately defining both the independent and dependent variable.[38]

> Of particular significance for research on casework, as well as for other in-
> tervention, is the development of research techniques that make it possible to
> conduct rigorous experiments with individual cases or series of cases. . . . The
> spreading application of these designs in social work indicates that the two prob-
> lems of specification are solvable.

The requirement that the independent variable be operationally defined is relatively straightforward. It means that the practitioner or researcher who is providing the treatment being tested must describe the technique so that it can be applied by others. In other words, the researcher-practitioner must find a way to standardize the treatment. This requirement raises some questions about how treatment procedures are described and disseminated for use by others.

There are several useful ways of standardizing treatment procedures. One is for practitioners to follow the instructions in implementation manuals. These are precise checklists or how-to-do-it guides written in enough detail that users may replicate specific treatment procedures. Manuals can be supplemented by such media components as slides, films, audio tapes, or any similar methods of instruction about implementing treatment uniformly. Researchers and practitioners also might attend training workshops to study such teaching techniques as modeling and case demonstrations with simulated or actual clients. Workshops often build on the skills outlined in the implementation manuals and frequently use videotapes and other records to demonstrate standard procedures. Videotapes of trainee performances can be used as critiques of learners' progress, as well.

The dissemination process described here may lie well beyond the range of activities possible for any single practitioner or research worker. Yet the requirements for dissemination are essentially the same as for experimental research: The research worker must describe the treatment procedure in enough detail that others may accurately replicate it. The ideal method of achieving this demand is to produce a concise record of the treatment process. Written descriptions as well as other mechanical and electronic means may be employed. For the procedure to meet the criterion of replication, it must consist of observable activities, which, under the proper conditions, others should be able to repeat with a high degree of accuracy.

The practitioner and the research worker are accountable jointly for developing exact, measurable descriptions of practice procedures and techniques. To an ever-increasing extent, practitioners must assume responsibility for both the delivery of social work service and for conducting ongoing research on social work services. Single-subject designs can be incorporated into normal practice routines. Attention to the requirements of practice-oriented research will allow practitioners to contribute significantly to the advancement of practice knowledge.

Summary

The independent variable—often called the treatment or the experimental condition—is a major element in social work experimentation. The typical experiment employs one of three approaches: (1) provide the independent variable to one group and withhold it from another, (2) provide assorted degrees of the independent variable to different groups, or (3) present entirely different conditions to separate groups. The central idea in experimental research is that some subjects, under certain controlled conditions, are exposed to the independent variable and their reactions are then studied.

Research workers must retain control of the independent variable. They must apply it to the right subjects at the right time and place. Yet, too often, social work research workers do not achieve the required degree of control because they fail adequately to define the independent variable. Too frequently, practitioners and researchers apply dissimilar, ill-defined variables to experimental subjects; hence, few if any worthwhile conclusions can be drawn from most studies. Unless the time, quantity, and intensity of treatment are all specified and kept constant throughout a project, any findings become valueless. Further, if the dependent variable is not carefully described, it will be impossible for others to replicate the research.

The logic of evaluation research in social work requires the researcher to establish a control group, an experimental treatment, and reliable and valid outcome measures for comparing the reactions of various subjects. Where most social work researchers fall short is at the middle stage. They fail to describe the treatment in sufficient detail, believing somehow that most intervention plans are essentially similar. Such an assumption, however, is not consistent with experimental research.

Adequately describing treatment tactics is difficult; and the less structured a treatment is, the harder it is to describe and replicate. Specific techniques for isolating and describing dimensions of treatment include using (1) prestructured treatment stimuli, (2) treatment typologies, (3) selected practitioner variables, and (4) operationally defined treatment methods.

1. Prestructured treatment stimuli may or may not require practitioner involvement. Totally prestructured stimuli commonly take the form of tapes, movies, and self-help books; the practitioner need not be involved. Such stimuli often are used to teach clients to relax as a means of relieving stress, which is believed to cause problems like headaches, depression, and tiredness. Self-help manuals often aim to help people control habits like smoking and overeating.

Partially prestructured stimuli, such as practitioner handbooks, involve the therapist in the treatment to some degree. For the research worker, the more highly structured treatments are easier to replicate. Structured self-help materials usually benefit the client as well. A drawback is that some professionals, for various reasons, dislike prestructured treatment. Also, research workers cannot control how closely different practitioners follow manual instructions.

2. The treatment typology describes the essential attributes of a treatment package. It should help practitioners select the best type of intervention for a specific case. The basic idea in typology is that treatments may be classified and described according to their methods, characteristics, and governing theories. Although treatment typologies have been popular for describing practice techniques, they have not proved especially useful for social work research. To use the typology approach properly, the research worker must have an accurate description of what transpires during treatment—and accurate accounts are usually difficult to acquire. Further, typologies do not always allow classifying all aspects of treatment; too many are based on abstract concepts that cannot be observed in treatment.

3. Practitioner variables are important but create problems for social work research. Some investigators feel that the only such variables that are important are the professional's techniques, skills, and methods. But many others consider significant such additional characteristics as practitioners' experience, sex, race, and social standing. As yet, few concrete conclusions about the effects of practitioner variables on the success of treatment have been drawn. Some evidence suggests that certain therapist characteristics are more important in certain kinds of treatment than in others. Probably most are significant to some degree. But studies have not clearly demonstrated the connections between selected practitioner variables and specific treatment outcomes.

4. Operationally defining the independent variable means that the practitioner or research worker must standardize the technique being studied and must describe it so that others can apply it and replicate it. Instructions for precisely fulfilling these requirements may be acquired from a number of how-to guides (or implementation manuals) and other sources. For a procedure to meet the criterion of replication, it must consist of observable activities, which, under proper conditions, others may repeat with a high degree of accuracy.

Sources of Material

Self-help materials—videotapes, audiotapes, films, manuals—are available from a number of sources. The following list contains a sampling of these sources.

- Potentials Unlimited, 2545 Berwych, S.W., Grand Rapids, Mich., 49506. This firm has a large catalog of audiotapes.
- Guilford Publications, 200 Park Avenue South, New York, N.Y., 10003.
- Psychological Associates, 2005M South Kimball, Caldwell, Idaho, 83605.
- BioTemp Products, P.O. Box 88370, Indianapolis, Ind., 46208.
- Thought Technology, Ltd., 2193 Clipton Avenue, Montreal, Quebec, Canada, H4A 2N5.
- Weight Reduction Cassettes, W. Hodges, 754 First Street, Suite 203, Macon, Ga., 31201.
- Hypnosis Cassettes, Human Potential Company, 2953 Vineland, S.E., Grand Rapids, Mich., 49508.
- Research Press, 2612 N. Mattis Ave., Champaign, Ill. 61820.
- Plenum Publishing Company, 227 W. 17th Street, New York, N.Y. 10013.
- Brooks-Cole Publishing Company, 555 Abrego, Monterey, Calif. 93940.
- American Personnel and Guidance Association, 5203 Leesburg Pike, Falls Church, Va., 22041. Ask for 16mm film and audio cassette catalog, *Parent Training*, order #77578.

End Notes

1. Campbell, Donald T., and Stanley, Julian C. *Experimental and Quasi-Experimental Designs for Research.* Chicago: Rand McNally & Co., 1966.
2. Sundland, D. M. "Theoretical Orientations of Psychotherapists." In *Effective Psychotherapy*, edited by A. S. Gurman and A. M. Razin, pp. 189–219. New York: Pergamon Press, 1977.
3. Meyer, Henry, Borgatta, Edgar F., and Jones, W. C. *Girls at Vocational High: An Experiment in Social Work Intervention.* New York: Russell Sage Foundation, 1965.
4. Macdonald, Mary E. "Reunion at Vocational High." *Social Service Review* 40 (June 1966): 186–187.
5. Briar, Scott. "Family Services and Casework." In *Research in the Social Services: A Five-Year Review*, edited by H. S. Maas, p. 114. New York: National Association of Social Workers, 1971.
6. Powers, E., and Witmer, H. *An Experiment in the Prevention of Delinquency.* New York: Columbia University Press, 1951.
7. Brown, Gordon E. *The Multiproblem Dilemma.* Metuchen, N.J.: Scarecrow Press, 1968.
8. Briar, "Family Services," p. 115.

9. Reid, William J., and Shyne, A. W. *Brief and Extended Casework*. New York: Columbia University Press, 1969.
10. Briar, "Family Services," p. 116.
11. Rakos, R. F., and Schroeder, H. E. *Self-Directed Assertiveness Training*, Bama Audio Cassettes (New York: Guilford Publishing Company), 1976.
12. See, for example, catalog for Research Press, Champaign, Ill. Also see the following sample therapist manuals: Rodney Miller, "A Comparison of Brief Relaxation Therapies: Self Report and Psychological Indices." Master's thesis, unpublished, University of Montana, Department of Psychology, 1976; or Paul J. Bach, "A Cognitive/Behavioral Treatment Program for Use with American Indian Alcohol Abusers." Master's thesis, unpublished, University of Montana, Department of Psychology, 1979.
13. Miller, "A Comparison of Brief Relaxation Therapies," pp. 83–84.
14. Mungas, Dan M. "Pretesting and Therapist-Client Sex Matching Effects in Social Skills Training." Master's thesis, University of Montana, Department of Psychology, 1977, p. 102.
15. Germain, Carel. "Casework and Science: A Historical Encounter." In *Theories of Social Casework*, edited by R. W. Roberts and R. H. Nee. Chicago: University of Chicago Press, 1970, pp. 22–23.
16. Hollis, F. "Explorations in the Development of a Typology of Casework Treatment." *Social Casework* 48 (June 1967): 335.
17. *Ibid.*, p. 337.
18. Reid, William J. "Client and Practitioner Variables Affecting Treatment." *Social Casework* 45 (December 1964): 586–592.
19. Turner, F. J. "A Comparison of Procedures in the Treatment of Clients with Two Different Value Orientations." *Social Casework* 45 (May 1964): 273–277.
20. Briar, "Family Services and Casework," p. 119.
21. Reid, William J. "A Test of a Task-Centered Approach." *Social Work* 20 (1975): 3–9.
22. Rossi, R. B. "Helping a Mute Child." In *Task-Centered Practice*, edited by W. J. Reid and L. Epstein. New York: Columbia University Press, 1977.
23. Tolson, E. R. "Alleviating Marital and Communication Problems." In *Task-Centered Practice*, edited by W. J. Reid and L. Epstein. New York: Columbia University Press, 1977.
24. Rogers, C. R. "The Necessary and Sufficient Conditions of Therapeutic Personality Change." *Journal of Consulting Psychology* 21 (1957): 95–103.
25. Truax, C. B., and Carkhuff, R. R. *Toward Effective Counseling and Psychotherapy*. Chicago: Aldine, 1967.
26. Rogers, "Therapeutic Personality Change."
27. Carkhuff, R. R. *Helping and Human Relations*, 2 vols. New York: Holt, Rinehart, 1969.
28. Strupp, H. H. "A Reformulation of the Dynamics of the Therapist's Contribution." In *Effective Psychotherapy*, edited by A. S. Gurman and A. M. Razin. New York. Pergamon Press, 1977, p. 9.
29. Briar, S., and Conte, J. "Families." In *Social Service Research*, edited by H. S. Maas. Washington, D.C.: National Association of Social Workers, 1978, p. 26.
30. Fiske, D. W. "Methodological Issues in Research on the Psychotherapist." In *Effective Psychotherapy*, edited by A. S. Gurman and A. M. Razin. New York: Pergamon Press, 1977, pp. 23–43.

31. Garfield, S. L. "Research on the Training of Professional Psychotherapists." *Ibid.*, pp. 63–83.
32. Auerbach, A. H., and Johnson, M. "Research on the Therapist's Level of Experience." *Ibid.*, pp. 84–102.
33. Parloff, M. B., Waskow, I. E., and Wolfe, B. E. "Research on Therapist Variables in Relation to Process and Outcome." In *Handbook of Psychotherapy and Behavior Change*, 2nd. ed., edited by S. L. Garfield and A. E. Bergin. New York: John Wiley and Sons, 1978.
34. *Ibid.*, p. 273.
35. *Ibid.*, p. 264.
36. Sattler, J. M. "The Effects of Therapist-Client Racial Similarity." In Geirman and Razen, *op. cit.*, p. 284.
37. Parloff, Waskow, and Wolfe, "Therapist Variables," p. 273.
38. Briar and Conte, "Families," p. 27.

Experimental and Quasi-Experimental Research Designs

7

A research design serves as a plan to direct observations. It helps investigators to collect data and eventually reach conclusions about the problem under investigation.

A variety of designs for guiding the conduct of research is available to the practitioner–researcher. The selection of a specific research design depends on the purpose of the research. For investigators seeking to test, evaluate, and compare practice methods, and for those who wish to evaluate service programs, one of the experimental research designs should prove most useful. These range from the most rigorous designs—those that satisfy all the conditions for classification as fully experimental designs—to the less rigorous quasi-experimental designs.

Fully experimental designs employ two (or more) groups of people: persons exposed to an experimental condition are compared to control groups who receive no treatment. Research workers then assess the effects of different experimental and control conditions. This form of design can be used to evaluate practice methods or service programs.

Other research designs, such as single-subject plans (also called within-subject designs), are intended primarily for testing and evaluating the effectiveness of specific treatment methods. In the single-subject design, the subject serves as his own control. This research strategy involves comparisons between different time periods, in which separate treatment or control conditions are applied to the subject.

The practitioner-researcher who is interested in a problem that requires further exploration and clarification may use nonexperimental designs, such as the exploratory study. Exploratory research helps practitioners determine more precisely the nature and form of a problem, so they then may formulate and test more specific research questions.

This chapter explores in detail these and other basic research designs. It also provides practical examples of the various designs for review and illustration.

Experimental Designs

Experimental and Control Group Pretest and Posttest Designs

The research design using experimental and control groups, pretested and posttested, is a classic design for conducting true experimental research. It probably is one of the most powerful, hence most desirable, of the experimental designs. It is the deluxe model; it also is one of the most difficult and most costly to use.

This design assesses the effectiveness of a treatment or intervention by systematically comparing specific changes in two or more carefully selected groups. Normally these groups are designated as the experimental group and the control group.

The experimental group is exposed to the treatment; the control group is not. The population for this design is selected carefully and assigned randomly to one group or the other. A "pretest" measure is taken of the dependent variable. The treatment then is applied to the experimental group but not to the control group.

During the "treatment" phase, the experiment is monitored carefully to see if anything happens that might distort or contaminate the findings. Such potential distortions should be controlled if possible. If such control is not possible, research workers must identify and estimate the effect of any contamination on the experiment.

After the treatment, both groups again are measured for the final "posttest." The pretests and posttests then are compared for both experimental and control groups. Finally, the experimenter must try to identify any other possible explanations of differences between the two groups. Although this experimental model is designed to identify the effects of a treatment on a group of people, there always remains a possibility that some special event or factor other than the treatment has affected one group and not the other. The control group helps to identify those changes attributed to the treatment being studied; it also helps investigators isolate any changes that may be caused by the experiment participants.

Research workers long have been aware that participants themselves sometimes can alter research results. These reactive changes often are described as the Hawthorne effect. The Hawthorne effect was first noted by a team of researchers studying effects of changing the working conditions of Western Electric Company employees.[1] They were interested in learning if certain alterations could improve worker productivity. As part of the study, they added brighter lights to the work area and found that posttest productivity increased over pretest productivity. They further brightened the work area, and noted even greater increases in productivity. Finally, they lowered the lighting, reversing the treatment from brighter lights to dimmer lights. Yet worker output again increased!

The research team concluded that the workers were responding to the attention they were getting rather than to changes in their work environment. The very process of participating in research, then, may confound the results; the research worker sometimes may be unable to determine if the changes are due to the treatment alone or to the effects of the experiment itself.

The control group, in addition to controlling for the effects of the experiment itself, has a second important function. It must control for factors not contained in the experiment itself. For example, the research worker conducting an experiment concerning identification and treatment of child abuse probably would find that the news media regularly publish information on that topic. This ongoing public coverage could well affect the behavior of participants in this kind of survey. Newspaper and magazine articles, television documentaries, and dramatic presentations (movies, plays, and television programs) all could greatly influence study participants. Because the research worker rarely can control the exposure of an experimental population to such influences, the control group lets the experimenter gauge the effects of these and any similar variables.

The control group should provide a measure of any confounding effects. However, to achieve a scientifically acceptable research design (see Table 7–1), the investigators must meet an essential condition: the experimental and control groups must be comparable. The optimum approach for assuring comparability between experimental and control groups is a method called *random assignment.*

Subject Assignment

For two groups to be comparable, researchers should strive to make them as alike as possible except for the actual experience of participating in the experiment. A systematic random assignment procedure ensures that each person in the population to be studied has an equal chance of being assigned to

TABLE 7-1. Pictorial Representation of the Experimental Control Group Design Using Pretests and Posttests

Group	Before Treatment Measure (independent variable)	After Treatment Measure (dependent variable)	Difference
Experimental	A_1	A_2	$A = A_2 - A_1$
Control	B_1	B_2	$B = B_2 - B_1$

Definitions of Variables

A_1 = pretest results for experimental group
A_2 = posttest results for experimental group
B_1 = pretest results for control group
B_2 = posttest results for control group
A = $A_2 - A_1$
B = $B_2 - B_1$

Final treatment effect = $A - B$

To determine the effects of a treatment, subtract the pretreatment measure (A_1) for the experimental group from that group's posttreatment state (A_2). Perform the same operation for the control group: subtract B_1 from B_2. Finally, subtract B (the control group's outcome) from A (the experimental group's outcome). This result, $A - B$, is the effect of the experimental treatment.

either group—experimental or control. The word *random* is used here in a specific way. It does not mean haphazard. Random assignment means that everyone in the research population has an equal chance of being selected for either group. Experimental and control groups assigned by random methods will differ from one another only by chance. Thus, if the sample is of adequate size, for comparison purposes the groups may be considered equal.

To attain a scientifically acceptable control group, the research worker must employ carefully controlled methods for assigning subjects into experimental and control groups. All subjects should stand an even chance of being assigned to either group. The use of random assignment and similar techniques for assignment of subjects into experimental and control groups assures comparability. If the two groups are not comparable, then it is difficult to attribute to the independent variable any differences revealed by the experiment. It is necessary, then, for research workers to ensure that the experimental and control groups are as similar as possible.

The most common method of ensuring comparability of groups is randomization. One way the experimenter can achieve random samples is first to allot a number to each subject, then to assign persons holding odd numbers to one section and people with even numbers to the other. This method achieves the same end as tossing a coin for each subject to determine assignment.

Another means of subject assignment is matching subjects. In matching, research workers choose, for inclusion in both groups, subjects who are matched for relevant characteristics. For example, if the research is studying the effects of a training program on a population, the subjects' IQ scores and previous work experience would be a matter to control because both those factors can affect how well people benefit from a training program. The experimenter would want to use matched pairs of subjects having similar IQs and employment backgrounds, then assign each person to experimental or control by random methods. The result of matching should be the same as for random assignment: the control group and the experimental group will be comparable. Thereafter, any differences found probably can be attributed to the treatment.

For experiments involving several research groups (such as the Solomon group designs, discussed later in this chapter), the best randomization of participants might be achieved by the use of a computer to assign subjects to various groups. In any case, whatever method of subject assignment is used, the primary research concern is to guarantee that all subjects have an equal chance of being assigned to any one of the groups involved in a project.

Measuring Changes in Subjects

The classic control group design is presented here in a rigid manner to illustrate its basic features, but several variations may be imposed on the basic plan without invalidating the design. The classic design involves four basic measurements of change: the pretest and posttest for the experimental group, and the pretest and posttest for the control group.

It is possible to measure results for both groups at intervals during the course of the experiment. If the investigator decides to use such multiple measurements, though, he must determine if the measurement process itself is responsible for any of the changes being measured.

Some measures may not cause any response in subjects. These generally are called *nonreactive*. The measurement process is considered nonreactive when it does not produce an effect that can be attributed to the measurement itself.

For example, the research worker investigating the social work treatment of parents who abuse children may well need to employ multiple measurements of progress. In this instance, the selection of a measurement procedure is extremely important; one procedure likely will influence child-abuse patterns directly, whereas another measure might have no effect on abuse patterns. The research might aim to identify the most effective treatment for reducing child abuse, yet the measurement technique could confound the results and create confusion over which treatment method is most effective.

One measurement process likely to influence child abuse is a regular physical examination of the child in the parents' presence. Daily or weekly physical examinations probably will deter a child-abusing parent; thus, the physical examination as a measure of child abuse is a highly reactive measure. On the other hand, the child's schoolteacher may be trained to recognize indicators of abuse and then make daily observations of the child. This sort of measure, if the teacher's reports are unobtrusive, is unlikely to influence the parents. The second measure, therefore, is more likely to be nonreactive and will give a better picture of the effects the researcher is studying.

Another well-known research phenomenon is one that is similar to the Hawthorne effect. The placebo effect has been observed when people are treated with inert or otherwise nonpotent methods yet show improvement anyway. The placebo effect is common in medical research, often in testing the effects of drugs by means of an experimental design similar to the classic control group experiment just described. Research workers have observed that people often experience improvement even when they receive nonpotent drug substitutes, such as sugar pills. Thus, changes frequently can be achieved in the physical and psychological conditions of people who expect that a given treatment will help them.[2] That is, if a person believes that a pill is going to help in some specific way, such as reducing pain, that individual may in fact experience less pain.

Consequently, it is not always desirable to use a control group that receives no treatment. Instead, to control for the confounding effects of participating in a treatment program, research workers may have to provide a placebo treatment for the control group. It is advisable to employ a placebo when the experimental group is exposed to a treatment that obviously should influence its members' expectations for change. For example, if an experiment is testing the use of a counseling service for depressed persons, the experimental group can expect less depression just because participants expect to improve with counseling. To offset the possible results of this confounding effect, testers may need to design for the control group a placebo that approximates the conditions of the counseling being tested. For example, the control group could be converted to a placebo group by providing them with a group experience that resembles the treatment group but merely provides attention rather than treatment per se. This is known as an attention placebo.

In social work research, the potential for a placebo's confounding effects is especially great. Most, if not all, of the methods common to social work practice are subject to this influence. Thus, the social work research investigator must devise methods that will help separate placebo effects from actual treatment results. The attention placebo is suitable for many kinds of social work research.

An example of placebo research is contained in a study of insomnia by Carr-Kaffashan and Woolfolk.[3] They compared the relative effectiveness of relaxation training and of a placebo in treating sleeplessness. The false treatment used was a form of attention placebo designed to elicit an expectation for improvement comparable to that of the actual treatment, relaxation training.

The research workers decided that, to ensure equal credibility between active and placebo treatments, a placebo would be used according to the same rationale and procedure as those of the relaxation training. By random methods they assigned insomnia sufferers to two groups. One group received active treatment consisting of modified progressive relaxation training. The second received an attention placebo.

Subjects receiving the attention placebo "were told that sleep disturbance is a problem in which bedtime stimuli elicit intense emotional responses that are incompatible with sleep."[4] They were given a "modified desensitization" to learn. This involved the imagined pairing of bedtime stimuli with neutral (nonarousing) stimuli. According to the authors, "This procedure should be inert with respect to insomnia, since the imagined pairing of bedtime stimuli with neutral images should not change the presumed functional relationship."[4] The instructions given the placebo group were similar to those provided the treatment group. Both, for example, were told to practice twice a day at a certain time.

The results of this research project indicated that, as a method of reducing the amount of time persons suffering from insomnia require to fall asleep, relaxation training was significantly superior to the placebo treatment. (The research workers later did provide relaxation training to those who received the attention placebo.)

In designing an attention placebo, it is important that experimenters develop an alternative treatment similar in rationale and procedure to the treatment being tested (as did Carr-Kaffashan and Woolfolk). Subjects should be encouraged to expect as much improvement from the attention placebo as from the treatment. The research worker also must consider the ethical responsibility of treating the placebo group at some point, if an effective treatment is found.

Many professionals regard the use of placebos and other "no-treatment" strategies as ethically unacceptable. This difficult ethical problem has several sides. On one hand, professionals may object to the use of the essentially dishonest strategy of the placebo design. A strong argument can be made for therapists' ethical responsibility always to select and use the most effective treatment methods. On the other hand, practitioners often may be unable to determine honestly if a standard professional treatment is indeed more effective than a placebo. Probably, individual practitioners themselves must determine which, in each case, is the overriding considera-tion: the immediate needs of the client, or the value to many future clients of scientific findings gained from studies of subjects whose treatment was ex-perimentally postponed.

The Double-Blind Experiment

The research worker whose behavior might influence subjects' expectation for improvement presents another potential source of research error. For ex-ample, if a medical research worker is testing the effects of a drug, the use of a placebo may not be enough to determine if the drug alone is responsible for change in the subjects. The investigator can influence the subjects' expecta-tions in a variety of ways.

If the medical investigator knows which persons in an experiment are receiving the placebo, the information may be inadvertently communicated to some patients, thus influencing the subjects' expectations. For instance, the research worker may know that Mrs. B. is receiving sugar pills instead of the experimental drug. Because of this knowledge, the investigator probably will not expect her to improve and unintentionally may communicate this presumption to the subject in a variety of ways, both verbal and nonverbal. If Mrs. B. perceives that the physician does not expect her to improve, she really may not expect to improve herself.

In this case, the placebo effect is lost because the person is not con-vinced that the placebo will help. Unless the experimental subjects all are treated in the same manner, the experimenter will have lost one of the essen-tial elements of a controlled experiment—the requirement that the two groups be comparable.

To avoid this problem, a variation of the classic control group design, known as the double-blind experiment, was developed. The double-blind approach introduces two special conditions into the experiment. With this technique, neither the research worker nor the research subjects know who is receiving the treatment and who is receiving the placebo. In effect, the treatment and placebo are provided in a "blind" manner to both experimen-tal and control subjects.

Although the double-blind experiment is used widely in medical research, it has found only limited application in social work and in the related social and behavioral sciences. Granted, designing a double-blind ex-periment for social work research would be difficult. The research worker would not only need to select a placebo treatment that was convincing to the client–subject, but also would have to design the pseudotreatment so that the social work practitioner employing the treatment did not know whether a placebo was being used. In practice, achieving such a design would be dif-ficult but not impossible. Such a technique would add a measure of credibil-ity to social work research.

Classic Experimental Control Group Designs

Pretest, Posttest

Example.   One example of the use of the classic control group design in social work research is described in the book *Girls at Vocational High*.[5] (This experiment is also discussed in chapters 5 and 6.) This research project attempted to study the effects of a program of social work services on a group of adolescent girls who were troubled, unmanageable, and prone to delinquency. Subjects for experimental and control groups were assigned by random procedure from a population of problem girls entering a vocational high school.

Over a four-year span, 189 girls were chosen for the experimental group and 192 were selected as control subjects. Those in the experimental section were provided casework and group work services; members of the control group did not receive services. Pretests and posttests were taken on a variety of measures for both groups. The researchers then compared the groups on the basis of differences in their two measures.

Investigators used sixteen measures for comparisons. Despite the large number of measures, however, the results of this study revealed few statistically significant distinctions between the experimental and control groups.

The *Vocational High* experiment exemplifies the use of the classical control group design. It also provides an important illustration of some common problems in experimental social work research.

This experiment suffered from several major deficiencies. One is a lack of specificity in identification of the independent variable. The research design did not provide enough information about what constituted this crucial element. Some subjects were given casework services; others were provided with group work services. There is no assurance that all received the same treatment, nor is content of the actual treatment specified.

Social work services are not a unitary method; they may vary greatly from one practitioner to another. The only variable specified in the *Vocational High* experiment is that the subjects received some kind of social work services. That claim is not specific enough—either to provide any useful information to others who may wish to replicate the research, or to help practitioners identify the potentially useful effects of social work treatment. This deficiency is hardly unique to this research project; it unfortunately is a common feature in much of social work research.

A second flaw in this investigation stems from the selection of outcome measures for the dependent variable. Sixteen measures were used in this study to determine if there were differences between the experimental subjects and the control subjects. But the outcome measures were not carefully selected to reflect the objectives of the research. Further, the

103

variables measured in the pretests and posttests were not carefully scrutinized to assure that both tests were reliable and valid measures.

Posttest Only

According to Campbell and Stanley, it is not essential to employ the pretest in a true experimental design.[6] Provided that subjects of the experimental and control groups are assigned randomly, it is not necessary to prove that the groups were "equal" before the experiment. In fact, achieving pretest conditions for controlled experiments frequently is impractical and difficult. The pretest may sometimes be undesirable because it is reactive. When a pretest is suspected of causing reactivity, the research worker may then expect that a pretest effect would contaminate the research. Therefore, when pretests are impractical or impossible, the posttest-only control group design is acceptable. Indeed, the posttest-only control group actually may be more suited to social work research than the experimental control pretest and posttest method.

The post-test-only control group procedure involves the selection and assignment of subjects to groups by means of a random technique. Because the equivalency of groups must be assured, the most acceptable method for guaranteeing it is randomization.

With this technique, two or more groups may be selected and compared. The trial treatment is applied to the experimental group, then both control and experimental groups are given a posttest to measure the dependent variable. The posttest measures then are compared to determine the treatment's effectiveness.

This design is a simple and effective experimental approach (see Table 7–2). Its key is in the random assignment of experimental and control groups, which allows the investigator to assume comparability of groups. In addition, the control group allows the research worker to control for other confounding effects, such as Hawthorne or placebo effects. Because there is no pretesting, the reactive risks of a pretest are eliminated.

Because of the lack of pretesting, however, the research design suffers from a possible flaw. Group differences after the application of the experimental condition may be the result of the differential selection of subjects. Random assignment of subjects probably should eliminate this flaw, however. Random assignment is even more likely to ensure the equality of groups as the sample size increases. With large samples, the investigator can be more confident of equality (but absolute assurance of group equality is not possible without the pretest).

Example. An example of a modified post-test-only research project has been reported by Brown.[7] In this project, the research worker studied the effectiveness of casework methods in helping multiproblem families. A total of

TABLE 7–2. Pictorial Representation of Post-test-only Control Group Design

Group	After Treatment Measure (independent variable)
Experimental	A
Control	B

Definition of Variables
A = posttest measure of experimental group
B = posttest of control group
Final treatment effect = A − B

150 families were randomly assigned to an experimental group or to one of two control groups. The experimental group and one of the control groups were subjected to pretest and posttest measurements. The second control group was subjected to the posttest only and was designated as a hidden control group.

The experimental group received intensive casework services from professional social workers; families in the two control groups received regular, nonintensive services. The outcome measures selected as dependent variables were based on two scales used to measure the results of social work services. The research findings revealed no significant differences in outcome between the experimental group and the two control groups.

Of special interest, however, in this research project is the similarity in the two control groups. The pretest of the hidden control group demonstrated that the pretest measures, because they did not influence the experiment's outcome, may be considered nonreactive. The hidden control group design is especially useful when the research worker is not sure if the pretest is potentially reactive. It allows the research worker to test the reactivity of a measure. It can be somewhat expensive, however, because it involves three groups. When there is good initial reason to believe that a measure is reactive, the investigator may wish to use the post-test-only design, involving only two groups.

The Solomon Four-Group Design
The Solomon four-group design combines features of the pretest/posttest experimental control group design and the post-test-only control group design.

The Solomon plan allows evaluation of the effects of the pretesting used in pretest/posttest designs. Because those models use pretests on both experimental and control groups, the design contains a possible limitation. The research subjects may react to the pretest (hence the experiment may measure this reaction rather than the effects of the experimental treatment). Although the post-test-only design avoids this pretest contamination, it does not provide complete assurance that groups are comparable on specific measures before treatment.

The Solomon four-group design allows greater control. It provides pretests and posttests for half the subjects, the posttests only for the other half. In this design, each subject is randomly assigned to one of four groups: pretest/posttest experimental, pretest/posttest control, post-test-only experimental, or post-test-only control group.

The pretest is carried out on the pretest experimental and control groups. The experimental condition next is applied to the two experimental groups; finally, the posttest is given to all four groups. These results are analyzed for differences between experimental and control groups. The pretest/posttest groups then are compared with the post-test-only groups to determine if the pretest had any effects.

The Solomon design is probably the strongest of the basic experimental designs. Although it does not really control any more sources of error than other designs, it does permit the research worker to determine the possible reactive effects of testing. Further, should research workers desire, the Solomon design may be used with larger numbers of groups; it is not limited to four-group modes. This experimental method is, however, one of the more expensive in terms of time, personnel, and total resources required.

The Solomon design is especially strong in that it contains a built-in control for contamination resulting from the pretest. Most important, because it is conducted with at least two experimental and two control groups, the design allows replication of the experiment. The importance of replication in developing a scientific approach to social work practice cannot be overemphasized.

Example.   Using a Solomon six-group design, Ware and Barr examined different approaches to group treatment.[8] These researchers studied the effects of using two separate leadership styles for conducting personal growth groups. Subjects first were assigned by random methods to one of three units: (1) a group provided with structured leadership, (2) a group provided with unstructured leadership, or (3) a nonparticipating control group. Subjects were further assigned by random methods to pretest groups or post-test-only groups, to create a total of six groups. Three received both pretests and posttests, three received the posttest only. Measures of self-concept and self-actualization were used for both tests.

The experiment results indicated that both the structured and unstructured groups attained significantly higher self-actualization scores than did the control group. No significant differences in the level of self-concept were found between the structured and unstructured groups. Finally, in this case, comparisons between subjects who received both pretests and posttests and those who received only the posttest indicated that the pretest did not significantly affect the results.

Factorial Designs

The foregoing classic control group experimental designs are intended to explore the effects of one independent variable. Social work practice, however, often consists of more than a single treatment. A practitioner may use a variety of treatments on different clients, or on the same client at different times. In addition, the manner in which a specific treatment is used may vary considerably from one practitioner to another.

The social work investigator in practice confronts a variety of complex questions, such as determining which treatments are most effective for a specific client population, or whether experienced practitioners are more effective than beginners in their use of a particular treatment. With the factorial design, investigators may systematically explore these and similar issues.

A factorial design allows the research worker to study the effects of two or more variables in a single experiment. It allows the study of the combined effects of multiple variables—which is called *interaction*. The interaction of variables is little understood in social work.

An interaction occurs whenever the diagnostic, preventive, or therapeutic action of a professionally induced treatment is modified by another factor. The interaction may be caused by another treatment induced by the practitioner or by some factor in the client's environment that affects the treatment. Interaction may (1) enhance the treatment, adding to its effects on the client; (2) inhibit the effects of a treatment, thereby reducing its effects on the client; or (3) have no effect at all.

Factorial designs let the research worker test and evaluate the treatment even when interaction is present. For example, many social workers deal with "captive clients," people such as parolees, or residents of public institutions or hospitals, who have no choice about receiving social work services. The evaluation of clients who do not elect to receive social work services raises multiple questions, such as: Are there differences in the treatment effects provided by social workers using different treatment methods? How does Glasser's Reality Therapy approach compare with behavior modification in treating institutionalized versus noninstitutionalized delinquent boys? Can the two treatments be used together? Will one treatment enhance the other or will it detract from it? Perplexing questions of this nature abound in social work practice.

107

TABLE 7-3.   2 × 2 Factorial Design: Pictorial Example

Treatments

	Behavior Modification	Task-Centered Casework
Male Practitioners		
Female Practitioners		

In its most simple form, the factorial design consists of two variables, each tested under two conditions. This technique is known as a 2 × 2 design (see Table 7–3). With it, research workers could compare the effectiveness of two different treatment methods as applied, for example, by male and female practitioners.

In this example, research workers may compare the effects of two treatments—task-centered casework and behavior modification—applied by practitioners of either sex. In some research (for example, in studies of methods of helping battered women) the treatment method and the sex of the practitioner may both be important variables. The 2 × 2 design allows the research worker to study the interaction of such factors.

An advantage of the factorial design is that it allows the researcher to assess the effects of a number of variables in a single experiment. The design may be expanded to explore several variables at the same time. As the number of factors increases, however, so do the complexity of the design and the number of subjects and subject groups.

The factorial design furnishes unique information about the combined effects of more than one independent variable. Because the effects of interaction in social work research are little understood and poorly documented, further investigation needs to be done in this area.

Example.   An excellent example of a 2 × 2 factorial design in social work research was reported by Pilivian and Gross.[9] Their research examined the effects, on public assistance clients, of the separation of social services and income maintenance services. (In the United States, only since 1970 have public welfare agencies undertaken the separation of financial aid from the provision of social services. Before the separation, workers would initiate visits with welfare recipients. During visits, they both assessed need for continued financial aid and offered social services that they believed clients needed.)

In the Pilivian and Gross study, the separation of aid and services involved two major changes. The first was assigning social services delivery to one group of social workers and assigning public assistance eligibility determination to another group (designated as eligibility technicians). The second change concerned methods of initiating services. Under the separate-services arrangement, social workers normally have no contact with public assistance clients unless the clients specifically request meetings.

Using the factorial design, Pilivian and Gross examined (1) how the separation of services affected clients' patterns of using those services, and (2) the degree of client satisfaction with each of several combinations of services. The research attempted to study the comparative effects of providing services under four different conditions. Conditions 1 and 2 involved the separation of income maintenance and social services; conditions 3 and 4 concerned who originated a request for services:

1. Combined income maintenance and social services.
2. Separate income maintenance and social services.
3. Service contact initiated only at the request of the client.
4. Service contact initiated by worker and client.

Clients were divided by random selection into four service groups. Each group received services described under one of the four conditions. Table 7–4 is a pictorial representation of the four service conditions.

A fifth group, receiving no special service conditions, was used as a comparison group. Subjects for all groups were selected by randomization.

TABLE 7-4. Alternative Conditions for Receiving Service

	Income Maintenance and Services Combined	Income Maintenance and Services Separated
Service Contact Initiated Only at Recipient Request	1 (N = 70)	2 (N = 75)
Service Contact Initiated by Worker as well as Client Initiative	3 (N = 72)	4 (N = 73)

(Reprinted from "The Effects of Separation of Services and Income Maintenance on AFDC Recipients," *Social Service Review*, by I. Pilivian and A. E. Gross by permission of The University of Chicago Press. Vol. 51, No. 3, copyright 1977.)

To assess the effects of different service conditions, the research workers studied two outcome measures: the frequency of new client requests for casework services and financial aid, and (by use of a questionnaire) client expression of relative satisfaction with the public welfare service.

Table 7–5 presents the findings concerning the frequency of service requests. The table provides an excellent example of reporting the results of a factorial research design. The chart makes it clear that, under conditions of separation, client requests for casework services decrease significantly compared to requests in the combined service condition.

The research workers reported additional results. They found that recipients in the combined condition tended to feel more strongly that service workers were concerned with helping them.[9] They also reported an interaction effect: clients in the separated and client-initiated service groups had a less positive view of worker helpfulness than did recipients in the other groups.

Finally, request-for-service rates and client satisfaction measures for the four groups were compared with results from the control group. No significant differences were found between the separated client-initiated service group (who most resembled the control group) and the control group on the basis of either measure.

In summary, the research with a factorial experimental design determined that the division of service and eligibility had important impact on public welfare services. "Specifically . . . under the circumstances of separation, recipients tend to reduce requests for services and to perceive service

TABLE 7–5. Effect of Experimental Manipulations on Recipient Requests for New Services Across All Contacts

	Monthly Request Rates			
Type of Request	Combined Service Condition (N = 70)	Separated Service Condition (N = 75)	Worker Initiated Service Condition (N = 72)	Client Initiated Service Condition (N = 73)
Recipient Requests for New Financial Services	.260*	.140*	.200	.191
Recipient Requests for New Non-Financial Services	.343	.262	.398*	.207*

*Difference significant at the 1 percent confidence level.
Source: Reprinted from "The Effects of Separation of Services and Income Maintenance on AFDC Recipients," *Social Service Review*, by I. Pilivian and A. E. Gross by permission of the University of Chicago Press. Vol. 51, No. 3, copyright 1977.)

workers as less helpful."[10] Removing income maintenance responsibilities from service workers led to a reduction of requests for financial aid. Similarly, demand for nonfinancial services dropped when agencies provided those services only when clients requested them.

Quasi-Experimental Designs

Essentially, the quasi-experimental design differs from the true experimental design in that it does not satisfy all the conditions for the experimental design. Quasi-experimental designs have the advantage of offering practical research solutions to real problems when it is not possible or feasible to achieve full experimental status.

Time Series Experiments

The time series design couples an experimental condition with periodic measures of a group or individual. This design need not involve a control group. Typically it entails the taking of a series of measurements before, during, and after the experiment. By comparing intermediate and before-and-after measures, any change or rates of change may be identified.

Consider a child abuse prevention program, for example, designed to reduce the incidence of child abuse among known child abusers in a community. To test the program using a time series design, research workers first would measure child abuse rates (the number of abuse incidents) among a group of known child abusers. Next, the persons being studied would be exposed to the new child abuse prevention program—the experimental condition. Following the program, the researcher would take postprogram measures of child abuse. Finally, the examiner would compare preprogram rates to postprogram rates to determine the degree of subject improvement.

On the graph in Figure 7–1, note the difference between rates T_2 and T_3. The rates before T_2 and after T_3 are stable, indicating a strong possibility that the experimental program is responsible for the change.

Because this design has some weaknesses, the research worker must attempt to segregate other plausible explanations of any changes that occur, since causality cannot be directly inferred from this design.

Nonequivalent Control Group

The nonequivalent control group design dispenses with random assignments to experimental and control groups. Instead, individuals or groups with similar characteristics are used as controls. For instance, a research worker

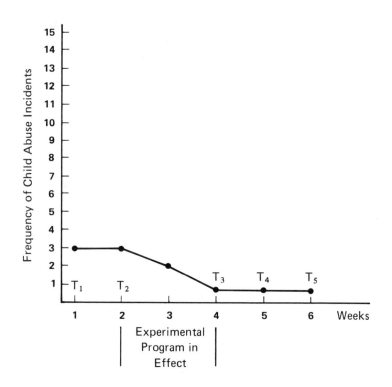

FIGURE 7-1. Pictorial representation of the time series design.

might designate the children in the fourth grade of School A as an experimental group and School B's fourth graders as the control. Before and after measures would be made for both groups, and the results would be compared for differences.

Because random selection is lacking, this is a weak design. From it, consequently, only limited inferences may be made about causation. The nonrandomized controls generally are referred to as "comparison groups."

Example. An example of the nonequivalent control group design has been described by Geismar and Krisberg.[11] This study, like several others conducted during the same period (late 1960s), focused on the multiproblem family. Thirty such families were provided extended social services; the research studied the effects of those services on family functioning.

The multiproblem families in the experimental group all lived in one low-income housing project. Specialized services provided to these experimental subjects consisted of intensive casework services, nursery schools for preschool children, a youth neighborhood center, scouting and 4-H activities, adult activity groups, and other organized community activities.

The experimental families were compared to fifty-one multiproblem families living in other low-cost housing projects in the community. The special services were not available to them. Because experimental subjects and those used for comparison purposes were not selected by random methods, the comparison group constituted a nonequivalent control group.

This research project used premeasures and postmeasures for both the experimental and comparison groups. The two groups were compared on the basis of three outcome measures: delinquency rates, economic dependency, and scores on a family functioning scale. The experimental group scored statistically higher on the family functioning scale. On the two remaining measures, however, the differences between experimental and comparison groups were not conclusive.

Matched Pairs Nonequivalent Control Group Design

A variation of the nonequivalent control group design is the "matched pairs nonequivalent control group design." This design attempts to make the control group resemble the experimental group. The procedure pairs members of the experimental group with control persons who share similar characteristics. Some of the more common features on which people are often matched include sex, age, education, IQ scores, occupation, marital status, and similar variables. Often it is difficult to determine, for matching, which characteristics are most important.

Example. An example of the matched pairs design is contained in a study reported by Sze, Keller, and Keller.[12] In this project, researchers studied the effects of teaching a portion of the social work undergraduate curriculum under different conditions. They compared the different effects of using social work faculty members as instructors in the human behavior and social environment courses to the results of using faculty from other departments. Four schools were involved.

Students who received instruction from social work faculty (designated as the "in" departments) in two universities were compared to students receiving instruction from non-social-work faculty (the "out" departments) in two other universities. All students were tested on their knowledge of the content area. In each school, the test was given to beginning undergraduate students and to graduating seniors. Researchers desired to establish a baseline against which they could compare the performance of the graduating seniors. The beginning students in a sense became the pretest; the seniors became the posttest.

In this case, the authors reported that instruction by faculties from different departments caused no statistically significant differences in the quality of knowledge students gained.

113

Retrospective Research

Investigators using retrospective research attempt to study the relationships among variables after the fact. In practice, the research worker often is unable to manipulate and control the independent variable directly, and just as often finds it impossible to assign subjects randomly to different experimental treatments. When these situations prevail, whatever the cause, the best alternative is to conduct retrospecting research. Some authors refer to retrospective research as *ex post facto research* or *causal-comparative research.*[13]

A major difference exists between retrospective research and the post-test-only research design. In retrospective research, the research worker does not plan the manipulation of experimental and control conditions, does not arrange an experiment, and does not control independent variables. Typically, retrospective research involves a study of two groups already known to differ on the basis of a dependent variable measure. The research worker attempts to determine which antecedents may be related to that difference.

A great many research investigators study alcoholism, for example, using retrospective research. Investigators typically begin with two groups, one of which is composed of alcoholics. Next, they comb the backgrounds of all the participants for factors that appear to promote alcoholism or discourage it. Research workers hope to identify significant traits in the histories of one group, then to find those factors lacking in the backgrounds of the other subjects.

Another common form of retrospective research is to examine two groups of people who differ on the basis of a specific experience. An investigator may compare the high school dropout, for example, to the graduate. After-the-fact comparisons might be made, using such criteria as income levels, occupational success, or marital stability.

Retrospective research also is commonly used to study so-called natural experiments wherein entire communities are exposed to natural disasters such as floods, tornadoes, or volcanic eruptions. The effects of the disaster may be studied by comparing the reactions of the stricken community to conditions in nearby unaffected communities. Such factors as mental health problems, stress reactions, and birth rates are often used as bases for comparison.

Retrospective research can be an extremely useful form of investigation. When populations are affected by disease or other misfortunes, this type of research allows professionals to identify possible causes and to determine how best to help the afflicted populace.

Retrospective research cannot be used to establish a cause-and-effect relationship, however. Causality cannot be established beyond a doubt because the event took place in a natural setting and because control of the variables is lacking. Direct manipulation of the independent variable does not occur, and replication is not possible. Therefore, causal inferences cannot be made with confidence. In contrast to causal relationships, some research workers prefer to discuss functional relationships between variables in retrospective research. Ary, Jacobs, and Razavien state:

> A functional relationship is one in which it has been demonstrated that a change in one variable is accompanied by a change in the other, but the relationship is probably based on a complex system of interactions rather than being directly caused.[14]

Retrospective research, when used and interpreted appropriately, can yield a great deal of information. Its major utility lies in the study of functional relationships among variables as they occur in natural settings—when experimentation cannot be used because of ethical issues, or when controls would contribute to an artificial or simplistic relationship among variables.

Some of the basic weaknesses in the retrospective design include: (1) lack of direct control over the independent variable, (2) possibility of extraneous variables or unidentified sources of causation that may account for group differences, (3) selection of subjects who may not be representative, (4) inability to replicate the research, (5) uncertainty of including the causative factor among the factors being studied, and (6) uncertainty of cause-and-effect relationships.

Retrospective research has been called *the reverse approach to experimentation.* Instead of starting with two equivalent groups and exposing one to experimental conditions, it begins with two groups that are different and tries to identify the antecedents responsible for their differences.

Summary

A research design serves as a plan to direct investigators' observations. The design used for a particular project depends on the purpose of the research. The two primary classes of design are experimental and quasi-experimental. There are varieties of each.

The classic research design uses experimental and control groups whose members are tested both before and after the experiment. This basic model assesses the effectiveness of a treatment by comparing specific changes in two or more carefully selected groups: an experimental group whose members are exposed to treatment, and a control group. Subjects are assigned to groups by random methods.

Experimenters must constantly guard against the chance that some external factor may affect the research, including the possibility that subjects may, to some degree, be responding to the attention they receive (a phenomenon called the Hawthorne effect). The control group should provide a measure of such confounding effects.

Research also must try to ensure that the members of experimental and control groups are comparable—that they are as alike as possible. To do this, investigators use various random assignment procedures designed to give everyone in the research population an equal chance of being selected for either group. One common method is to give each participant a number, then assign subjects to the groups using a table of random numbers. Another approach is to match subjects according to factors important to the particular project (e.g., such traits as IQ or work histories).

When choosing measures (pretests, posttests, and any desired interim measures) for research groups, experimenters must be careful to use measurement procedures that are nonreactive—that is, research workers should test subjects' change by means that will not somehow affect participants' target behaviors. Investigators also must be aware of the placebo effect, a phenomenon that occurs when people treated experimentally with inert or nonpotent methods show improvement anyway. Although the placebo effect can have therapeutic usefulness, it can confound the aims of research. Thus (especially in much social work research), investigators often must provide control groups some form of placebo treatment—some approximation treatment that actually should neither worsen nor improve subjects' conditions. Experimenters designing an attention placebo should develop an alternative treatment with a rationale and procedure that resemble the treatment being tested. Participants should be encouraged to expect as much improvement from the attention placebo as from the active treatment. (The use of attention placebos means research workers and practitioners must weigh the inherent ethical considerations, however.)

If the attitude or actions of a research worker might somehow affect the reactions of subjects receiving placebos, experimenters might consider using a double-blind approach, with neither investigator nor subject knowing who is receiving treatment and who is receiving the placebo. Although this strategy is common in medical research, designing such an experiment for social work remains considerably more difficult.

When a particular experiment should not employ a pretest, because doing so might cause reactivity, a posttest-only design may be used. Experimental and control group members still must be selected carefully by random means to ensure equivalency. In cases where the research worker desires to employ a pretest, yet fears its reactive effects, the Solomon four-group design may be used. This design splits control and experimental participants into two divisions—half receiving both pretests and posttests, half receiving only posttests. After the experiment, investigators compare and analyze results from subjects in both divisions to determine if the pretest had any effects. The Solomon design is a strong research plan: it contains a built-in control for pretest contamination and also enhances experimental replication.

Factorial research designs are appropriate for the study of effects of two or more variables in a single experiment. These allow the study of the interaction of variables. An interaction occurs whenever the diagnostic, preventive, or therapeutic action of intervention is modified by some other factor. The factorial design lets research workers test and evaluate the treatment even when interaction is present. Its simplest form, the 2×2 design, consists of two variables, each tested under two conditions. As the number of factors increases, so does the complexity of the factorial design.

Quasi-experimental methods do not satisfy all the conditions of the fully experimental designs, but they often allow the solution of actual problems that do not permit full experimentation. One such plan, the time-series design, couples an experimental condition with periodic measures of subjects; it need not involve a control group. Research work compares intermediate and before-and-after measures to discover any changes and rates of change. Causality may not be directly inferred from the time-series design.

The nonequivalent control group design employs as subjects groups or individuals having similar characteristics. It dispenses with random assignments to experimental and control groups, which makes it a fairly weak design from which only limited inferences about causation may be made.

An offshoot is the matched pairs nonequivalent control group design. Although random assignment still is lacking, experimenters attempt to make the control group resemble the experimental group by pairing group members according to similar characteristics. Commonly matched variables include sex, age, education, IQ, and occupation.

To study after-the-fact relationships among variables, researchers employ a quasi-experimental design called retrospective research. That is, they attempt to determine causation by studying the recent history of a phenomenon. Retrospective research differs from posttest-only designs in that the research worker cannot plan the experiment or the manipulation of experimental and control conditions, but only examines present conditions and their antecedent causes. A typical retrospective research project compares two groups already known to differ on the basis of a dependent variable measure. Investigators often use such studies to try to learn the social and psychological causes of alcoholism, for example. Retrospective studies are frequently employed in studying people who differ on the basis of a specific experience, such as education level. Retrospective research, further, is commonly used to explore such natural experiments as the effects of a natural disaster or an epidemic on a stricken populace.

Retrospective research cannot establish causality, however, because the events studied occurred in natural settings wherein control of the variables was lacking. It does allow the examination of functional relationships among variables. Despite its drawbacks (including the inability to replicate a given study) retrospective research, when used and interpreted appropriately, can yield a great deal of information.

End Notes

1. Roetheisberger, F. J. and Dickson, J. W. *Management and the Worker.* Cambridge, Mass.: Harvard University Press, 1939.
2. Frank, J. D. *Persuasion and Healing,* 2d ed. Baltimore: Johns Hopkins University Press, 1973.
3. Carr-Kaffashan, L., and Woolfolk, R. L. "Active and Placebo Effects in the Treatment of Moderate and Severe Insomnia." *Journal of Consulting and Clinical Psychology* 47 (1979): 1072–1080.
4. *Ibid.,* p. 1075.
5. Meyer, Henry, Borgatta, Edgar F., and Jones, W. C. *Girls at Vocational High: An Experiment in Social Work Intervention.* New York: Russell Sage Foundation, 1965.
6. Campbell, Donald T., and Stanley, Julian C. *Experimental and Quasi-Experimental Designs for Research.* Chicago: Rand McNally & Co., 1966.
7. Brown, Gordon E. *The Multi-problem Dilemma.* Metuchen, N. J.: Scarecrow Press, 1968.
8. Ware, R. J., and Barr, J. E. "Effects of a Nine-Week Structured and Unstructured Group Experience on Measures of Self-Concept and Self-Actualization." *Small Group Behavior* 8 (February 1977): 93–101.
9. Pilivian, I., and Gross, A. E. "The Effects of Separation of Services and Income Maintenance on AFDC Recipients." *Social Service Review* 51 (1977): 389–406.
10. *Ibid.,* p. 403.
11. Geismar, L. L., and Krisberg, J. *The Forgotten Neighborhood: Site of an Early Skirmish in the War on Poverty.* Metuchen, N. J.: Scarecrow Press, 1967.
12. Sze, W. C., Keller, R. S., and Keller, D. B. "A Comparative Study of Two Different Teaching and Curricular Arrangements in Human Behavior and Social Environment." *Journal of Education for Social Work* 15 (1979): 103–109.
13. Van Dalen, D. B., and Meyer, W. J. *Understanding Education Research.* New York: McGraw Hill, 1966. Also see: Issac, S., and Michael, W. B. *Handbook in Research and Evaluation.* San Diego: Robert Knapp Publishers, 1974.
14. Ary, D., Jacobs, L., and Razavien, A. *Introduction to Research in Education.* New York: Holt, Rinehart & Winston, 1972, p. 72.

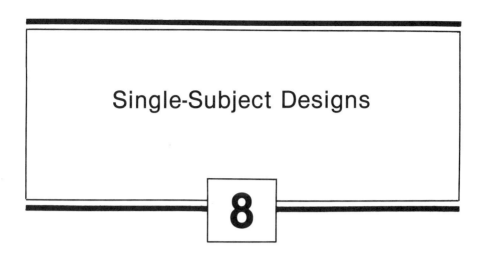

Single-Subject Designs

8

Single-subject methodology, a recent innovation in social work, offers practitioners a badly needed alternative to traditional between-group research designs. Many single-subject designs are well suited to studying the kinds of problems now confronting social workers. This chapter explores a number of these research designs.

In single-subject designs, the subject serves as his or her own control: research workers compare treatment and control results taken at different times for the same person. Also called within-subject designs, single-subject plans evolved through the application of features of the time series design (see chapter 7) to the single case.

Single-subject designs allow examination of the effects, on single cases, of clinical applications of theory and practice methodology. Single-subject methods allow investigators to develop, evaluate, and refine techniques rapidly for treating a variety of problems that arise in social work practice. These designs provide professionals with immediate and practical feedback on their work. They are less expensive and less complicated than between-group designs.

Although this chapter focuses on the application of within-subject designs to single subjects, the same basic designs can be used to study groups of people. Other than for convenience and expense, there are no logical or practical reasons to confine the within-subject designs to single subjects when groups are involved in a research project.

Indeed, several limitations restrict the group research designs. Sometimes the research work needs as many as four control groups to develop effective group designs involving between-subject methodologies. The time, facilities, and number of subjects required make these designs costly and somewhat inflexible. Traditional between-group designs allow only for minimal treatment of control groups until the follow-up is completed.

Some problems under study do not permit the luxury of a delayed follow-up, especially when life-threatening behavior is an issue. If a social worker were investigating the most effective treatment for a family involved in child abuse, for instance, any deferment of services to those involved would raise ethical and legal questions. In this and similar cases, the delay imposed by use of a no-treatment control group poses important ethical questions.

Furthermore, most social agencies simply do not budget the time or staff to conduct ongoing research as part of their services. Therefore, because of the expense and effort required, agencies are not prepared to conduct group research involving between-subject designs. For the average practitioner, group designs constitute a relatively esoteric, expensive, and remote type of research design. The average practitioner needs a research design that is inexpensive, easily understood, and relevant to ongoing social work practice. The single-subject design offers these qualities. It is a practical design that can easily be incorporated into social work practice.

Single-subject designs can demonstrate logically that a specific treatment results in the experimental control over a target behavior. The objective of these research designs is to determine if a causal relationship exists between the dependent and independent variables.

Single-subject designs consist of phases, during which measurements of the dependent variable are taken. Each program involves one or more control phases, called *baselines*, in which the dependent variable is measured but during which no experimental intervention occurs. Each design also involves one or more experimental phases that combine the experimental intervention with measurement of the dependent variable. The baseline condition provides a control that can be used for comparisons with subsequent experimental conditions. The resulting different experimental designs simply are different arrangements of the basic phases of control and experimentation.

The sequence of the different phases of single-subject designs is limited by the underlying logic of the design. For example, a cardinal rule, identified by Hersen and Barlow, concerns the use in the single-subject design of more than one variable. Hersen and Barlow suggest that only one variable at a time be changed when proceeding from one phase to the next.

They point out, "When two variables are simultaneously manipulated, the experimental analysis does not permit conclusions as to which of the two components (or how much of each) contributes to improvement in the target behavior."[1]

Two essential phases are present in all single-subject designs. Users can create different designs by varying the sequential order of the phases. The first phase, designated by the letter A, is the pretreatment stage, in which investigators collect baseline information on a specific problem behavior. The second, or B phase, is the treatment period. Practitioners introduce the treatment variable while monitoring the behavior. These two features, no-treatment (baseline) and treatment, are the basis of all the variations on the single-subject design. They are generally characterized by the letters A and B respectively.

The Baseline

Before implementing treatment procedures, the social work practitioner must obtain definitive information about the strength of the problem behavior. This knowledge will allow the practitioner not only to assess precisely the strength of the problem behavior, but also to evaluate how the treatment procedures affect it. That is, knowing the strength of the problem behavior before treatment will provide the social worker a base against which the effects of treatment may be compared. This data collection period, which immediately precedes the implementation of treatment, is called the *baseline*.

The fundamental task in collecting baseline information is to determine the strength of the problem behavior, which is designated as the dependent variable. Of course, many behaviors have an enormous range of variability. The problem of variability makes obtaining accurate and reliable measures of the dependent variable difficult. To secure a reliable estimate of the problem behavior, research workers should make repeated measurements of the dependent variable. The resulting product—repeated measurements that characterize the preintervention phase—becomes the baseline.

The baseline, then, is a precise record of the frequency of a target behavior before any treatment methods are implemented. The amount of initial observation necessary varies from one case to another, or may vary with one client's different behaviors.

The length of time over which baseline information is collected depends on the fluctuations in the target behavior. Ideally, to produce a stable baseline, investigators should gather baseline information until they observe only small variations in frequency of the behavior. A stable baseline is one in which periodic changes in behavior are not excessive. Admittedly, this definition is vague; fulfilling it requires a judgment on the part of the practitioner.

Bloom recognized the problem of variability in baseline data collection; he has suggested a procedure for producing a baseline that reflects a typical range of behaviors.[2] Bloom recommends restricting the range of problem behavior occurrences to those events within the middle two-thirds of a normal curve. To construct a comparative baseline, his scheme thus eliminates the high and low extremes.

Another solution to the problem of developing a stable baseline measure may be to examine apparent trends in the baseline data. Consider the example of Tom, a nine-year-old boy who hits other children regularly while at school. The school social worker plans to develop a behavior modification treatment procedure designed to reduce his hitting. Accurate baseline information is required before the treatment procedure is initiated. The baseline data will be collected by two observers who will watch Tom continuously during school hours. Table 8–1 is a sample recording of observations during the first four days.

If treatment began on the fifth day, it would be most difficult to evaluate whether the treatment was responsible for any further decline in the behavior because it already was decreasing. Additional observations over more days might have revealed the normally expected range of Tom's behavior, after which the effects of a treatment program would be more apparent.

A stable baseline is one in which no marked ascending or descending trends in the target behavior are evident, and in which fluctuations in the target behavior are not excessive. If a baseline record is descending or ascending, the effect of treatment procedures will be difficult to evaluate unless the treatment is intended specifically to reverse the trend.

Conducting Baseline Observations

To record behavior with which to establish baselines, a variety of methods is available. Three useful techniques include frequency counts, interval recording, and time sampling.

TABLE 8–1. Frequency of Tom's Hitting Other Children During School Hours

Day	Occurrences Observed from 8:30 A.M. to 12 noon	Occurrences Observed from 12:01 P.M. to 3:00 P.M.	Total
1	100	40	140
2	90	40	130
3	20	40	60
4	20	10	30

Frequency Counts. Observers conducting frequency counts record the number of times a behavior occurs. Recording the times Tom hit another child, for example, is a simple frequency count. Paper-and-pencil tallies often are used to collect this kind of information, especially when more than one behavior is being observed. When a single behavior, such as Tom's hitting, is being surveyed, mechanical devices such as a golf counter are very convenient. Observers can even use a technique as simple as transferring beans from one pocket to the other each time a specified behavior occurs.

Interval Recording. Interval recording provides more information than do frequency counts because it gives an indication of both the duration and the frequency of a behavior. It furnishes baseline information regarding sustained behaviors. Again consider Tom, who not only habitually struck other children but also was out of his seat without permission much of the time. An intervention plan in this case might try to increase the intervals when Tom is properly seated.

To obtain a baseline using the interval method, one approach would involve planning several ten-minute observation periods during each day. To increase accuracy, observers could divide each survey period into smaller spans, such as twenty intervals of thirty seconds (there are twenty thirty-second spans in ten minutes). Instead of recording Tom's "in seat" behavior for ten-minute periods, observers would check it in thirty-second intervals.

On a recording sheet, observers can note whether Tom is in his seat (I) or out (O) for each thirty-second interval. Before observation begins, however, the criteria for registering an I or an O must be defined. For purposes of scoring this case, these standards were used: an I was recorded if the subject was in his seat at least twenty-nine seconds of each thirty-second period; an O was marked if he was entirely out of his seat for more than one second of each thirty-second period.

In this way, observers armed with a stop watch, an observation form, and a pencil can assemble accurate records regarding Tom's preintervention in-seat and out-of-seat behavior. The sample observation form in Table 8–2 illustrates interval recording.

Interval recording can be expanded to incorporate more than one behavior. By adding other columns and by using other symbols, an observer can record the duration and frequency of several behaviors, thus producing a multiple baseline.

The length of the interval—thirty, twenty, ten, or even two seconds—depends on the usual frequency of the behavior. Very frequent activities require short intervals, whereas less frequent activities may be observed over longer spans.

Time Sampling. Time sampling is a third technique for gathering baseline data. Although it resembles interval recording, time sampling features an important difference: Observers record behavior only at the end of each time span, rather than throughout each period. For example, with interval recording, young Tom was surveyed continuously for thirty seconds, and an I or an O was recorded. With the time sampling technique, Tom would be checked at the end of each thirty-second interval to see if he was in his seat or out. The time sampling observer, then, merely records whether a subject is performing a specified behavior at the end of each designated time span.

Time sampling observation sheets may take several forms. They can easily be adapted to include several behaviors and even can be constructed to describe the conditions when each behavior occurs.

The length of the observation interval depends on what frequency is expected for a specific behavior. For example, investigators may find how often a school child with learning problems pays attention to a specific task by observing the child's behavior once every two minutes. Over a thirty-minute period, once every two minutes the teacher or other observer will record whether the pupil is studying at a desk or is engaged in other activities. A specific number of these thirty-minute terms can be arranged for different tasks at other times during the day.

TABLE 8-2. Interval Recording

Interval	Interval Score
1	I*
2	I
3	O†
4	I
5	I
6	O
7	O
8	O
9	I
10	I
11	I
12	I
13	I
14	O
15	I
16	I
17	O
18	I
19	I
20	I

*I = In-seat behavior sustained for at least 29 seconds
†O = Out-of-seat for more than 1 second

Summarizing Baseline Information by Graphing

After observers have gathered enough information during the baseline period, they customarily summarize the data in the form of a line graph.

A line graph shows the relationship between two or more variables. Generally, the two variables represented are time and behavioral frequency. The horizontal axis (the abscissa) represents time; the vertical axis (the ordinate) represents frequency. Each point on the graph represents a recurrence of the particular behavior. For example, the earlier sample recording form in Table 8–1 chronicles how often Tom hit other children during school hours. The data cover four days of observations.

The form may be converted to a line graph. See the sample baseline graph in Figure 8–1. Time, in number of days, is depicted along the horizontal axis. The numbers from one to four each represent one day. The occurrences of Tom's problem behavior (hitting other children) are depicted along the vertical axis. Because of the high frequency in this case, Tom's behaviors are numbered in units of ten. Every point on the graph represents the total occurrences of the target activity on a particular day. On Day 2, for example, 130 incidents of hitting were recorded. To show change from day to day, the points are connected by straight lines.

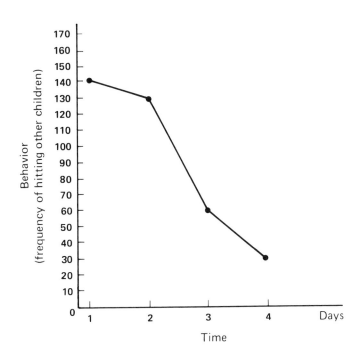

FIGURE 8-1. Sample baseline graph. Observations on the frequency of Tom's hitting other children during school hours.

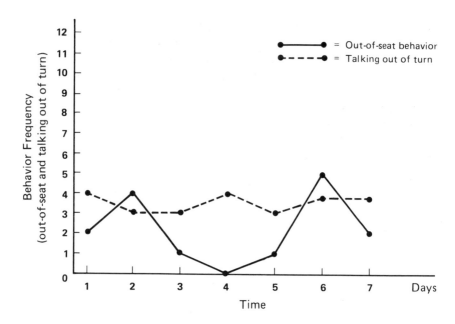

FIGURE 8-2. Sample multiple baseline graph. Out-of-seat and talking out of turn behavioral frequencies for Tom.

Each axis of a line graph must be labeled. A caption should describe what data the graph contains. If more than one behavior is diagrammed, different kinds of lines (dots, solid lines, dashes) and connection points should be used for each different behavior. Each behavior represented should be labeled in the corner of the diagram so that the reader knows exactly what is depicted. For example, the sample baseline graph in Figure 8-2 depicts baselines for two of Tom's school-related problem behaviors: (1) talking out of turn and (2) out-of-seat activity. The sample multiple baseline graph represents each of the two problem behaviors with distinctive lines and different connection points.

Extending the Graph Beyond the Baseline

After the baseline phase has been completed, practitioners initiate the treatment phase. In single-subject research designs, the procedures for observation recording and graphing in the baseline stage also are used to characterize any subsequent phases (Figure 8-3). The line representing the baseline (phase A) simply is extended to include the treatment (phase B) as well as any subsequent phases. The separate time phases of baseline and treatment are divided on the graph by vertical dotted lines. Figure 8-3 shows a sample AB baseline and treatment graph. The baseline and treatment phases are labeled clearly. The baseline phase ends on Day 7; the treatment phase starts on Day 8.

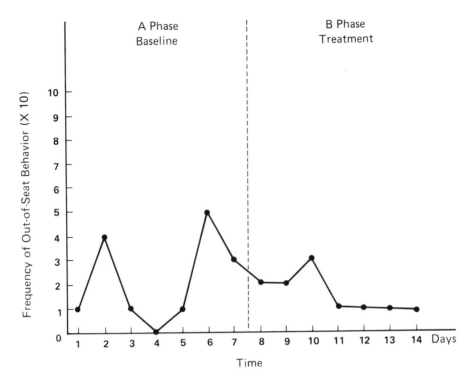

FIGURE 8-3. Sample baseline and treatment graph. Out-of-seat behaviors for Tom.

This technique of graphic presentation conventionally is used to describe the results of single-subject research designs. The same pattern can be repeated for different single-subject programs in any sequence a specific design requires. The same graphic methods also can be used to characterize multiple baselines and multiple interventions.

Methods for Assuring Baseline Data Reliability

The first step in the precise observation and recording of behavior is defining the behavior accurately. The key to an accurate definition is determining if others also can understand and apply the definition in a consistent manner. How can a practitioner be confident that his or her observations will agree with some other person's observations of the same behavior occurring under the same conditions?

A practical answer is to use more than one person to observe and record the target behavior. This procedure assures the reliability of data collected during different phases, including baseline and intervention.

There are several systems of calculating the extent of agreement between two observers. But the relatively simple method of figuring the

127

percentage of agreement is adequate: the higher the percentage, the greater the agreement. Calculating two observers' percentage of agreement involves a simple formula:

$$\text{Percentage of agreement} = \frac{\text{record of observer with lower count}}{\text{record of observer with higher count}} \times 100$$

For instance, suppose two social workers record the frequency of Tom's out-of-seat behavior in school. Figure 8–4 is a sample observation chart. In this example, social worker A counts fifty-two out-of-seat behaviors during the observation period. Social worker B tallies fifty-five out-of-seat instances for the same time. Their observations are not in perfect concurrence. How closely they agree can be determined by dividing the lower count by the higher count, then multiplying the result by one hundred. The calculation in this example:

$$\text{Percentage of agreement} = \frac{52}{55} \times 100 = 94.5\%$$

Since 100 is the highest possible percentage of agreement, the level in this case probably is satisfactorily high.

When interval or time sampling procedures are used, research workers determine the percentage of agreement between observers differently. They compare the number of intervals in which the observers agree that the target behavior occurred.

Assume that two observers watched Tom for one-minute intervals. The sample observation chart of Tom's out-of-seat behavior (Figure 8–5) shows that Tom was observed for ten separate periods of one minute each. The disagreement column indicates that in three of the ten instances the observers disagree about the extent of out-of-seat behavior. To calculate the

Frequency of Tom's Out-of-Seat Behavior

Name of Client	Tom Doe
Behavior Observed	Out-of-Seat Behavior in School
Observation Period	One Hour

Frequency Score: Social Worker A	Frequency Score: Social Worker B
52	55

FIGURE 8–4. Sample Observation Chart

percentage of agreement, the number of intervals of agreement is divided by the total number of intervals and multiplied by one hundred:

$$\text{Percentage of agreement} = \frac{\text{number of intervals of agreement}}{\text{total number of intervals}} \times 100$$

$$\text{Percentage of agreement in sample} = \frac{7}{10} \times 100 = 70\%$$

The sample indicates that the observers are in agreement 70 percent of the time. Although there are no absolute standards regarding what constitutes satisfactory agreement, anything lower than 80 percent normally is considered unacceptable. When lower levels occur, as they do here, efforts should be made to improve observer reliability. This improvement can be achieved by defining the behavior more precisely, by training the observers, and by extending the number and periods of observation. Remember, the research is only as good as the data!

Frequency of Tom's Out-of-Seat Behavior—Ten One-Minute Intervals

Name of Client	Tom Doe
Behavior Observed	Out-of-Seat Behavior in School
Length of Each Interval	One Minute
Number of Intervals Observed	10

Interval No.	Interval Score Social Worker A	Interval Score Social Worker B	Disagreement
1	I	I	
2	O	O	
3	O	I	D
4	I	I	
5	O	I	D
6	O	O	
7	I	O	D
8	I	I	
9	I	I	
10	O	O	

I = Interval where in seat for more than 31 seconds.
O = Interval where out of seat for more than 31 seconds.
D = Disagreement between observers regarding interval score.

FIGURE 8-5. Sample Observation Chart

Design Structures

The AB Design

The AB design is the most simple of the single-subject designs. In the A phase, no treatment is introduced; observers merely collect information about the frequency of the problem behavior. The information gathered is plotted on a two-part graph (see Figure 8–3). The first part becomes a preintervention record, which can be compared with the B, or treatment, phase.

One example of an AB design is a case involving Jim, a thirteen-year-old boy who was absent from school frequently. Jim's school attendance was monitored for four weeks to establish a preintervention baseline (phase A). Then treatment was introduced. The treatment consisted of a positive reinforcer, horseback riding, a privilege made contingent on school attendance. For each full day of school attendance, Jim was allowed to ride horses at a local stable for an hour and a half. Figure 8–6 depicts the results of this intervention plan.

Leon, an eleven-year-old boy who had a bed-wetting problem, provides a second AB case example. Leon had been examined by a pediatrician who found no organic basis for bed-wetting. Phase A consisted of a two-week preintervention baseline. In phase B, a treatment, consisting of a twin-signal conditioning device originally developed by Mowrer,[3] was applied.

The Mowrer approach employs a urine-sensitive pad, which is placed

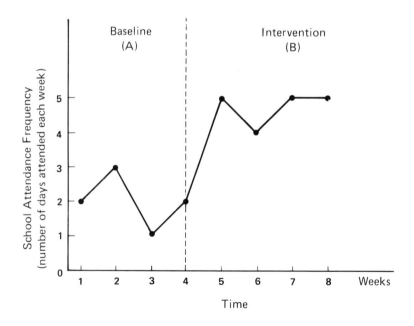

FIGURE 8-6. AB example of school attendance intervention.

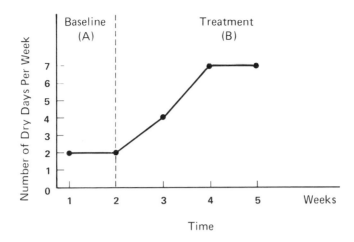

FIGURE 8-7. AB design. Treatment of enuretic child with twin-signal conditioning device.

under the child in bed. When the child begins to urinate, the urine serves as an electrical conductor, closing a circuit in the pad and triggering a relay circuit with an electric bell and a light. The bell and light wake the child and parent. They proceed to the bathroom where the child is encouraged to finish urinating. The apparatus is reset when the child returns to bed. Figure 8-7 illustrates the outcome of this experiment.

In another AB design example, foster grandparents were taught specific training skills to help severely handicapped foster grandchildren achieve greater independence.[4] The experiment aimed to improve head and neck control. Skills to be acquired were turning the head to the right or left when the child's name was called from either side, and turning the head upward when the name was called from above.

The baseline (phase A) involved daily observation of the foster grandparent and the foster grandchild together. During baseline, an observer recorded the number of times the target behaviors occurred. Next, each foster grandparent was shown specific teaching procedures designed to enhance head and neck control and then asked to try to use these techniques to improve the child's head and neck control. The results of the experiment are depicted in Figure 8-8. The chart shows a baseline rate of near zero. The treatment phase shows a marked increase in head and neck control.

The AB design has several limitations, however. It does not allow the experimenter to conclude with any certainty that the treatment is responsible for observed changes. Because no other variables are controlled, a number of different explanations could account for the change. Because of this limitation, the AB scheme is considered a weak design, to be used only when no practical alternatives exist.

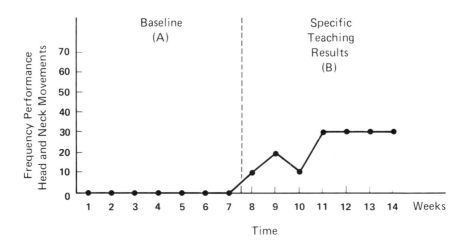

FIGURE 8-8. Modification of head and neck behaviors.

The ABA Design

The AB design is strengthened somewhat if another phase is added to it. Research workers employ a third stage, in which the treatment is withdrawn. The ABA design allows investigators to view the results of applying, then removing, a treatment. If withdrawing treatment results in deterioration, the conclusion is more certain that the treatment is the agent responsible for any observed changes.

An important distinction should be made between two technically different procedures that can be used in the ABA design. Hersen and Barlow distinguish between withdrawal of treatment and reversal of treatment. Withdrawal involves removing the experimental treatment (B phase) and returning to a no-treatment baseline condition after a behavior change has been successfully demonstrated. Reversal involves an alternate step. According to Hersen and Barlow,[5]

> A major difference in the "reversal" and withdrawal design is that in the third phase of the reversal design, following instigation of the therapeutic procedure, the same procedure is now applied to an *alternative* but incompatible behavior. By contrast, in the withdrawal design, the A phase following introduction of the treatment . . . simply involves its removal and a return to baseline conditions. (Emphasis added)

Many research reports do not specify which of the two procedures have been used in particular cases. Some argue that in practice the reversal design is extremely cumbersome.[6] They claim the withdrawal design, in contrast, is better suited for investigations that are not confined to the operant conditioning theoretical framework.

Moreover, the ethical problems stemming from the use of a reversal procedure are not easily solved. On one hand, the practitioner is responsible for selecting and using treatment procedures that have been demonstrated to be effective. When no evidence exists to guide the selection of effective methods, the practitioner is further responsible for carefully evaluating the effects of the procedures used.

It is one thing to apply a procedure and evaluate it; it is quite another thing to attempt to produce a deliberate reversal—which from a practice perspective might be defined as a deliberately induced deterioration.

Some research workers argue that the reversal procedure results in a stronger research design. Yet, given the ethical and practical problems with reversal, the withdrawal procedure is recommended as the generally acceptable method for any projects that require extension beyond the initial AB phase.

The withdrawal procedure also may be unacceptable to some practitioners. Some may believe that the withdrawal of treatment, for the second A phase, could result in irreversible deterioration. Hersen and Barlow find no evidence supporting this argument, however. They point out that, in fact, multiple withdrawals and reinstatements of treatment in extended ABAB designs often result in treatment carryover effects: the problem behavior never returns to the initial low level for the baseline. Although this phenomenon may produce a problem for the investigator, it is a highly desirable condition from the perspective of the client and the practitioner. Research workers, after all, should never let the need for better research take precedence over the true objective of social work practice.

The ABA design can be illustrated with the case of Jim, the thirteen-year-old boy with a school truancy problem. That study of school attendance intervention can be extended to an ABA design by simply adding a third four-week period to the original AB plan. During this period, the intervention program is discontinued: conditions are allowed to return to the baseline or preintervention state.

The frequency of Jim's school attendance is recorded and plotted for this extra period. Figure 8–9 shows an increase in school attendance for the intervention phase (B) and a decrease during the second baseline phase (A). This graph strongly suggests that the intervention effectively produced a temporary increase in Jim's attendance, and that withdrawal caused a corresponding drop.

The ABA design suffers from several limitations. The strongest objection to its use stems from the ethical problem caused by ending a case on a no-treatment phase. Practitioners thus deny the client the potential benefit of any continued treatment. Once again, it is important that practitioners

133

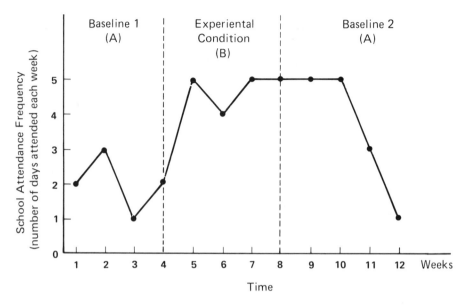

FIGURE 8-9. ABA example of school attendance intervention.

remember that treatment should be initiated and ended according to the needs of the client and abilities of the practitioner—not according to the requirements of a particular experiment.

The ABA design also is impractical to use on any condition that is not reversible. As an extreme example, consider using single-subject design methods to evaluate treatment intended to reduce teenage pregnancies. Obviously, because pregnancy is not a reversible condition, the ABA design would be inappropriate. Another example could be found in the use of a short but very intense and effective behavior modification treatment program that reduced a specific problem behavior, such as Tom's out-of-seat conduct. A practitioner might have produced relatively enduring changes in the problem behavior as a result of treatment. If those changes are relatively nonreversible, use of the ABA design would not be feasible.

The ABAB Design

The ABAB design is the ABA design carried one step further. Instead of ending on a no-treatment phase, the ABAB design ends with treatment. One of the strongest arguments for using the ABAB design is that, because it offers two opportunities to test the effects of treatment, it can provide more convincing evidence.

Jim, the thirteen-year-old truant, again can exemplify the design. On the sample ABAB chart (Figure 8–10), the ABA scheme is extended to an ABAB design with the resumption of intervention at the thirteenth week. The chart shows an increase in school attendance in the final phase of intervention, suggesting a consistent treatment effect.

The ABAB design depends on continuous assessment of the problem behavior. The logic of this design depends on comparisons of the target behaviors (and the trends in those behaviors) across the various treatment and no-treatment phases. In each phase experimenters use the data to (1) characterize the current status of the client, and (2) especially predict the client's behavior under circumstances of either addition or withdrawal of treatment. This design should reveal any difference in the level of problem behavior when treatment is reintroduced, as compared to the no-treatment (baseline) phase.

The logic of the ABAB design is that it can demonstrate a causal relationship by showing that the problem behavior varies according to the presence or absence of a specific treatment. The design's two-stage feature (ABAB) can indicate a pattern of response strongly suggesting a causal relationship. However, these features also somewhat restrict the use of this design.

One problem of using it with nonreversible behavior is that withdrawing treatment does not always result in a reversion of subject behavior. Similarly, for studying behaviors that, once altered, do not revert

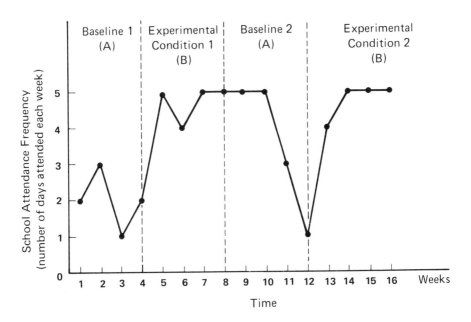

FIGURE 8–10. ABAB example of school attendance intervention.

to baseline levels, the ABAB design may not always be practical. In one sense, of course, this circumstance is ideal from the standpoint of both the client and the practitioner. The limitation in such cases, however, is that the practitioner can make no inferences about causality.

Secondly, the ethical problem of withdrawing treatment, especially following improvement, again may not easily be resolved. Both the client and the practitioner may find unacceptable the idea of making things worse, even on a short-term basis.

The BAB Design

The BAB design does not employ a preintervention baseline (phase A). Rather, the treatment (phase B) becomes the first phase studied. The second phase (A) is the withdrawal of treatment; in the final phase (B) the treatment is reapplied. The advantage of this design is that the experiment is terminated positively, during a treatment phase. Researchers sometimes select the BAB design when it is necessary to begin treatment at once, without the delay involved in collecting the initial baseline information.

A report by Bassett and Blanchard provides a good example of a BAB design.[7] The experiment took place in a prison. In this instance, the BAB design was used with a group of people, rather than on a single subject.

The authors studied the effects of removing direct supervision from a prison's behavior-management program—its "token economy," so-called because prisoners' good behavior is rewarded with tokens, which inmates can exchange for tangible, useful items like cigarettes.

The researchers used the BAB design to evaluate the effects of different types of supervision on the token economy's operations. This BAB research began with the treatment program—the token economy—established. It is shown in the Figure 8–11 charts as the first column (Program Director Present). In the A phase (Program Director Absent), program supervision was removed. In the last B phase (Program Director Present) supervision was returned to the program.

The dependent variables studied in this research were the number of different behavioral categories used in the token economy and the total number of "fines" imposed by the staff. The results of this experiment are depicted on the two charts in Figure 8–11.

The lower chart indicates the total number of response categories available for use in the token economy. During the initial B phase, there were five response categories. In the second phase, A, when supervision was removed, the number of response categories added to the system increased dramatically. Finally, in the third phase, B again, the number of response categories was maintained at the high level established in the A stage, but was not increased.

The upper graph represents the total number of response costs, or

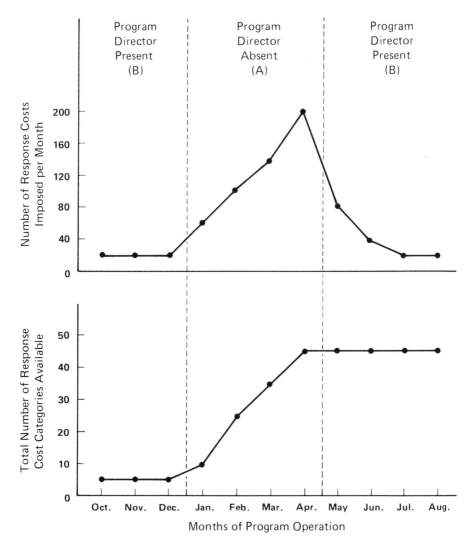

FIGURE 8-11. BAB Research design example. *(Source: From J. E. Bassett and E. B. Blanchard. "The Effect of the Absence of Close Supervision on the Use of Response Cost in A Prison Token Economy,"* Journal of Applied Behavior Analysis, *10 (1977): p. 377. Copyright 1977 by the Society for the Experimental Analysis of Behavior, Inc.)*

"fines," imposed per month. During the first B phase, the number of fines imposed was quite low. In the second phase (A), when on-site supervision was removed, observers found a marked increase in the frequency of fines. In the final B phase, with the return of on-site supervision, the number of fines returned to the original level.

In other words, the authors found that without on-site management, the token economy deteriorated. When the prisoners were without supervision, the staff extended the number of behaviors that were included in the token economy and increased the use of fines. Thus, during the middle phase, the token economy was changed from a self-management program for inmates to a program whereby staff increasingly emphasized punishing misbehaviors and gave less emphasis to reinforcing positive behaviors.

The Multiple Baseline Design

Because of some of the important limitations of the withdrawal designs, including the ABA and the ABAB designs, other designs have been devised. These designs allow the practitioner to evaluate the effects of different treatments without needing to withdraw treatment to produce a return to baseline conditions. The major limitations of withdrawal lie in the ethical problem of sacrificing therapeutic gains, and in the practical problem of attempting to reverse nonreversible behavior.

Baer, Wolf, and Resley suggested the multiple baseline technique,[8] which offers an alternative to the withdrawal designs. Their approach was to identify several different target behaviors, repeatedly measuring each to establish baselines against which changes could be evaluated. The authors outline the next steps: "With these baselines established, the experimenter then applies an experimental variable to one of the behaviors, produces a change in it, and perhaps notes little or no change in the other baselines."[9] Next the research design applies the same treatment or experimental condition to a second target behavior and notes any changes. This procedure is repeated in a sequential manner until the treatment has been applied to all the target behaviors.

The multiple baseline technique may be used as a single-subject design procedure or to compare different groups. It measures and monitors more than one target behavior. The experimenter can establish baselines for each of the target behaviors and then apply the experimental variable (treatment) to a single behavior. In this way, the experimenter can determine if the target behavior has changed and observe the other behaviors for changes as well.

After applying treatment to the first target behavior and observing changes, experimenters next introduce treatment in sequence to each of the remaining target behaviors. They note changes in any of the behaviors, both those subjected to the treatment and those not treated. Experimenters thus can measure possible interaction between variables. The sequential technique can be viewed as a series of separate AB designs, each using the same treatment; behaviors treated later simply have an extended baseline.

The sequential technique also allows the experimenter to observe the differential effects of the same treatment on several target behaviors. If interaction occurs, however, the results are obscured for each of the variables, because often it is difficult to determine which effects are due to the treatment and which are caused by the interaction.

The issue of treatment interaction is important in using the multiple baseline technique, because it assumes that the target behaviors are independent of each other. If interaction occurs, there is no effective way to separate the effects of treatment versus interaction; thus, the experimenter is unable to infer definite results from the experimental treatment.

The multiple baseline design is recommended as the design of choice for social work practice. It allows the practitioner to avoid the problems inherent in the reversal programs. It also offers research workers a powerful alternative design by which they can evaluate treatment effects. This design approaches the problem of demonstrating causality by using two discrete variables and applying treatment sequentially. If the practitioner can demonstrate two appropriate responses in two different variables using a specific treatment applied in sequence, he or she then can make a strong case for assuming a causal relationship.

One example of a multiple baseline design in use involves treating the penchant of many children for disturbing products on supermarket shelves. This research involved a program to instruct parents in the use of behavior modification procedures—so they in turn, while shopping, could change the problem behavior of their children.[10] The two specific target behaviors selected for modification:

1. Proximity, the percentage of time the child remained within reach of the parent while shopping.
2. Product disturbances, how often the child handled or disturbed store products.

Separate baselines for the two behaviors were established for three boys: Andy, Barney, and Marty. Their mothers were trained in observation and recording procedures to monitor the problem behaviors. An independent observer was used to verify the mothers' records.

The mothers also were trained in behavior modification procedures that employed a home-based token economy point system. The research design involved a sequential approach to the two target behaviors. After establishing baselines, the treatment package was applied to the proximity problem, while baseline monitoring continued on the product disturbance problem. After the proximity behavior was stabilized, the treatment package was extended to the second behavior, product disturbance. The results of the multiple baseline AB designs for Andy, Barney, and Marty are shown in Figures 8–12, 8–13, and 8–14.

The vertical axis on the charts represents the percent of each time interval that the child was behaving in the desired manner. To establish this

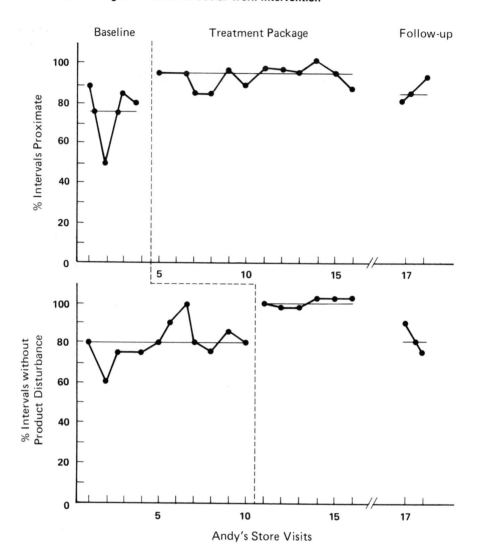

FIGURE 8-12. Percent of intervals in which Andy remained proximate and refrained from disturbing products during store visits. *(Source: From J. D. Barnard, E. R. Christophersen, and M. M. Wolf, "Teaching Children Appropriate Shopping Behavior through Parent Training in the Supermarket Setting,"* Journal of Applied Behavior Analysis, *10 (1977): p. 53. Copyright 1977 by the Society for the Experimental Analysis of Behavior, Inc.)*

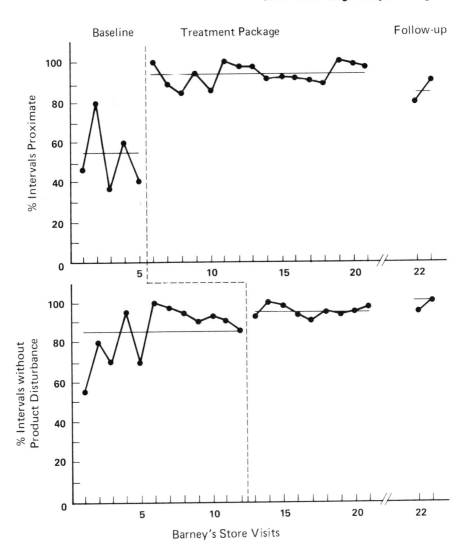

FIGURE 8-13. Percent of intervals in which Barney remained proximate and refrained from disturbing products during store visits. *(Source: From J. D. Barnard, E. R. Christophersen, and M. M. Wolf, "Teaching Children Appropriate Shopping Behavior through Parent Training in the Supermarket Setting," Journal of Applied Behavior Analysis, 10 (1977): p. 54. Copyright 1977 by the Society for the Experimental Analysis of Behavior, Inc.)*

141

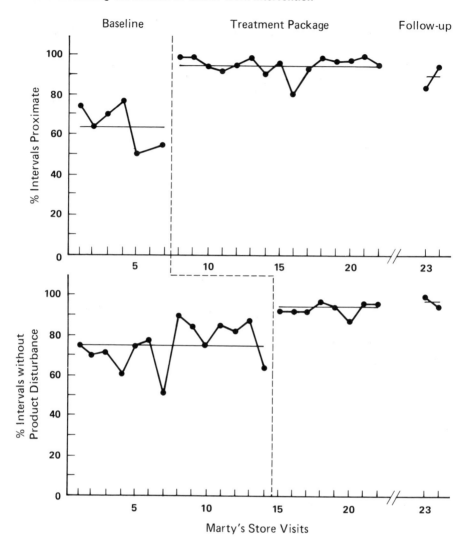

FIGURE 8-14. Percent of intervals in which Marty remained prox-imate and refrained from disturbing products during store visits. *(Source: From J. D. Barnard, E. R. Christophersen, and M. M. Wolf, "Teaching Children Appropriate Shopping Behavior through Parent Training in the Supermarket Setting,"* Journal of Applied Behavior Analysis, 10 (1977): p. 55. *Copyright 1977 by the Society for the Ex-perimental Analysis of Behavior, Inc.)*

measure, time sampling procedures were used to determine occurrences of target behaviors for each interval. The three charts present clearly the results of the experiment.

Andy's chart reveals that during baseline he remained proximate to his mother during an average of 75 percent of the observation intervals. The product disturbance baseline, which covers a longer time period, reveals that he behaved without product disturbance 80 percent of the time. After experimenters introduced the first treatment package, levels of both behaviors improved. Andy's proximity behavior averaged 96 percent, and his product disturbance score, even before the second treatment was applied, also increased.

Once the second treatment package was introduced, Andy's product disturbance score improved to 99 percent. Later, after treatment was discontinued, researchers performed a follow-up survey to determine if the treatment retained its effectiveness. The follow-up revealed that Andy's proximity behaviors remained at treatment levels, but that his product disturbance scores had declined.

For Barney, proximity during baseline had averaged 51 percent of the observed intervals, and his product disturbance level had averaged 85 percent during baseline. Treatment increased his proximity score to an average of 95 percent. Some gain in Barney's product disturbance score occurred during the extended baseline period, when treatment was applied to the proximity problem and before the product disturbance treatment began. A further improvement in the product disturbance score, to 96 percent, took place after treatment was applied to that problem. Follow-up data revealed that the levels of both behaviors were maintained.

Testers noted similar changes in Marty's shopping behavior. During baseline, his proximity behavior averaged 65 percent, and the average percent of intervals without product disturbances was 75 percent. With treatment, Marty's behavior for both behaviors increased to 95 percent.

The product disturbance baseline data for the children reveals that, for each, the treatment for proximity also affected handling of products. This result is especially noticeable for Barney. In each case, actual treatment for product disturbances further increased the boys' scores for that behavior. These results suggest either that the two behaviors are not entirely independent, or that the experiment's first treatment unintentionally affected the second behavior.

In either case, in this study a treatment interaction occurred, making nearly impossible any definitive explanation of the effects of treatment. On a positive note, this experiment suggests that parents, with little or no instruction, may be able to generalize principles of treatment to their children.

The Changing Criterion Design

The changing criterion design demonstrates the effect of an intervention by showing that the criterion for performance can systematically be altered, with consequent variations in subject behavior.

The design begins with a baseline phase. In the second phase, experimenters introduce the treatment and choose a specific level of performance as a criterion for the client. Then, on days when performance meets or exceeds the criterion level, the response consequence, usually some form of reinforcer, is provided. When the subject's performance remains consistently at or above the criterion level for a given period, such as a week, the criterion is raised. The response consequence thereafter is rewarded only for meeting the new standard. In this step-like fashion, the criterion periodically is raised throughout the treatment phase until the objective is reached.

As the criterion level rises, so does the subject's ability to perform the target behavior. How well the subject ultimately learns to perform the target task will demonstrate to the research worker the effectiveness of the experimental condition.

The case files of a sheltered workshop provide an example of the changing criterion design. A retarded man named Ralph was learning to assemble chairs. The procedure consisted of six sequential steps, each requiring the successful completion of the preceding step. Figure 8–15 demonstrates how the changing criterion design was applied to Ralph.

Money was used as a positive reinforcer to train Ralph. For each step successfully completed in the proper sequence, he received immediate payment. After Ralph reached and maintained one selected level of performance, the criterion for payment was raised. Three criterion levels were used.

In the chart, Ralph's baseline performance is at zero. During the sec-

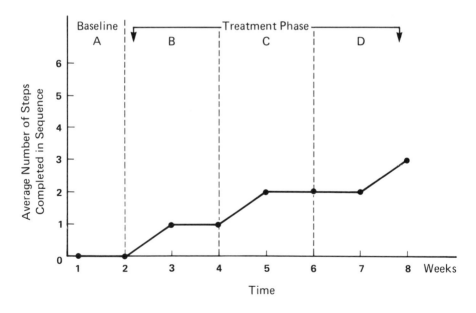

FIGURE 8–15. Changing criterion design. Chair assembly progress for Ralph.

ond phase (B), he successfully completed the first step in chair assembly and performed satisfactorily for a week. The requirement then was raised to successful completion of two steps in sequence, which he achieved and maintained. Again the criterion level was raised, to the successful completion of three steps in the chair assembly process.

In contrast to the discrete behaviors that are the focus of many of the other research designs, the changing criterion design appears to be well suited for modifying performance levels. It also is suited to extended treatment programs directed at incremental, gradual changes. For example, it could be adopted for use in studying gradual changes in poor habits like nail biting, smoking, or overeating. It also could be used to evaluate different teaching and learning procedures.

Multiple Schedule Designs

When using the multiple baseline design, experimenters test the effects of treatment by observing the changes it may cause in any of several target behaviors. In the multiple schedule design, they subject the same target behavior to different treatments.

According to Leitenberg, "This design is based on discrimination learning principles; that is, if the same behavior is treated differently in the presence of different physical or social stimuli, it will exhibit different characteristics in the presence of those stimuli."[11] In other words, the design assumes that a behavior can vary in unlike situations if it is treated differently each time. The basic idea is that, under different circumstances, people learn to discriminate between ways they act out a given behavior. For example, what may be appropriate verbal behavior for a child at home may be inappropriate for the same child at school.

One example of a multiple schedule design at work is contained in a research report by Garlington and Dericco.[12] In this study, the research workers studied the effects of two separate experimental variables on the beer drinking rate of male college seniors.

The independent variable was the rate at which the students drank beer. The experimenters decided that an important determinant of young people's drinking rates is peer example. They speculated that imbibing students would conform to the drinking rate set by peers. They established the baseline rates for their subjects, then introduced the two experimental conditions. One consisted of providing the students with a drinking companion who consumed beer at a rate one-third faster than the subjects' base rates. This phase was designated the *fast rate* condition (B). The second experimental condition (C) provided a drinking partner who quaffed at the *slow rate*, one-third less than the subjects' baseline rates.

The research strategy used in this experiment is an ABACA reversal design. The results for three subjects of the report are depicted in the charts in Figure 8–16.

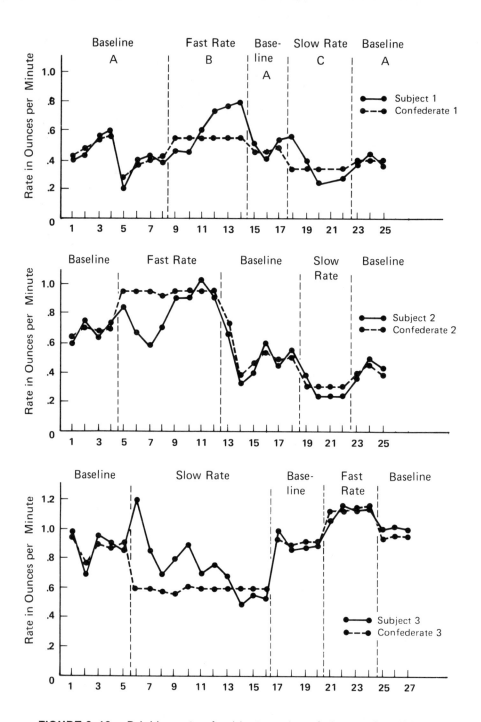

FIGURE 8-16. Drinking rate of subjects and confederates for all baseline and experimental conditions. *(Source: From W. R. Garlington and D. A. Dericco, "The Effect of Modeling on Drinking Rate,"* Journal of Applied Behavior Analysis, *10 (1977): p. 210. Copyright 1977 by the Society for the Experimental Analysis of Behavior, Inc.)*

In the baseline condition, A, the drinking companion matched his drinking rate to that of the subjects. In the first intervention, B, companions of two of the three students independently drank at the fast rate; the confederate paired with the third student independently drank at the slower tempo. Conditions were then returned to baseline A.

The next intervention introduced the second condition, C. For the first two drinking companions, this stage involved drinking at the slow rate, and for the third, at the fast rate. In the two interventions, then, the confederates attempted to get the students to match the pace of their drinking to the experimental fast and slow rates.

The three charts present the rates of beer consumption for the subjects and confederates during all conditions. The results of this experiment indicate that the increases and decreases in subject beer consumption rates roughly paralleled the rates established by the drinking companion. When the confederate drank fast, the subject drank fast; when the confederate drank slowly, the subject tended also to drink at a slow rate.

The multiple schedule design allows the research worker to test the influence of different treatments or stimuli on a specific behavior in diverse situations. It offers some unique advantages for investigating treatments designed to teach people to behave differently in various situations. Techniques of this sort are especially appropriate for use with persons preparing to leave institutions in order to return to community life, and for children who experience difficulty in making the behavioral transition from home to school.

Advantages and Disadvantages

A variety of research designs has been discussed, but this is not an exhaustive listing of possible single-subject designs. Indeed, possible combinations of different phases are limited only by the ingenuity of the research worker and by the practicalities of conducting research. The various configurations of A and B phases can be extended, staggered, or reordered to suit the demands of research.

Single-subject research methodology offers the social work profession some unique advantages. Among the most important is the convenience with which single-subject methods can be learned and applied to the demands of everyday practice. Although the single-subject design to date has been used most extensively in behavior modification programs, there is no reason it should not be used in other theoretical and practice situations. Leitenberg suggests that it might be used with a variety of psychotherapeutic orientations.

The single-subject plan also is compatible with most of the major theoretical practice orientations in social work. For example, it may easily be adapted to Reid and Epstein's Task-Centered Casework approach.[13] It also fits well into Compton and Galaway's problem-solving model.[14] The design has been well integrated into recent social work practice textbooks such as Jayaratne and Levy's *Empirical Clinical Practice*[15] and Fischer's *Effective Casework Practice.*[16]

But single-subject methods also suffer from some disadvantages. One relates to the withdrawal and reversal designs. When therapeutic gains already have occurred, it is difficult to make a convincing case for withdrawal of treatment. The use of reversal procedures is even less defensible. Both practical and ethical objections to these methods were discussed earlier. Before using these designs, practitioners first must deliberately and consciously consider their inherent drawbacks.

A further methodological problem also relates to the withdrawal and reversal procedures—specifically, to the possible nonreversal of some behaviors even after treatment is withdrawn. Some behaviors simply will not reverse. This fact confounds the experimental nature of the design, because no single explanation will account for it.

Another disadvantage is that the design does not help to identify the specific population for which a treatment is most effective. To achieve this finding, research workers would need to repeat the same experiment with different populations, such as women, children, or minorities.

Thomas has identified an additional limitation of the single-subject design. He points out that some basic differences exist between the roles of the researcher and practitioner. The potential conflict of the two possibly could cause compromises of either the research or the service.[17]

Despite the limitations, though, the single-subject design probably has more benefits than drawbacks. Many objections to use of the single-subject strategy can be resolved. The design's advantages are especially appealing to the practitioner in developing continuing evaluation of the services provided each client.

In a recent review of the use of single-subject research designs in social work, Gambrill and Barth concluded that single-subject programs offer the social work profession a number of advantages. These writers propose an interesting and pragmatic approach to the use of single-subject designs in social work practice. "Research designs lie on a continuum ranging from designs that are exploratory in nature and offer tentative data concerning the impact of a given intervention," they note, "to intensive single-case study designs that permit the researcher to draw inferences about the causal effects of interventions."[18]

Gambrill and Barth suggest that it is unnecessary and impractical to expect all research designs to yield data that result in explanations of causality. Instead, they believe that all the single-subject designs can provide information that to some degree is useful. The full range of designs assumes an important standing in social work practice.

Gambrill and Barth suggest, for instance, that even the AB plan, though one of the weakest single-subject designs, nonetheless can provide important information to the profession and should not be overlooked. They point out that it allows for replication when a single intervention method is used with different clients having similar problems. A series of such replications could demonstrate the possible general applicability of an intervention method. A successful AB design also might be viewed as a necessary form of exploratory research—as an initial study providing preliminary data needed for further exploration by more rigorous research designs. Gambrill and Barth concluded, "The accumulation of studies using designs that are exploratory in nature can inform the selection of questions to be pursued with the use of more rigorous designs."[19]

Practitioners should consider using follow-up methods with single-subject designs and with other evaluation methods. There is a temptation to regard the task of evaluation as completed when the case is closed or when the requirements of the single-subject design are satisfied. Practitioners should investigate systematically the durability of change resulting from intervention. The basic data-gathering procedures used in single-subject designs offer an excellent basis for extending evaluation beyond the confines of the design; they also provide a useful frame of reference for later comparison. This opportunity for longitudinal research should not be overlooked. It constitutes an obligation to both the profession and the client.

Use of the single-subject design highlights the conflicts in social work between practice and research. The profession's fundamental responsibility to select and apply the most effective practice methodology sometimes conflicts with the perceived need to provide immediate service to the client. The research methods provided by the wide range of single-subject designs offer many options. These choices allow the well-trained practitioner to satisfy both practice and research objectives: to provide service and to evaluate the effectiveness of that service.

The obligation to evaluate practice effects has been overlooked by many practitioners, simply because methods of conducting evaluation have been impractical for use in day-to-day practice. Single-subject designs offer the practitioner a realistic alternative method for actively evaluating his or her practice. The ultimate beneficiary of such evaluation is the client.

Summary

Single-subject methodology offers practitioners an alternative to the more expensive and more complex between-group research designs. In single-subject designs, the subject is his or her own control. Research workers thus compare treatment and control results taken at different times for the same person. Single-subject methods provide professionals immediate, useful feedback on their work. They are easy designs for individual practitioners to use, and they can demonstrate the efficacy of a specific treatment as it is used on a specific behavior. They even may be used with groups.

Single-subject designs employ from two to several phases of control and experimentation, normally (but not always) beginning with a baseline measurement of a problem behavior, or dependent variable. The first phase usually is the A stage, the baseline period. The second phase, B, is the first treatment period. Depending on practitioner aims and the needs of a given case, various combinations of treatment and nonintervention (AB, ABAB, BAB) may be used. One cardinal rule is that, when moving from one phase to the next, only one variable should be changed; if two or more variables are altered at once, determining the cause of any client improvement becomes nearly impossible.

Taking an initial baseline measurement—collecting data about the strength of a problem behavior—provides the therapist a base against which to compare the effects of treatment. Usually the practitioner must take several measurements of the behavior, ideally gathering baseline data until only small variations in the behavior's frequency are observed. One method of constructing usable baselines is to eliminate the extremes and consider only the events within the middle two-thirds of a normal curve; another is to examine apparent trends in the target behavior.

Three techniques for recording behavior are (1) frequency counts (simply observing and recording the number of times a behavior occurs in a given time), (2) interval recording (monitoring sustained behaviors over several short observation periods), and (3) time sampling (recording the subject's behavior at the end of each time interval, but not throughout that span). For the last two approaches, the length of the observation interval depends on the frequency expected for a specific behavior. Once observers have gathered enough baseline data, they usually summarize that information on a line graph. Then, after treatment begins, the line may be extended on the graph to provide a visual depiction of the effects of intervention.

To ensure the precise observation and recording of behavioral data, the behavior first must be defined accurately. Using more than one observer, then calculating the percentage of their agreement, is one practical technique when the recording method used is frequency counting. With interval or time sampling procedures, the research worker can compare the number of intervals in which observers agree the target behavior occurred. In all cases, the most accurate baseline data can be attained by following three rules: precisely defining the behavior, using trained observers, and observing the behavior for sufficient periods. The value of the research depends entirely on the precision of the data.

The AB design is the most simple. In the first phase, observers collect information about the problem behavior; in the second stage, they introduce treatment. Then research workers compare the two stages. Because the AB design controls for no variables other than treatment, it is a relatively weak scheme.

The ABA design allows examination of effects of withdrawing treatment. If a client's behavior reverts, the likelihood is great that the treatment affected it. In this design, withdrawing treatment is not the same thing as reversing treatment—applying it to a separate behavior. However, the use of either withdrawal or reversal implies ethical concerns to some social workers, who fear such manipulation of treatment for experiment's sake might harm clients. Another criticism of the ABA strategy is that it ends intervention on a no-treatment phase. It also is worthless for studying irreversible conditions.

The ABAB design ends in a treatment phase. This design's logic depends on comparisons of the target behaviors and their trends across the four phases. It can demonstrate a causal relationship by showing that the problem behavior varies according to the presence or absence of a specific treatment. Drawbacks with the ABAB plan are that some client behaviors may not revert much in the second A phase, and that (again) even temporary withdrawal of treatment might present ethical problems in some cases.

The BAB design begins with treatment. This design can be useful when it is necessary to begin treatment at once with no delay to collect baseline information.

Multiple baseline designs allow practitioners to evaluate the effects of different treatments without needing to withdraw treatment to produce a return to baseline. Experimenters first measure all a client's target problem behaviors, then apply the same treatment in sequence to each, measuring changes in the process. This technique may easily be used either as a single-subject design or to compare different groups. In effect, it is a series of separate AB designs. When the target variables are independent, researchers can measure the results of the treatment on each. However, if interaction occurs among the various behaviors, the results may be obscured because separating the effects of treatment from those of interaction may be impossible.

The multiple baseline design may be the best for both social work and research. If the practitioner can demonstrate two appropriate responses in two different variables using a specific treatment applied in sequence, a strong case can be made for assuming a causal relationship.

The changing criterion design demonstrates the effects of intervention by systematically raising the criteria for performance to produce increasing alterations in subject behavior. The design begins with a baseline. Next, experimenters introduce treatment and name a specific level of client performance as a criterion. Then, as performance improves, the criterion level necessary for the client to earn a reinforcer is raised. Increases usually are introduced at given periods, such as weekly, throughout the treatment phase until the objective is attained. How well the subject ultimately learns to perform the target task demonstrates the effectiveness of the experimental condition. This design is well suited for modifying performance levels, and for extended-treatment programs designed to effect gradual changes in habits like nail-biting or smoking.

With the multiple schedule design, research workers subject one target behavior to several treatments. This design assumes that a behavior can vary if treated differently in different situations. Thus, it allows research workers to test the influence of different stimuli on a specific behavior on diverse occasions. The multiple schedule strategy is useful for teaching people, such as those preparing for discharge from an institution, how to behave in various situations.

Experimental designs and phases may be linked in any combination desired by the research worker or dictated by the demands of research. Although to date, single-subject designs have been most used in behavior modification, they are applicable to numerous other theoretical and practice situations. Further, they can be adopted to use with most of the major practice orientations in social work. The principal drawbacks of single-subject designs concern ethical considerations of withdrawal and reversal, possible conflicts between the roles and aims of the research worker and the practitioner, and the use of these designs when they may not help identify the specific population for which a treatment is most effective.

Yet the benefits outweigh the drawbacks. Probably all of the single-subject designs can provide information that is useful to some degree. Even the weakest, the AB plan, allows for replication when a single treatment is used with several clients having similar problems. All the designs are especially appealing to practitioners desiring continuing evaluation of their services to clients. The full range of single-subject designs represents an important tool for both research workers and practitioners in social work.

End Notes

1. Hersen, M., and Barlow, D. H. *Single Case Experimental Designs: Strategies for Studying Behavior Change.* New York: Pergamon Press, 1976, pp. 82–83.
2. Bloom, Martin. *The Paradox of Helping.* New York: John Wiley and Sons, 1975, p. 183.
3. Mowrer, O. H. "Apparatus for the Study of and Treatment of Enuresis." *American Journal of Psychology* 51 (1938): 163–66.
4. Farby, Pamela A., and Reid, Dennis H. "Teaching Foster Grandparents to Train Severely Handicapped Persons." *Journal of Applied Behavior Analysis* 11 (1978): 111–23.
5. Hersen and Barlow, *Single Case Experimental Designs*, pp. 93–94.
6. Leitenberg, H. "The Use of Single Case Methodology in Psychotherapy Research." *Journal of Abnormal Psychology* 82 (1973): 87–101.

7. Bassett, J. E., and Blanchard, E. B. "The Effect of the Absence of Close Supervision on the Use of Response Cost in a Prison Token Economy." *Journal of Applied Behavior Analysis* 10 (1977): 375–379.
8. Baer, D. M., Wolf, M. M., and Resley, T. R. "Some Current Dimensions of Applied Behavior Analysis." *Journal of Applied Behavior Analysis* 1 (1968): pp. 91–97.
9. *Ibid.*, p. 94.
10. Barnard, J. D., Christophersen, E. R., and Wolf, M. M. "Teaching Children Appropriate Shopping Behavior Through Parent Training in the Supermarket Setting." *Journal of Applied Behavior Analysis* 10 (1977): 49–59.
11. Leitenberg, H. "Single Case Methodology," p. 93.
12. Garlington, W. K., and Dericco, D. A. "The Effect of Modeling on Drinking Rate." *Journal of Applied Behavior Analysis* 10 (1977): 207–212.
13. Reid, William J., and Epstein, Laura. *Task-Centered Casework*. New York: Columbia University Press, 1972.
14. Compton, Beulah R., and Galaway, Burt. *Social Work Processes*. Homewood, Ill.: Dorsey Press, 1975.
15. Jayaratne, S., and Levy, R. L. *Empirical Clinical Practice*. New York: Columbia University Press, 1979.
16. Fischer, Joel. *Effective Casework Practice*. New York: McGraw-Hill, 1978.
17. Thomas, E.J., "Research and Service in Single-Case Experimentation." *Social Work Research and Abstracts* 14 (1978): 20–31.
18. Gambrill, E. D., and Barth, R. P. "Single-Case Study Designs Revisited." *Social Work Research and Abstracts* 16 (1980): p. 15.
19. *Ibid.*, p. 17.

Adjunctive Aspects of
Social Work Research

PART

III

Sampling Concepts
and Techniques

9

A sample is a small representation of a whole. In research, the observation or study of a phenomenon in its entirety would be tedious and time-consuming and would produce a massive amount of data. Fortunately, a substantial body of theory has demonstrated that research workers need observe or interview only some of the people or phenomena involved—a sample—to gain a usable idea of the characteristics of all the subjects.

The most basic considerations in sampling are size and representativeness. The size must be adequate so that estimates about the characteristics of phenomena are made with reasonable precision. The sample must also include phenomena that are representative of the whole.

The first step in drawing a sample is to determine the size—the adequacy of the sample. Considerations affecting the size of the sample include homogeneity, sampling procedure, time, money, and the personnel available to conduct the research.

Homogeneity is the degree to which the subjects under investigation resemble one another with respect to the characteristics being studied—income, for example. The more alike the people are, the smaller the sample can be.

The kind of sampling procedure employed in a study also affects sample size. Types of samples called *nonprobability* samples include accidental samples, quota sampling, and purposive samples. The basic varieties of *probability* samples are the simple random sample, the stratified sample, and the cluster sample.

Important factors in any investigation are the time, money, and personnel available to conduct the research. The amount of time and money allotted to hire assistants, collect information, and process data directly affects sample size. The research itself must be compatible with the resources available. It is impossible to study all social workers in one state, for example, if the study must be concluded in a month or if the research worker has limited funds and no assistance.

Types of Samples

Nonprobability Sampling

Nonprobability sampling is not the preferred approach. It is likely to be less accurate and less representative than probability sampling. Yet a majority of samples in most disciplines, particularly social work, are nonprobability samples. There are three principal methods of nonprobability sampling: accidental, quota, and purposive.

Accidental Sampling. Frequently, an event requires a quick research response or provides an opportunity for which a research worker must develop a quick response. In such cases, the data must be gathered from available persons. The primary difficulty of this method is that the critical variables of the available subjects may not be typical of the subject population.

One type of accidental sampling that occurs frequently among students develops when their professor (or professor's colleague) distributes a questionnaire to a class. The students' "accidental" presence in that particular class causes them to be included in a sample.

This is the weakest form of sampling. When the phenomena being investigated are homogeneous within the population, however, the bias may not be too great. The converse is true with heterogeneous populations. The significant problem is that the investigator cannot evaluate the presence or absence of bias and must be cautious in analyzing, interpreting, and generalizing from accidental samples.

Quota Sampling. Here, the research worker uses known data about the population to provide representativeness. Quota sampling receives its name from the establishment of quotas for the strata from which data are to be collected. A research worker who knows about the population under investigation can be fairly certain that its subgroups are proportionately represented in the study.

A likely example of quota sampling is one such as this: An investigator decides to study social work students at ABC University. The social work undergraduates at ABC U. number 1,500. The investigator has determined that 350 is a desirable sample size within the resources of the study. To use accidental sampling, this research worker might attend a student social work association meeting or distribute a questionnaire in a few social work classes. However, to use quota sampling, some facts about the student population must be kept in mind:

- Males number 500 (33.3%)
- Females number 1,000 (66.7%)
- First-year students number 800 (56.3%)
- Second-year students number 400 (26.7%)
- Third-year students number 300 (20%)

This information should guide the selection of respondents in the sample of 350. The quotas would be met by selecting the correct percentage of male or female respondents within the sample frame of 350. Male respondents should number 116 or 117 (33%); female respondents should number 232 or 233 (67%). These numbers are the quotas for the male and female categories. The procedure for class breakdown should be the same.

The procedure for quota sampling is not difficult, and determining quotas requires little time or effort.

Purposive Sampling.   In this form of sampling, the research worker uses his or her knowledge about the population to select cases to be included in the sample. The criterion for including certain subjects in the sample is only the research worker's belief that they possess "typical" characteristics. Purposive sampling is not a recommended approach.

Probability Sampling

Probability sampling specifies that the sample findings should not differ from the true population values by more than a certain amount. A good probability sample does the following:

1. Provides ways to determine the number of respondents needed
2. Specifies the chance (probability) that any person will be included in the sample
3. Permits investigators to estimate how much error results from selecting some people or events instead of all of them
4. Lets research workers determine the degree of confidence that can be placed in population estimates made from the sample.[1]

The three most commonly used probability sampling methods are simple random, stratified random, and cluster sampling.

Simple Random Sampling.   This method underlies all probability sampling designs. The principal features of a simple random sample are that it (1) gives each unit of a population an equal chance of being selected and (2) makes the selection of every possible combination of the desired number of cases equally likely.

In other words, a random sample is so drawn that the research worker has no reason to believe a bias will result. The units of the study's "universe" must be so arranged that the selection process gives "equiprobability" (chance) of selection to every unit in that universe. The research worker acknowledges that the universe is not sufficiently known to duplicate exactly in the sample but attempts to "randomize" his or her ignorance about that universe.

The universe must be defined as carefully as possible. One problem in acquiring a sample of social data is that a list guaranteeing a complete definition of the universe may not be available. Suppose the research worker is examining the distribution of welfare services in a community. One problem in working with social services records is that they usually comprise "open" and "closed" files. The open file contains current active cases. From these files, however, no assumptions can be made about time. Some cases may have been opened long ago; others may have been closed recently. The research worker must specify this information to produce a more accurate sample.

The mechanics of selecting a random sample are not complex. The procedure involves selecting cases that depend on chance alone. One method is to number every unit of the universe, record the numbers on identical slips of paper, then place them in a receptacle. They are thoroughly mixed, then the needed amount is drawn. The sample will be random. This method is tedious and time-consuming, however.

A better method is using a table of random numbers. This procedure still requires each item in the universe to be numbered. Each item's number must have an equal number of digits—for example, 0001, 0002, 0003.

The third method is to sample a list by fixed interval or fixed position. That is, every second, fifth, or twentieth name on a list might be selected for the sample. This method should be used only when position on the list does not somehow affect randomness.

Stratified Random Sampling.   This method is based on random sampling but is combined with another method to increase representativeness. The added feature of representativeness enables the use of a smaller sample than does random sampling, saving in time and money.

The stratified method assumes that a universe is composed of homogeneous subuniverses whose attributes could be gender, age, or occupation, for example. Thus, the research worker's first step is to divide the universe into homogeneous subuniverses. This process of categorization into subuniverses must be directly correlated with the variables being studied. Too many subuniverses must not be created because doing so would necessitate an increase in the sample size over that needed for simple random sampling.

The typical procedure employed in stratified sampling, after grouping (the creation of subuniverses) has been done, is to select subjects from among the subuniverses using a table of random numbers. In many cases, to keep the sample makeup in proportion to the composition of the universe as a whole, the research worker must select uneven numbers of persons or units from the subuniverses. For example, suppose the investigator wishes to select from among minority groups (who are of unequal size in the subject population) the correct proportions of blacks, Japanese-Americans, and Irish-Americans. If the universe under study is composed of 3,000 blacks, 7,000 Japanese-Americans, and 15,000 Irish-Americans, the sample should reflect these numbers. Therefore, the sample size for each group should approximate the distribution of this principal variable. Stratified sampling guarantees the appropriate representation of each segment of the universe.

Stratified sampling increases the precision and representativeness of the final sample. When it is desirable to obtain reliable information about subuniverses with relatively small membership, stratified random sampling provides a means to include a sufficient number of cases in the sample. However, the research worker who lacks information on the critical variable of the study will find that stratified sampling is not feasible. Further, stratified sampling requires more knowledge and labor than does simple random sampling.

Cluster Sampling. For large surveys, the typical procedure is to use cluster sampling. This form may be used when acquiring a list of all the elements of a universe is not possible. For example, if a study group were to contain all the full-time social work students in the country, it would be impossible to list and enumerate them all for the purpose of drawing a simple or stratified random sample. The cost would be prohibitive. For such reasons, large-scale surveys seldom use simple random samples or stratified random samples.

In cluster sampling, successive random samples are selected from the units. The first sample is drawn from the large unit, or cluster. To study all social work students, for instance, the investigator might first select universities by the random procedure. Next, selection from within would take place, from the largest (most inclusive) unit, to less inclusive units, and finally to the most basic unit of the population being studied. This procedure often is referred to as *multistaged sampling*.

Sample Size
Typically, a major problem confronting the first-time research worker concerns the number of respondents needed in a sample. What size should the

sample be? With probability sampling techniques, it is possible to determine in advance the appropriate size for accuracy of the sample. However, no single formula can ensure precision because sample size is affected by the heterogeneity of the variables under study, the sampling procedure used, and the type of estimating procedure used. (This technical topic is discussed in advanced statistical textbooks.)

The research design should try to use the largest sample possible. When in doubt, research workers should exceed what they perceive as minimum requirements. The larger the sample, the more representative of the universe it is likely to be. The larger the sample, the smaller the sampling error.

Elements of Measurement

When gathering research information, investigators must pay considerable attention to the methods by which data will be measured.

The process of measuring independent variables is crucial to research. For some disciplines and their particular needs, measurement is not complex. Height and weight, for example, are easily measured. However, such things as alienation, despair, and depression are more subtle and complex; no convention or agreement exists regarding the measurement of such conditions. Yet most variables studied in social work are intangibles, commonly referred to as sociological or psychological variables. Most social workers and social scientists agree that the problem of measurement may be the most significant concern in social science research.

The process of specifying variables contains two steps: quantification and measurement. Quantification is the process of establishing a standard amount of a phenomenon and labeling it. Isolating standardized units increases the power of description and analysis. When Farenheit proposed the idea of degrees of temperature, for example, he made possible much more useful descriptions of heat and cold than had previously existed.

Quantification in social science and social work assumes two forms: discrete and continuous. Discrete quantification can lie only at separate points on a scale. That is, it counts the units of a phenomenon. For example, the number of people in a room may be expressed only in whole numbers—zero, one, two, three, or four, for instance. In the same fashion, a vote is a discrete and specific act that can be counted in a conventional manner. A continuous variable, on the other hand, is one that can be represented by any value or fractional value between points on a scale. One can count the number of years in a person's age, but the quantification of that age is an expression of an ongoing process. A person might be 43.1234 years old on a given day, for instance. Even smaller units could express smaller fractions of such a variable, assuming the measuring instrument permits it. Therefore, no matter how small the unit of measurement, a continuous variable can always (in theory, at least) be made smaller; a discrete value can fall only at separated points of the scale.

Levels of Measurement

There are four generally recognized levels of measurement: (1) nominal, (2) ordinal, (3) interval, and (4) ratio.

1. Nominal Measurement.   The nominal scale orders observations in an either/or fashion. It is the most fundamental scientific measuring design in use.

To assign objects to nominal categories is merely to measure them according to some fundamental likeness or difference, such as race, religion, eye color, blood type, or nationality. Investigators using nominal measurement assign subjects numbers with which they can classify characteristics or attributes into categories. Suppose a research worker wishes to identify all the black items in a room. Such a study keys on one of the many attributes of the objects in a room; it isolates items that are black. In distinguishing black from non-black objects, the research worker is using the most rudimentary of measurements, nominal scales.

The number of categories depends on the variability and distinctness of the phenomenon. Because they are distinct and exclusive, such categorical differences are sometimes referred to as being qualitative or discrete.

Categorization or classification is common in social work and other social sciences. Much social work research consists of responses solicited from people. Thus, a question is asked, and the response is then categorized. A "yes" or "no" response would constitute a nominal measurement. Such data as "male" or "female," "married" or "unmarried," or "separated" or "divorced" constitute other nominal measurements.

All such cases provide nonquantitative organizations of observable phenomena. Classes of phenomena are identified, then objects are either assigned to a category or not. If numbers are assigned to categories of variables, their use is arbitrary, with no quantitative implication.

To achieve a proper nominal scale, two basic requirements apply. All the members of one level of the attribute must be assigned the same numeral. No two levels may be assigned the same numeral. In other words, the properties of exclusiveness and exhaustiveness must be realized. To ensure exclusiveness, a research worker assigns to Category X only objects that possess Characteristic X. For exhaustiveness, a category must exist for each distinct phenomenon.

2. Ordinal Measurement.   The ordinal measurement scale can be applied when some sequence of degree exists—when one degree, point, or value precedes another or when a rank order of the phenomenon may be created.

Assume that a respondent has already provided a yes-no (nominal scale) response. Now the investigator wishes some expression of the degree to which the respondent agrees or disagrees with a statement. The alternatives might be set up as follows:

Strongly agree	Agree	Slightly agree
Slightly disagree	Disagree	Strongly disagree

Thus, the ordinal scale offers a sequence or ordering of categories or classes. Several such ordinal scales are in common use.

3. Interval Measurement.   Interval measurement occurs when the classes are of equal size. The research worker must be able to specify the degree or amount of variation among them along some measurable dimension. Also, a fixed unit of distance must be established between each of the points along that dimension or continuum.

The interval scale satisfies all the properties of ordinal scales, and more. An interval scale not only allows investigators to make statements about "more" or "less," but also allows them to determine how much more or less of a given attribute one subject possesses. IQ tests furnish the best example of an interval scale in the social sciences. The difference in intelligence between 110 and 100, for instance, should equal that between 100 and 90. These numerical classes are supposed to be equally spaced. The respondent makes a decision on the basis of a hypothetical zero category.

Another property of the interval scale is additivity. All the scale's intervals are equal. Therefore, the distance between points A and B plus the distance between points B and C, for example, should equal the distance between points B and C plus the distance between points C and D. Any combination of equal numbers of distances or intervals on an interval scale should be equal. For instance, $A + B + C = D + E + F$.

4. Ratio Measurement.   A ratio scale has a zero point. Measures on a ratio scale provide information concerning (1) the rank order of objects, (2) the interval between the objects, and (3) the absolute magnitude of the attribute for the object. Most physical measures of a person provide ratio data, for example.

Measurements of education or income typify ratio scales encountered in social work. A client may have a zero education or a zero income. Or social workers might speak of an education of six years being twice as great as one of three years, or of $5,000 income being twice as great as $2,500.

Numerous mathematical operations may be performed on the various scaling techniques. They have been explored in more advanced texts. This chapter aims only to introduce the student to the concepts of measurement and scaling.

Summary

A sample is a small representation of a whole. Samples allow research workers to gain a worthwhile idea of certain characteristics of an entire population by studying only a few of its members. The sample must be truly representative of the whole, however, and its size must be large enough to allow reasonable generalizations to be made. Several considerations affect the size of the sample, including the time, money, and personnel available for the study; the subjects' homogeneity (how closely they resemble one another); and the sampling procedure used.

The two types of sampling procedures are probability and non-probability.

Nonprobability sampling is not the preferred approach because it is usually less accurate and less representative than probability sampling. However, it is the strategy most used in social work. There are three principal nonprobability sampling methods.

Accidental samples are obtained from readily available subjects. Accidental sampling might be used when speed is important or when the research opportunity is a fleeting one. These tend to be the weakest form of samples, but sometimes their use is necessary.

In quota sampling, researchers establish sample quotas for the subgroups that constitute the larger population being studied. Investigators must possess prior knowledge about key categories within the subject universe.

The research worker using the purposive sampling method merely uses personal knowledge about the population at large to select study subjects with presumed typical traits. The purposive approach is not the most reliable sampling scheme.

Probability sampling specifies that sample findings should not differ from the true characteristics of the population by more than a certain degree. There are three common methods.

In the simple random sample, every unit and combination of units of a population has an equal chance of being selected for study. Randomness is guaranteed by one of several methods of selecting project participants.

The stratified random design provides increased representativeness but uses smaller samples. To use this strategy, research workers must divide a universe into homogeneous subgroups according to such attributes as gender or occupation. Next, they select participants, using random selection methods, and conduct the research. Users of the stratified random sampling design must be careful to correlate their subuniverses closely with the variables being studied.

Cluster sampling is useful for large-scale surveys, when populations are simply too large to permit samples to be chosen by other means. The research worker successively selects smaller units in stages, until a sample group is representative and of a small enough size to be workable.

One of the largest problems in the social sciences is measuring variables. No scales exist by which investigators may measure precisely the degrees of such human conditions as hopelessness or alienation. To specify such sociological or psychological variables as well as possible, scientists use two steps. The first step is to quantify the phenomenon, or establish for it some sort of yardstick. Discrete quantification employs only whole numbers. Variables quantified in a continuous fashion, in contrast, may be presented for study in fractions as small as desired.

The second step is the actual measurement. There are four common methods.

When using nominal scales, numbers are assigned to subject areas; then subject attributes are categorized according to those numbers. Nominal scales merely classify objects according to some fundamental likeness or difference, such as religion, race, or shoe size. Research using nominal scales must attain exhaustiveness and exclusiveness. Categories must be provided for each phenomenon or characteristic being studied, and only objects possessing that characteristic are assigned to each category. The nominal scale orders observations in an either/or manner. Objects possess a trait or do not; there are no finer distinctions.

Ordinal measurements may be used when some sequence of degrees exists or when phenomena or attributes may be ranked in some way.

Interval measuring allows comparison of classes of equal size along points on a scale. The distance between each set of points on the scale should be equal. Interval scales are more exact than ordinal measurements.

A ratio scale begins at zero. It can provide information about the ranking of objects, the interval between them, and the absolute magnitude of a certain attribute of each object. Typical ratio scales used in social work measure client education or income.

End Note

1. Hansen, Morris H., Hurwitz, William N., and Madow, William G. *Sample Survey Methods and Theory. I. Methods and Applications.* New York: John Wiley and Sons, 1953.

Survey Methods
in Data Collection

10

Most social work students are familiar with the survey as a technique for collecting research data. Surveys can identify the incidence, distribution, and interrelation of sociological and psychological variables in populations. From relatively small samples, the survey can furnish fairly accurate information on whole populations.

Most survey research is descriptive. Descriptive surveys generally focus on the incidence and distribution of the opinions and characteristics of a small but representative sample of people. Businesses and governments use surveys to help formulate policies and actions. Probably the best-known type of survey research is the census.

The two data collection techniques survey researchers use most are the questionnaire and the structured interview.

The Questionnaire

The questionnaire probably is the most widely used research technique in social work and the behavioral sciences. It is fairly economical to use with a large, geographically dispersed study group, and administering it requires little skill. A questionnaire is merely a list of questions the investigator wants answered, to which the respondent replies personally. It differs from observation, in which the investigator both makes the judgment and records the data. Anonymity enables respondents to express themselves freely. To be effective, though, a questionnaire must be designed specifically for the educational level of its respondents. For example, what may be an excellent device for surveying caseworkers who are college graduates may not be at all appropriate for persons whose education ceased at the eighth grade.

Constructing the Questionnaire

The questionnaire must be thoughtfully constructed if it is to elicit the specific information sought. Questions must be appropriate. They may be of two types: structured (or closed) and unstructured (or open-ended). When answering an unstructured question, the respondent provides any answer felt most appropriate. In contrast, the structured format provides all the possible responses; the respondent must choose one.

The following sample question typifies an unstructured question:

1. How did you feel about your treatment at the Hill Mental Health Center?

The second question is a typical structured item; the respondent must select one of the options:

2. Did your treatment here help you to solve your problem?
   Yes _____ No _____
   If no, what additional services would have helped?
   a. More interviews _____
   b. Medication _____
   c. Hypnosis _____
   d. Nothing would help _____
   e. Other _____

When research workers possess prior knowledge of the possible responses to a particular question, they usually use the structured form. Without previous evidence, they would probably use an open-ended format. Structured queries are used most often in explanatory or descriptive research (defined in chapter 2). Unstructured questions, which are more difficult to evaluate, are used more frequently in exploratory research.

If the research worker is not certain about the possible responses to a question, it should be left unstructured. Consider this structured item:

The most important quality in a caseworker is
Intelligence ___
Empathy ___
Appearance ___
Other ___

Here, the research worker has had to guess at the possible responses. In this case, it would be better to allow respondents to express their own thoughts.

Is it possible to construct accurate structured questions before administering the questionnaire? There are two primary approaches to this problem. One is to study similar previous research; such an inquiry may suggest some possible questions. An existing questionnaire may suffice, in fact. The Survey Research Center at the University of Michigan's Institute for Social Research has developed questionnaires for a variety of purposes. Research workers may find that one of the SRC's forms meets their special needs.

The other approach is the pilot study, which is a good tool for determining if questions are appropriate. By using only open questions in the pilot study, the research worker can formulate better structured questions for the final questionnaire. No leading or threatening questions should be used, however.

Suppose an unstructured question on caseworker qualities elicits ten different responses from eighty-two respondents. The respondents rated caseworker traits as follows:

Personality	14
Empathy	17
Good listener	21
Intelligence	9
Unselfishness	6
Emotional stability	7
Appearance	2
Assertiveness	3
Vocabulary	1
Good looks	2
	82

The research worker, in designing the final questionnaire, would include the most frequently mentioned responses based on the pilot study. The item might read:

Rank the most important qualities of a caseworker:
Empathy ___
Good listener ___

169

> Personality ____
> Intelligence ____
> Emotional stability ____
> Unselfishness ____
> Other (please specify) _____

The question in this case has been changed slightly; instead of forcing respondents to pick only one caseworker trait, it now allows them to rank the most important qualities. The infrequently named responses are eliminated, but the "other" category has been retained to allow for a more exhaustive listing. Thus, the research worker creating a questionnaire first solicits responses about a particular issue from a small sample population, then uses that information to design the final instrument. This process yields a better questionnaire than that produced when the research worker merely makes educated guesses about possible answers.

Another way to refine a questionnaire is to administer it as a pretest to a small sample group. Because the primary concern is creating clear questions, the investigator asks the sample group members to identify any defects or questions they do not understand. Space should be provided next to each question for respondent comments. This pretest should supply the examiner enough information to rewrite or eliminate ambiguous or offensive questions.

Completing the Questionnaire

Questionnaires that get a high rate of return generally are easy to fill out and are not too long. They are interesting, attractively designed, simple to return, sponsored by a prestigious group, and personalized to the respondent.

The cover letter accompanying the questionnaire should be on official letterhead. It should briefly describe the purpose and value of the study.

Unfortunately, even under the best circumstances, a large percentage of questionnaire recipients fail to return the forms. Two practices—setting a reasonable but firm date for the questionnaire's return, and offering to send respondents a report of the study's findings—may tend to improve response rates. Also, a follow-up letter sent a few days after the completion deadline often stimulates a response. The first letter can be followed by a second, and ultimately by a phone call.

Research workers should be aware that nonresponders could sometimes cause a bias in the study results; persons who have had a bad experience with the agency may be less likely to respond to a questionnaire than those whose experience has been favorable. Thus, research results might become unrealistically weighted toward the positive end of a norm. To avoid this possibility, a random sample of nonresponders might be personally interviewed. This step is time-consuming and expensive, however.

The Interview

When collecting data through interviews, the research worker interacts directly with members of the population being studied. The interview may be a face-to-face encounter or a telephone conversation. Both versions employ similar guidelines. Most projects of any size require more than one interviewer.

A distinct advantage of the interview is that it generally evokes a higher response rate than the questionnaire. It also usually yields more detailed information. For one thing, the research worker, not the respondent, records the answer. The interviewer, besides asking standard questions, can note such things as the respondent's manner of speaking, home and neighborhood, dress (if significant), and general reactions to the subject matter. By astute observation, the interviewer may even find that no more personal or delicate questions need be asked.

Because the interview usually contains more open-ended questions than the questionnaire, its use normally requires more skill. The interviewer must remain alert to ambiguities and deceptions in respondent answers. Further, if the respondent's native language is not English, the interviewer must take special care to try to determine intended meanings correctly.

Another problem with interviews is reliability, particularly when the investigation is large enough to require two or more interviewers. Investigators must ensure that interviewers use the same questions and must guard against interviewer bias or variation as well.

One solution to the problem of interviewer variation is using standardized interview schedules (as do public opinion polls). With these, interviewers ask every respondent the same questions in the same order. This format eases the investigator's job of comparing and analyzing the data. However, to standardize the data, investigators usually must sacrifice interview depth and opportunity to probe. As a compromise, most use an interview guide, which requires that certain standard information be obtained from all respondents but allows interviewers some leeway (for example, to decide when they should rephrase a question for a respondent, or whether to probe further on a specific question). Obviously, this sort of interviewing requires more skill than the standardized type.

Rules for Interviewing

The specific interview varies with the population being studied and the nature of the research. Some general considerations apply to most interviews.

The interviewer should not dress in a way that might intimidate respondents. Because first impressions are important, inappropriate dress could bias the respondent and complicate the interview. Questioners should be pleasant and relaxed. They should try to seem interested in getting to know the respondent without appearing to pry.

Interviewers should be familiar with the questions. Otherwise the study results could suffer. The list of questions should be kept reasonably short. Lengthy interviews can (1) cause respondents to lose interest and (2) result in the accumulation of too much trivial data, the evaluation and presentation of which may make project deadlines difficult to meet.

Interviewers should record responses as exactly as possible. Any attempt to summarize or paraphrase or to correct bad grammar might alter or lose intended meanings.

The Telephone Interview

Only recently has the telephone interview gained respectability among researchers, even though pollsters and marketing specialists have used this technique for some time. A major limitation is the cost of long-distance calls. For most research, this constraint limits the length of interviews. Also, because not everyone has a telephone, a sampling problem arises. Probably telephone interviews should be used mainly for exploratory rather than in-depth research.

Horton and Duncan point out that the telephone survey enables researchers to gather data quickly, allowing immediate investigation of an event, not weeks after the fact when memories are stale.[1] Though expensive, the telephone survey still costs less than field interviews. Finally, this method is convenient; the research worker can gather data on widely dispersed populations without leaving the office.

Summary

Surveys allow research workers to learn about the characteristics of large populations by investigating smaller sample groups. The two most used survey techniques are the questionnaire and the structured interview.

Using the questionnaire simply involves respondents' replying to a list of questions. Despite the ease of its use, however, the construction of an effective questionnaire may require considerable time and careful thought. To be most effective, a questionnaire must be designed with the educational levels of respondents in mind.

Questions may be structured or closed questions, which provide all the possible responses: The respondent must choose one option or must rank all options according to perceived order of importance. Unstructured or open-ended questions allow respondents to supply any answer they feel most appropriate.

Research workers often use the structured format when they are familiar with the likely responses to a particular question. The structured form is used most often in explanatory or descriptive research. When investigators are uncertain what responses a question might elicit, they are likely to choose unstructured queries. This format is employed most commonly in exploratory research.

Accurate structured questions can be developed in three ways. One is to study similar previous research; an existing questionnaire may even suffice. Another is to conduct a pilot study, using unstructured questions, to learn the most likely responses for each questionnaire item; then worthwhile structured questions can be developed from the results of the pilot study. A third approach is to administer a trial questionnaire to a sample group as a pretest. Any ambiguous or unsatisfactory questions then may be rewritten or eliminated.

Tactics that investigators can use to improve questionnaire response rates include setting a date for returning the form, telling respondents they will receive a report on the study, and using follow-up letters and phone calls.

Interviews may be conducted either in person or by telephone. Interviews usually can supply more detailed information than questionnaires, but interpreting the results may be correspondingly more difficult and laborious. Moreover, conducting interviews requires more skill than administering questionnaires.

Besides asking standardized questions, experienced interviewers can note other tangible information impossible to obtain through questionnaires—details regarding the respondents' speech, environment, dress, and reactions to the subject matter, for instance. Interviewers should be pleasant and relaxed. They should dress nicely, but should not wear clothes that would intimidate respondents. They should be familiar with their questions.

With interviews, reliability becomes a greater problem than in studies using questionnaires—especially (as in most surveys) when two or more interviewers are employed. Using standardized interview schedules can help ease this problem.

Telephone interviews allow researchers to gather data quickly and to investigate an event immediately. They are convenient. They can be costly, however, and because some people lack phones telephone surveys cannot reach everyone.

End Note

1. Horton, Robert L., and Duncan, David J. "A New Look at Telephone Interviewing Methodology." *Pacific Sociological Review* 21 (July 1978), 259–273.

Field Observation and Recording

11

The simple techniques of observation and recording are the basic tools of field research. Social workers throughout their training are encouraged to be astute observers. Therefore, they should find observation easily adaptable to research. It is a data-gathering technique with which most social workers are already familiar.

Because much of social work practice occurs in the home, neighborhood, and community, most of the observational methods discussed in this chapter apply primarily to real settings rather than to the laboratory.

Bickman notes, "Observation is not only one of the most pervasive activities of daily life, it is a primary tool of scientific inquiry." Scientific observation, states Bickman, contains four properties.[1]

> Observation becomes a scientific technique when it (1) serves a formulated research purpose, (2) is planned systematically, (3) is recorded systematically and related to more general propositions rather than being presented as reflecting a set of interesting curiosities, and (4) is subjected to checks and controls on validity and reliability.

Observation may be the most appropriate means of gathering data on two types of occasions: (1) when research workers are recording a pure description of the activity of a group, neighborhood, or community, and (2) when the location (a mental hospital or unique community setting, for example) inhibits the use of more formal techniques.

One primary advantage of observation is that it allows the gathering of data in the settings in which people live. Investigators can observe subjects under conditions of stress that are ethically impossible to duplicate in a laboratory situation (that is, it would be unethical to induce stress in someone artificially just to be able to study the subject's reactions).

Observation Roles

For scholars conducting field work, Buford Junker has differentiated four possible roles: complete participant, participant-as-observer, observer-as-participant, and complete observer.[2]

The complete participant interacts as naturally as possible with those being observed. The research worker's identity and purpose are not revealed to the subjects. A potential problem in this role is that the investigator might become one of the group and, consequently, might lose the necessary sense of objectivity. Also, retaining the information observed can become difficult if the interaction time is very long. The main advantage of this technique is that it offers possibilities for learning about aspects of behavior that otherwise might escape the field observer.

The participant-as-observer role differs significantly: the informants (those being observed) are aware of the field relationship. This role can allow the research worker to include interviews in formal observation. However, because the participants are aware of the research, they might tend to mask some behaviors, denying the investigator access to selected kinds of information. The social worker is more likely to use this role than that of complete participant. It is particularly appropriate for community organizers.

The role of observer-as-participant is more formalized and entails less personal risk than the previous role. However, it allows the research worker to participate only in limited interactions. This limitation affects the amount and type of data revealed to the investigator.

The complete observer has no interaction with the field subjects. In this role, the social worker must rely on observing and interpreting, and be left alone to determine the meanings and innuendoes of behavior.

Each of these roles offers advantages and disadvantages. Students might practice them in class to determine the information-gaining potential of each, and to determine in which role they are most comfortable.

These techniques are particularly appropriate when used in community organization. Other settings in which social workers may find ample

175

opportunity for research using these techniques include schools, mental institutions, halfway houses, and hospitals.

Although observation, on the surface, appears a relatively simple technique, its use presents some difficulties. Problem areas include defining one's role relative to the informants, knowing which data to record, and knowing how to record. Generally, the observer attempts to construct as complete and nonselective a description as possible. In some types of research, however, the research worker may wish to categorize the observed behavior. The approach and role must be determined before beginning the study.

Recording in the Field

Information in this section has been adapted from Lofland.[3]

A vital part of the observer's role is recording information. Only by taking comprehensive field notes is the observer likely to be able later to produce a qualitative analysis. Writing is the best aid to memory; the observer who does not take field notes might as well stay at home.

Like newspaper reporters, field observers should be concerned with discovering the "who, what, when, why, where, and how." Such matters as who was at the scene, their numbers, who said what to whom, and the order of events should all be noted.

One note-taking practice involves taking what Lofland calls *jotted notes*—cryptic comments concerning key phrases, quotes, and activities the observer has seen and heard during a day. Jotted notes can be a great aid to the observer writing more complete field notes at the end of an observation period.

A general rule for note-taking, whether or not the observer's role is known to those he is observing, is to take notes inconspicuously. Granted, sometimes it is almost impossible—during an interview, for instance, or on other occasions when considerable data simply must be recorded on the spot. But generally the research worker should take notes as surreptitiously as possible. Even when the observed persons are aware that they are being scrutinized, open note-taking may cause them to act unnatural and self-conscious. Thus, the observer should try to make notes when shielded in some fashion: in rest rooms, cars, or offices, for example. Sometimes, though, during meetings or under similar conditions when others also may be writing, observers can make research notes openly.

Field Notes

The observer should convert jottings into field notes as soon as possible. Morning observations should be written up in the afternoon; a day's or afternoon's observances should be expanded that evening, or the next morning at the latest. Forgetting is slow immediately after a learning experience; but as time passes, memory dissipates in near-geometric fashion. Thus, the observer who does not transcribe notes for a day or more is likely to forget a great deal of material. Because memory decays very little during sleep, it is reasonably safe to write up one day's observations on the following morning. But the wait should be no longer than that. New experiences can quickly obliterate the old.

The writing of field notes requires time and personal discipline and indeed may easily take as long as the observation. In fact, a reasonable rule of thumb is to expect to spend as much time writing as observing, but individual observers may well spend much more or much less time writing.

How many pages of notes should an observation period generate? Observers differ enormously. Some can produce forty pages describing a three-hour observation. Others might write only a few pages. There are no rules; observers and conditions differ greatly. One rough guide is that notes should be adequate enough to allow the writer, months later, to have a reasonably vivid picture of an event. In most cases, each hour of observation should probably generate at least two single-spaced typed pages.

Because field notes are private documents, the writer need not worry greatly about correct grammar and punctuation, if doing so will aid the flow of information onto paper. Propriety may be saved for the next stage—concerted analysis. The object in making field notes is to record immediately as much correct information as possible.

Ideally, an observer should know how to type. Typing is faster, easier to read, and easier to copy. Observers skilled in using dictation machines may save time by dictating field notes. Transcriptions, too, should be done as soon as possible. The author should then pore over the transcriptions and make any necessary further notes. Although talking may take less time than writing, it also tends to remove the observer from having to think as hard about his or her observances. For most people, writing seems best to stimulate thought.

Usually the observer should make at least two carbons of field notes. Some like to type each day's notes directly onto duplicating masters like dittos or mimeographs. Then, as many copies can be made as desired.

Content

What goes into field notes? Most contain a general chronological description of what happens, both to the setting and to the participants. Notes describe events, people, and conversations. Each new setting and person encountered, and any changes in them, should be recorded. Many observers draw maps into their field notes to indicate the approximate layouts of scenes, the placement of persons in them, and the movement of persons. The times at which various events occur can be recorded.

Lofland suggests two rules for writing running descriptions.

1. Be concrete. Avoid summarizing, avoid using abstract adjectives and adverbs. Try to stay at the lowest possible level of inference. Avoid being judgmental. Rather, try to capture the descriptive and interpretive terms of the participants themselves. If Person A thought Person B was happy or depressed, the observer should report Person A's reaction to Person B's behavior. The observer should try to avoid for the moment any judgment concerning B's "true state" or the "meaning" of his acts.

2. Recall distinctions when possible. Few people possess author Truman Capote's unusual ability to recall verbatim several hours of conversation. Most can recall only the general outline of an event. But the degree of exactness should be indicated in field notes. One group of observers[4] suggests (1) putting verbatim material within quotes, (2) putting less precise verbal material within apostrophes to indicate paraphrasing, and (3) using no markings for material recalled with a lesser degree of certainty.

Often the observer later remembers forgotten information. At the moment of remembrance, such previous data should be entered into the field notes, with the date, context, and any other pertinent information, recorded as well as the observer's memory will allow.

Analytic Ideas and Inferences

Frequently, the observer conceives ideas regarding observations: how occurrences are examples of some sociological concept, how small actions affect larger events, and so on. However trivial or far-fetched some of these notions may seem, the observer should set them off somehow as being ideas or inferences; typewriter characters like asterisks or brackets can be used.

Thus, the research worker, having left the setting to analyze the information, should possess more than raw field material. The analysis will be considerably easier if, during the field work, the observer already has begun to consider possible lines of interpretation. Most analytic ideas are of three varieties: (1) ideas about the main themes of the study, (2) middle-level pieces of analysis (important but not vital items uncovered during the observation), and (3) lesser topics.

The typical observer will probably collect many of these analytic memos in the field notes that never see the light of the final report. However, their inclusion during the note-writing doubtless guides the analytic period considerably. Preparing the final report then becomes only a matter of selecting and defining existing themes.

A given day's notes also may raise a series of observational questions. The observer may want to write these down while expanding the jotted remarks at the end of a day. They can serve as reminders of things to look for or questions to ask on the next day of observation.

Observers' Feelings

During a study, the observers likely will develop personal opinions and emotional responses to the situation. They should probably keep a private diary to record such involvements. When the setting or its participants cause observers to feel embarrassment or hate, or to receive praise or criticism, a separate record should keep track of such events. This record can serve two important functions: (1) Observers may find that their feelings parallel those of the participants, which may aid in later analysis. If a turn of events angers an observer, for example, it may later develop that many participants felt the same way. (2) Later review of both personal diary and field notes may allow observers to recognize any biases unknowingly held at the time of the study. Of course, any personal opinions, impressions, and so forth should have been labeled as such in the notes.

Special problems sometimes arise from the process of note-taking and analysis. The observer's relation to the people under observation is peculiar. While the participants are continuing with their lives, the research worker is dissecting and contemplating their world. In any study, participants do and say things they might prefer not to have publicized. Yet the observer, while writing up the notes, necessarily violates such participant preferences. The portrait the observer ultimately presents to other scholars is not likely to be the one the participants would choose.

In most studies, the observer forms personal attachments to some of the observed. Observer and observed become friend and confidante. Yet the products of such attachments and revealed confidences should go into the field notes and ultimately into the research report. In this regard, the observer can only try to remain aware of any relationship or empathy that may have developed and should try to serve both science and brotherhood as well as conscience will allow.

Once the observer has acquired the habit of jotting regularly and making disciplined field notes, the practice can develop a demand and a logic of its own. The observer begins to sense a compulsion to record almost any observation of any importance. When the observer begins to feel this strong a need to log information, he or she has become a true field researcher. Though field work has its share of drudgery and requires considerable patience and persistence at times, it also offers uncountable rewards and moments of insight and joy.

Structured Observation

Structured observation is useful when the research worker knows which aspects of the group activity are relevant to the research. In such cases, the investigator is in a position to plan for making and recording observations before collecting data.

Structured observation may take place either in the field or in a controlled laboratory experiment. This practice typically employs some form of checklist of categories that the investigator has developed or has adopted from previous research work. One valuable strategy for use in a laboratory situation was developed by Robert Bales and his associates at Harvard University.[5] The Bales approach is to collect a group of people in a laboratory in order to observe the development of a group structure. The subjects are given a problem to solve as a group and are observed (typically, through a one-way mirror) as they process the problem.

I.	A.	Shows solidarity, affection, liking for others, raises other's status, gives help, reward:	_____
	B.	Shows tension release, jokes, laughs, shows satisfaction:	_____
	C.	Agrees, shows passive acceptance, understands, concurs, complies:	_____
II.	D.	Gives suggestion, direction, implying autonomy for others:	_____
	E.	Gives opinion, evaluation, analysis, expresses feeling, wish:	
	F.	Gives orientation, information, repeats, clarifies, confirms:	_____
III.	G.	Asks for orientation, information, repetition, confirmation, explanation of behavior:	_____
	H.	Asks for opinion, evaluation, analysis, expression of feeling:	_____
	I.	Asks for suggestion, direction, possible ways of action:	_____
IV.	J.	Disagrees, shows passive rejection, formality, withholds help, doubts genuineness of behavior:	_____
	K.	Shows tension, embarrassment, asks for help, withdraws out of field	_____
	L.	Shows antagonism, anger, irritation, deflates other's status, defends or asserts self:	_____

Rate each category using the following scale:

0 = No response of this type occurred
1 = Very little occurred
2 = Some of this occurred
3 = Quite a bit occurred
4 = A great deal of this occurred
5 = Entire response was of this type

FIGURE 11-1. Interaction Process Categories. *(Source: From ANALYZING SOCIAL SETTINGS, A GUIDE TO QUALITATIVE OBSERVATION AND ANALYSIS by John Lofland. © 1971 by Wadsworth Publishing Company, Inc. Reprinted by permission of Wadsworth Publishing Company, Belmont, California 94002.)*

After observing many such groups, Bales identified twelve categories, which he asserts cover all the possible kinds of reaction and interaction that could take place in group settings (Figure 11–1).

An observer using the Bales design codes each verbal or nonverbal behavior into one of the twelve categories. The decision on coding the behaviors is the research workers'. According to Bales, each "bit" of information is:[5]

> the smallest discriminable segment of verbal or nonverbal behavior to which the observer, using the present set of categories after appropriate training, can assign a classification under conditions of continuous serial scoring. This unit may be called an act, or more properly, a single interaction, since all acts in the present scheme are regarded as interactions. The unit as defined here has also been called the single item of thought or the single item of behavior.

These data do not provide the sequence of interaction. Doing so would be simple, though, merely by using multiple recording sheets, each representing one or more minutes of observation.

To become an effective recorder requires practice. One way of increasing the information retained would be to use both audio and video equipment.

Users of Bales's structured observation method gain two distinct advantages. (1) Reliability may be increased in several ways. For example, two or more persons could record a session, compare their data sheets to resolve any differences, and produce an accurate report. (2) Because the categories are fairly exhaustive and standardized, the possibility of selective perception is greatly reduced.

The method's disadvantages also are two. (1) Generalizing from a laboratory activity is difficult. (2) Because the group is aware it is being observed, the likelihood increases of the participants' behavior being distorted and artificial.

Evaluation in the Natural Environment

The basic considerations that apply to gathering all research data apply equally to the process of collecting data in the natural environment. First, the research worker must determine if the process of observing and recording has an effect on the people being observed—called *reactivity* (explained in detail in chapter 5). The research worker also must ensure that the data collected are both reliable and valid.

Observation is widely used in family and home settings to collect information about interaction among family members. Patterson, and a number of other research workers and practitioners, make extensive use of this procedure to assess the effects of behavioral intervention procedures.[6] Haynes and Wilson reviewed more than forty different studies that used observers to collect data in naturalistic settings in conjunction with the evaluation of treatment.[7] Some used parents and other family members as observers; others used trained observers.

Some research workers reported that the use of trained observers (non-family members) produced reactive effects. Leitenberg and associates found that more reactive effects took place when outside observers were used than when family members collected the data.[8]

Kent and associates reported that when trained observers worked in institutional settings, such as schools and hospitals, reactive effects were minimal.[9] Still others investigating observer reactivity have revealed inconsistent and often contradictory findings. In an extensive review of research on this topic, Kent and Foster conclude: "There seems little reason to doubt that . . . an observer may, in fact, affect the behavior of those he observes. But the number of factors determining the magnitude and direction of behavior change may be so great that manifest reactivity is scattered and almost completely unpredictable."[10]

Investigators also have studied the reliability factors associated with using observers. All observers are subject to the same limitations in the collection of outcome data. Such limitations include inaccurate or biased observation and inaccurate or biased recording. Researchers have demonstrated that errors in data collection can be reduced with standardized data collection techniques and with trained observers. Patterson's standardized format for defining and collecting behavioral data demonstrated reasonable levels of reliability when used by trained observers and by parents who were trained in its use.[11] Reid used a similar approach to evalute family interaction.[12]

Much behaviorally oriented research and practice now involves the use of standardized behavioral codes and provides for the training of observers. Parents and others in the natural environment are often willing to learn complex procedures for observing and recording behaviors. However, many practitioners fail to realize that they also might profit from special training in data collection and recording.

The issue of how the data are collected remains controversial throughout the field of research in the natural setting. The central issue is the extent to which the observation procedure itself is responsible for modifying the behavior being studied. Because observation alone may create changes in the target behavior, the measurement procedure is potentially reactive. The research worker, then, has no way to separate the effects of measurement from the effects of a specific program of intervention.

Behavioral observation uses one or more independent observers to monitor a subject's behavior directly. It is an important tool for collecting data in both the natural environment and in simulated settings.

The major problems associated with behavior observation concern reliability, validity, and reactivity. Research workers such as Patterson have established high reliability for observational techniques in natural environments.[11] The Patterson Behavioral Coding System, reviewed in chapter 5, uses a highly sophisticated system for observing and classifying the behavior of family members in the home and elsewhere. Both the Patterson system and the Home Observation Assessment Method developed by Steinglass[13] (reviewed in chapter 5) employ trained observers to collect behavioral data about family interaction at home. A primary advantage of behavioral observation is that high reliability can be attained by using several observers, then comparing their reports.

Some of the problems of observer reliability have been resolved through the careful selection and training of observers. Other reliability problems have been minimized by carefully specifying and describing the behaviors to be observed. The problem of measurement reactivity when compiling observational data still is unresolved, however.

Observational data may also be collected from simulated or analogue settings in the clinic and laboratory. Because of the many problems (including reactivity, cost, and other practical limitations) associated with data collecting in natural settings, some practitioners and research workers create analogue conditions in the office or laboratory to measure client outcomes. These analogues, also known as simulations, attempt to simulate the natural environment and assess client responses to the simulation. Nay has identified five categories of analogue measurement.[14]

Paper and pencil analogues require the client to respond to a written scenario describing a particular circumstance or event.

A second form of simulation is the audiotape analogue, in which a tape-recorded narration describes a specific scene. The client listens to the tape and responds to the scene.

A third form of simulation is the videotape analogue. Similar to the audiotape analogue, it uses recorded visual scenes to evoke responses from clients.

A fourth type is the enactment analogue. In this format, the client interacts with relevant stimulus persons. Nay describes the enactment analogue: "An ordinary stimulus found in the natural environment is present in the contrived surroundings of the clinical setting. . . . Investigators require the client to respond, both verbally and physically, as he ordinarily would in the natural setting."[15]

The fifth form of simulation is role-play—probably the most commonly used analogue technique found in social work practice. In role-play, the client acts out a certain scene, either alone or in response to another person who also plays a specific role.

Summary

Social workers must constantly employ observation as a primary means of gathering data, in practice as well as in research. The primary advantage of observation is that it can be done in people's natural environments. It requires no laboratory apparatus, no instruments more complex than pencil and notebook.

The observer may assume one of four possible roles:

- Complete participant (mingles among the subjects; identity remains hidden)
- Participant-as-observer (identity of researcher is revealed to subjects)
- Observer-as-participant (more formalized; might restrict interaction)
- Complete observer (observes only; has no interaction with subjects).

Problems include defining the role of observer relative to informant, knowing which data to record, and knowing how to record. When observing, research workers should try to take notes as inconspicuously as possible, then expand them afterward into fuller field notes. Few rules apply to the making of notes; perhaps a rough guideline is to spend about as much time writing field notes as in making the observation. Field notes should be as complete as the observer can make them. They also should be concrete and as nonjudgmental as possible. Any analytical ideas should be recorded as they occur but should be set apart from the observations.

Structured observation is useful when the research worker knows which aspects of the group activity are relevant to the research. It usually involves observing subjects while marking items on a checklist. An important example of such a process is the laboratory procedure developed by Robert Bales. Controlled experiments offer standardization and high reliability, but generalizing from them may be difficult, and subjects may tend to act less natural than during field observations.

Observation in the natural setting is widely used to collect information about interaction among family members in the home. The procedure allows research workers and practitioners to assess the effects of behavioral intervention tactics.

For observers collecting data in the natural environment, a primary concern is guarding against reactivity—the effect of the observation itself on the conduct of subjects. The research design also must ensure that the data are reliable and valid. Reactivity in home settings is difficult to assess. It generally seems to be higher when outside observers, rather than family members, collect data. In institutional settings, however, reactivity from the use of trained observers is minimal.

Investigators can increase reliability (that is, reduce errors) by using

184

standard data collection techniques and trained observers. Often, parents and other family members can be trained in observation techniques.

Behavioral observation uses one or more independent observers to monitor directly a subject's behavior. The strategy can be used to collect data in both natural and simulated settings. It offers the advantages of high reliability because the observations of several observers can be compared. Reliability may be further enhanced by carefully selecting and training observers, and by carefully specifying and describing the behaviors to be observed. The problem of controlling reactivity remains unresolved, however.

Rather than observe subjects at home, some practitioners and researchers prefer to create artificial environments in the office or laboratory. They then observe clients in these simulations, or analogue situations, and collect information. There are at least five categories of analogue measures: paper-and-pencil, audiotape, videotape, enactment, and role-play.

End Notes

1. Bickman, L. "Observational Methods." In *Research Methods in Social Research*, edited by C. Selltiz, L. S. Wrightsman, and S. W. Cook. New York: Holt, Rinehart & Winston, 1976, p. 182.
2. Junker, Buford. *Field Work: An Introduction to the Social Sciences*. Chicago: University of Chicago Press, 1960.
3. Lofland, John. *Analyzing Social Settings: A Guide to Qualitative Observation and Analysis*. Belmont, Calif.: Wadsworth Publishing Co., 1971, pp. 101–108. Reprinted by permission of the publisher.
4. Strauss, Anselm, Schatzman, Leonard, Bucher, Rue, Ehlich, Danuta, and Sabshin, Melvin. *Psychiatric Ideologies and Institutions*. New York: Free Press, 1964.
5. Bales, R. F. *Interaction Process Analysis*. Reading, Mass.: Addison-Wesley Press, Inc., 1950, p. 37.
6. Patterson, G. R. "Naturalistic Observation in Clinical Assessment." *Journal of Applied Child Psychology* 5 (1977): 309–322.
7. Haynes, S. N., and Wilson, C. C. *Behavioral Assessment*. San Francisco: Jossey-Bass, 1979, pp. 82–87.
8. Leitenberg, H., Burchard, J. D., Burchard, S. N., Fuller, E. J., and Lysought, T. "Using Positive Reinforcement to Suppress Behavior: Some Experimental Comparisons with Sibling Conflict." *Behavior Therapy* 8 (1977): 168–182.
9. Kent, R. N., et al. "Expectation Biases in Observational Evaluation of Therapeutic Change." *Journal of Consulting and Clinical Psychology* (1974): 774–80. Also see: Wright, H. F. *Recording and Analyzing Child Behavior: With Ecological Data from an American Town*. New York: Harper and Row, 1967.
10. Kent, R. N., and Foster, S. L. "Direct Observational Procedures." In *Handbook of Behavioral Assessment* edited by A. F. Ciminero, K. S. Calhoun, and H. E. Adams. New York: John Wiley and Sons, 1977, p. 289.

11. Patterson, G. R., et al. *A Social Learning Approach to Family Intervention.* Vol. 1. Eugene, Ore.: Castalia Publishing Co., 1975.
12. Reid, J. B. *A Social Learning Approach to Family Intervention.* Vol. 2. Eugene, Ore.: Castalia Publishing Co., 1975.
13. Steinglass, P. "The Home Observation Assessment Method (HOAM): Real Time Naturalistic Observation of Families in their Homes." *Family Process* 18 (September 1979): 337–354.
14. Nay, W. R. "Analogue Measures." In *Handbook of Behavioral Assessment,* edited by A. F. Ciminero, K. S. Calhoun, and H. E. Adams. New York: John Wiley and Sons, 1977.
15. *Ibid.*, p. 255.

Other Methods of Research

12

Besides the research techniques discussed in detail in the preceding chapters, five other types of research are available to the student: case studies, secondary data analyses, exploratory-descriptive studies, historical research, and evaluation research.

The Case Study

Social workers use case studies extensively to perform in-depth investigations of individuals, groups, institutions, or communities. The case study examines the variables important in explaining the current status of the people or condition being analyzed. This format may require detailed study over an extended period. Basically, the case study attempts to learn why things are as they appear.

Case studies present advantages to the research worker. They are an excellent means of generating insights and hypotheses that can be tested with other research formats. Indeed, many scientists argue that this is the case study's most important function. For example, the case studies of Sigmund Freud's clients helped establish an elaborate system of psychological theory that still is of profound significance to social work and related disciplines. The intensive probing demanded by the case study format may reveal previously unnoticed relationships and exploratory systems. The case study may also clarify concepts and variables for further research. Because the research process generates considerable data, a comprehensive research report may contain information useful to investigators in several other areas.

The greatest advantage of the case study method is not only that it allows in-depth investigation, it also requires such exploration. However, the use of the case study as a method of research presents two major disadvantages. The single most limiting factor is that research workers cannot generalize from the study, although they can extrapolate specific data from the case in question. The other weakness is the potential for research bias, resulting in less objectivity. If, over a period of time, the investigator begins to acquire the attitudes, perceptions, and biases of the study group, a potential for distortion in the case study arises.

The appendix contains an example of a case study of a community. The reader should give particular attention to the types of data included in this sample study.

Secondary Sources of Data

Excellent sources of research information in social work lie in secondary data—existing knowledge collected as a result of other research. Each year, research activity gathers a tremendous amount of data, much of which may be useful to other research. Frequently, the investigator may test his or her hypotheses against such information gathered for other purposes. The three major types of secondary data are: expressive documents, mass media reports, and official records.

Expressive documents reflect the writer's perception and interpretation of events or activities. Good examples are case records, diaries, and logs. Mass media reports contain data taken from newspapers, magazines, movies, radio, and television. Official records include registration data such as births, deaths, marriages, divorces, crime records, voting statistics, and social service records; census data or surveys done by nongovernment personnel; and business and organization records.

Reliability (the extent to which a second observer would produce the same results) is relatively low for expressive documents. It improves somewhat for media reports, and increases considerably for official records.

Secondary data can be used to add to primary data already gathered, or as a check against other data. Secondary evidence may even constitute the sole source of information for a study. The research worker should always seek out secondary data. The probability of finding such information is high, and the likelihood of its being useful also is great.

The research worker can analyze secondary data in one of five ways:

1. Examine the variables analyzed in the previous study.
2. Explore different relationships of variables than were explored in previous research.
3. Examine a subsample contained in the previous study.
4. Conduct an examination using a different unit of analysis.
5. Use new methods to analyze previous research data.

Three examples of the kind of secondary data that social workers might find useful:

1. A major study of importance to anyone desiring facts about employment and unemployment in the social work field: In 1977, the National Association of Social Workers (NASW) commissioned a study of an apparent scarcity of social work jobs. This book reports the findings of the study. Some of the enlightening results were that the unemployed were more likely to be female direct-service workers, unemployment is higher on the coasts than in the nation's interior, and declassification may be contributing to the decline in available social work positions.[1]

2. A comprehensive national research study of the conditions under which independent, nonagency adoptions are carried out: The experiences of biological parents, adoptive parents, agencies, intermediaries, and law enforcement agencies. This study examines the elements of legal and psychological risk in independent adoptions and makes clear, practical recommendations for changes to reduce those risks. This study is a major contribution to adoption practice.[2]

3. A report on a study of existing social work quality assurance programs in health care: The NASW commissioned Claudia J. Coulton in 1977 to examine these programs; her report includes examples of the components of programs now in use. Some of the major findings described in the study are components of social work quality programs; social work information systems data elements; criteria for peer review systems; systems designed to assure social work access; minimizing costs of quality assurance programs; using quality assurance program findings; quality assurance programs and PSROs (Professional Standards Review Organizations); testing quality assurance program validity.[3]

Subsequent investigators could use the data of any of these three studies to test related hypotheses of their own. The major advantage of secondary analysis is that it is less costly and time consuming than original research. It allows the research worker to bypass the data-gathering steps in the research process. Further, when two sets of secondary data with similar variables are found, the research worker could perform a comparative analysis valuable for generating propositions, theories, or generalizations.

Probably the largest disadvantage of using secondary data is the lack of knowledge about quality control in the initial data-gathering process. The investigator using information collected by others can never be certain of the accuracy of such data.

Exploratory-Descriptive Studies

Most research models discussed in this text are designed to evaluate practice methodologies and programs. The experimental and quasi-experimental designs generally are used to test hypotheses and to deal with the logic of developing scientifically acceptable answers to research problems. However, in social work and related areas, investigators are not always able to conduct purely experimental studies. When a research problem is poorly understood or inadequately described, they must instead perform exploratory-descriptive research.

This sort of investigation becomes necessary when a poorly defined problem confronts the practitioner. Often, he or she initially possesses little objective information about the nature of a problem and the possible factors influencing it. In such cases, therefore, the practitioner or research worker first must objectively describe the problem before studying its causation and prescribing treatment.

To investigate child abuse adequately, for example, the problem must be fully described. What is child abuse? Does it consist only of physical abuse, or does it include mental abuse? How can it be recognized and reported?

These and other basic questions require answers before research can explain what causes child abuse and how it can be eliminated. Research workers must be able to recognize the different forms of child abuse before they can conduct further study; practitioners need the same information to diagnose a problem. Obviously, therefore, in many cases the needs of practice and research are identical. But until a problem has been well defined, neither the practitioner nor the research worker can consistently recognize its occurrence.

An example of descriptive research occurs in a study conducted by Robert Teare, who was concerned with describing the duties of the public welfare social workers in a state agency and with examining changes occurring over the years in such jobs.[4] As programs and problems evolve, so do job requirements. Yet, because the full range of social worker tasks had not previously been fully understood or described, it was impossible for the state agency to evaluate social workers' job performance. Without this information, the state agency could not rationally and fairly select the most qualified job applicants for social work positions. Nor could educators and staff development trainers provide the most relevant training for staff members.

Teare conducted a large-scale study of the tasks contained in social work. This research consisted of several phases, beginning with exploratory studies and ending with the final product, a descriptive study.

Teare conducted preliminary studies to obtain descriptions of the nature of social workers' tasks. These studies included a structured self-report questionnaire asking workers to describe their social work activities. Existing agency job descriptions also were used, as were other sources of information including audits of social worker activities.

When Teare had compiled a comprehensive list of all the tasks that could be included in the social work job, he began the exploratory phase. From the job descriptions, he developed a self-report questionnaire called the Job Analysis Survey. The JAS contained a section consisting of seventy-seven task statements: by responding to these, the social worker could describe his or her job. The JAS was pretested and modified, then it was administered to a large group of employees (approximately 16 percent of the agency work force) consisting of agency administrators, supervisors, social service workers, eligibility workers, and human service workers (paraprofessionals). The results were analyzed by statistical methods to determine which tasks and clusters of tasks were associated with different workers. Thus, the research effectively described the distinct tasks performed by members of each of the five worker groups.

The importance of this specific descriptive research becomes apparent when one considers the staffing requirements of a large state agency comprising thousands of social service workers and other employees. With this research information, administrators may relate specific job skills to each of the positions described and may select the best qualified persons for those positions. They can devise job evaluation procedures based on these job descriptions rather than on other less precise descriptions. Teare's study is only one example of exploratory-descriptive research.

Historical Research

Historical research is the systematic collection and critical evaluation of data relating to past events. The steps in historical research resemble those of other research: defining the problem, posing hypotheses or specific questions, collecting data in a systematic fashion, analyzing the data, and interpreting the findings. The focus in historical data collection is on past events, situations, and statements. The student or research worker using this method has no control over the documents, records, or artifacts available for study. Only records that have survived may be examined. The potential for bias is inherently great.

The student should not confuse historical research with reviews of literature. Historical research should attempt to explain the present or anticipate future events. It should not merely review what is already known about an issue or research problem.

A book by Jane Addams, *Twenty Years at Hull House*, is a good example of historical research in social work.[5]

Evaluation Research

Evaluation research is discussed to some degree in chapter 5. The primary purpose of evaluation research is to furnish investigators information with which they may judge the worth or quality of the topic under study. Such judgments are extremely important to social work. They allow administrators to make decisions about the inception of new social service programs and the possible discontinuation of existing programs.

Most social work professionals agree that a need exists for evaluative research. Most also agree that evaluation research poses several complex problems because of the number of different purposes it serves. Rossi et al. have defined the various purposes of evaluative studies.[6] They state that investigators undertake evaluation research projects for:

> . . . management and administrative purposes, to assess the appropriateness of program shifts, to identify ways to improve the delivery of interventions, and to meet the requirements of funding groups which have fiscal responsibility for allocation of program monies. They may be undertaken for planning and policy purposes, to help decide on either expansion or curtailment, and to reach decisions on whether to advocate one program or another. Finally, they may be undertaken to test a particular social science hypothesis or a professional practice principle. . . . For all these purposes, the key is to plan and implement an evaluation that is as objective as possible, that is to provide a firm assessment—an assessment [whose] results would be unchanged if done by another group or if replicated by the same evaluations.

Summary

Types of research not fully discussed in earlier chapters include case studies, secondary data, exploratory-descriptive studies, historical research, and evaluation research.

The case study examines in depth the important variables of a circumstance. The case study generates insights and hypotheses that investigators may test through other research formats. Its disadvantages are that generalizations cannot be made from the case study, and that a possibility for research bias exists.

Secondary sources of data are existing knowledge collected during previous research. Three major types of secondary data are expressive documents, mass media reports, and official records; their reliability ranges from low to high, respectively. The research worker should always seek secondary information regarding the research problem; such data often can be highly useful. Secondary analysis is less costly and time consuming than conducting original research. However, the user of secondary data can seldom be certain of its accuracy.

Exploratory-descriptive studies are needed when a research problem is poorly understood or inadequately described. To conduct any study effectively, the practitioner or research worker first must objectively describe the problem. When such a description is lacking, exploratory-descriptive research is the answer. It permits subsequent informed exploration of the object of study.

Historical research is the collection and analysis of data regarding past events. Historical research should not be confused with reviews of literature. It should attempt to provide a historical perspective on present or future events.

Evaluation research provides information with which research workers can further judge the worth or quality of the topic under study. Such research is important. For example, it provides administrators information valuable in deciding whether to begin, retain, or drop service programs. Evaluation research may serve a number of purposes.

End Notes

1. Hardcastle, David A., and Katz, Arthur J. *Employment and Unemployment in Social Work: A Study of NASW Members.* Washington, D. C.: National Association of Social Workers, 1979.
2. Meezan, William, Katz, Sanford, and Russo, Eva Manoff. "Independent Adoptions." *Child Welfare* 57 (1978): 45–52.
3. Coulton, Claudia J. *Social Work Quality Assurance Programs: A Comparative Analysis* (Washington, D. C.: National Association of Social Workers, 1979).
4. Teare, Robert J. "A Task Analysis for Public Welfare Practice and Educational Implications." In *The Pursuit of Competence in Social Work*, edited by Frank W. Clark and Morton L. Arkava. San Francisco: Jossey-Bass, 1979.
5. Addams, Jane. *Twenty Years at Hull House*. New York: Macmillan, 1959. [Original publication: 1910].
6. Rossi, Peter H., Freeman, Howard E., and Wright, Sonia R. *Evaluation: A Systematic Approach*. Beverly Hills: Sage Publications, 1979, p. 21.

Reporting, Writing, and Evaluating Research

13

One of the more difficult tasks associated with research is interpreting and writing the results. Unless the investigator completes this step, all the preceding phases will have been worthless: research is pointless unless others can benefit from its findings. The author of the report must be able to interpret statistics and results understandably and concisely. Creativity, intelligence, insight, and reasoning all are important. This chapter offers some general guidelines to help the investigator with the final step in the scientific process. It also furnishes a series of questions that students and research workers can use to evaluate each section of any research report.

The Report

Research reports are directed to various audiences, but the general form and content of research report writing in all the social and behavioral sciences is similar. The report should contain four major sections: the introduction, an outline of the study's methodology, a discussion of its findings, and a thorough analysis of the project. The research report tells readers the problem investigated, the methods employed to solve the problem, the findings of the investigation, and the conclusions inferred from those findings. The structure of the research report is the same as that of the research project itself. A general outline:

    I.   Introduction
        A.   The problem.
        B.   Theory, hypothesis, definitions.
        C.   Prior research.
   II.   Methodology
        A.   Sample and sampling method.
        B.   Measurement and definition of variables.
        C.   Data collection.
        D.   Methods of analysis.
 III.   Findings
 IV.   Discussion

The function of the research worker is not to convince or sell the reader on the virtues of the research. Rather, it is to report, as expeditiously as possible, what was done and why, the outcome, and the investigator's conclusions. The report should be so written that readers can reach their own conclusions about the adequacy of the research and the validity of the reported results and conclusions. (The student might benefit by reading library examples of research report writing in social work, sociology, psychology, and political science.)

Creating a well-done research report is no easy task. The author must present the right amount of detail, yet must retain objectivity and clarity. The best report is one with procedures that a knowledgeable reader could follow to replicate the project.

Interpreting the Results

The results of data analysis are numbers possessing little inherent significance. It is the research worker's responsibility to give meaning to the numbers. Interpretation is essentially a search for the broader implications of the findings of the study. Interpretation is guided by the general problem studied, the specific hypotheses tested, existing theory or frameworks, the findings of previous research, and the limitations of the research methodology employed.

When the findings confirm the hypothesis, interpretation is considerably easier than when the findings fail to support the hypothesis. When the hypothesis has been confirmed, in a sense the research worker has already prepared an interpretation; the hypothesis has conformed to the logical reasoning that preceded the data collection. However, it still is necessary to use caution in generalizing, even when the results confirm the hypothesis. Because hypothesis testing yields results that are probabilistic (i.e., are usually correct but are never infallible), care should be taken in generalizing the research findings to the overall population or universe studied. Even when the findings are in line with expectations, the research worker should exercise restraint in drawing conclusions.

Sometimes the research does not support the hypothesis. Beginning research workers, especially, frequently obtain results that do not confirm their initial reasoning. When this happens, two steps may be taken. First, the research worker should examine (1) the reasoning employed to derive the hypothesis, and (2) the sample and the methods. Something in these steps may provide an answer. The results of this procedure may allow the initiator or the other investigators to improve the methods or theory employed. A discouraged beginner must not underplay the significance of this procedure; it is the process by which knowledge grows in the field of social work. Sometimes the research worker can only state that no apparent relationship existed between the variables studied. Yet even this negative finding may considerably aid a later research project.

The Writing

Scientific writing is not easy. Several rewrites are usually necessary. A scientific report is a factual account of how and why a problem was selected and studied and what results were obtained. The author of a research report should avoid exaggerations or subjective, emotional statements. Any opinions should be clearly identified as such. The tone of the report should be as objective and impersonal as possible.

The goal in scientific writing should be to write simply and clearly. The use of pretentious words or jargon does little to improve the report. The purpose of a report is to communicate. The style should be concise and straightforward. It must contain correct grammar and spelling. Having it critiqued by a colleague or fellow student may help to produce a good report.

Some useful writing references include:

- *A Manual of Style*, 12th rev. ed. Chicago: University of Chicago Press, 1969.
- American Psychological Association. *Publication Manual of the American Psychological Association*, rev. Washington, D. C.: American Psychological Association, 1974. *The basic manual for writers of reports*

in psychological journals, especially APA journals. Particularly useful for mechanical details such as tables, typing, and so on. Note: Many journals, especially education journals, do not use the APA referencing system, preferring instead to list all references at the end of the report.

- W. Campbell, *Form and Style in Thesis Writing*, 3d ed. Boston: Houghton Mifflin, 1969. *A useful reference for thesis writers.*
- M. Nicholson. *A Dictionary of American-English Usage.* New York: Oxford University Press, 1957. *A valuable American revision of Fowler's classic*, A Dictionary of English Usage. *A good book for any writer.*
- W. Strunk, Jr., and E. B. White. *The Elements of Style.* New York: Macmillan, 1959. *This little gem, which every writer should own, is dedicated to clarity, brevity, and simplicity.*
- K. Turabian. *A Manual for Writers of Term Papers, Theses, and Dissertations*, 12th ed. Chicago: University of Chicago Press, 1979. *An invaluable reference. Can be called the handbook of the doctoral student. It is based on the* Manual of Style.

Evaluating Research

Social work is an applied profession. Social work research contributes to the knowledge base of the profession and produces potential practice information. Thus, its research findings are important to all social workers, not just to those interested in research. For this reason, social workers, as professionals, should possess the ability to evaluate research that relates to their practice.

Too often, readers of research literature in social work feel that merely because something is in print, it must be correct. However, most research contains weaknesses and limitations. The discerning reader should heed the results of research but at the same time be aware that it may have weak points.

The purpose of critical evaluation is not to search for flaws but to identify a report's adequacy, strengths, and deficiencies objectively. When drawing conclusions about the value of a study's findings, the reviewer should examine both its merits and its limitations. Thus, a good research critique involves objective and balanced consideration both of the study and of its significance to knowledge and practice.

The following steps involved in critical evaluation present questions that may be asked at each stage of a report. Some of these questions are general and apply to all research investigations; others are specific to particular research methods. Though not exhaustive, this list of questions should facilitate an orderly evaluation of any research report.

197

Evaluating the Introduction

The introduction sets the stage for the readers of a report. The manner in which the introductory materials are presented is vital to reader understanding of what the research worker has done and how he or she has done it. If the introduction does not adequately identify the problem and its importance, the reader may be unable to determine whether the solution was appropriate. A good introduction should provide favorable answers to the following questions.

The Problem

Is the problem clearly and concisely stated?

Is the problem too big or too complex to be solved in a single investigation?

Does the problem statement give precise information about the independent and dependent variables?

Can the research question be answered with empirical evidence?

Are the limits on the scope of the problem designated?

Is the significance of the problem discussed?

Are definitions of terms needed for a clear understanding of the study included?

Is the statement of the problem, definitions, and delimitations organized and presented in a coherent fashion?

Is the problem likely to have relevance and importance beyond the local scene?

Are the assumptions on which the study is based specified?

Are the assumptions reasonable and acceptable?

Review of Related Literature

Does the report tie the problem to related previous research?

Is the review of the literature comprehensive?

Are all the cited references really relevant to the problem under investigation?

Are the relationships between a prior study and the present investigation identified?

Is there an overdependence on secondary sources when primary sources could have been obtained?

Have any relevant references been omitted?

Is there an overemphasis on opinion articles or anecdotes and an underreliance on empirical work?

Is the review paraphrased adequately or is it a string of quotations from the original sources?

Is the review merely a summary of past work or does it critically appraise and compare the contributions of key studies?

Is the review so organized that the development of ideas is clear?

Does the review include recent literature?

Does the review conclude with a synopsis of the literature and its implications for the problem under investigation?

Conceptual Framework

Does the report attempt to link the problem to a theoretical or conceptual framework?

Is the theoretical framework tied to the problem in a natural way, or does the link seem contrived?

Has the theory been distorted or misrepresented by the research worker?

Would an alternative conceptual framework be more appropriate?

Are the deductions from a theory or conceptual framework logical?

Hypotheses

Does the report identify the hypotheses to be tested?

Does each hypothesis express a predicted relationship between two or more variables?

Do the hypotheses flow logically from the theoretical rationale or review of the literature? If not, what justification is offered for the research worker's predictions?

Can all the hypotheses be tested?

Are the hypotheses concisely and unambiguously stated?

Do the hypotheses identify which variables are independent and which are dependent?

Do the hypotheses indicate the general population of interest?

Evaluation of Research Methods

The heart of the research critique lies in the analysis of the procedures used to solve the research problems. For examining any research question, a vast number of alternative strategies exist. Each aspect of a study's methodology involves a decision. The methods of selecting subjects, measuring variables, controlling extraneous factors, minimizing threats to internal validity, and so forth are all selected by the research worker, who must therefore give considerable thought to choosing the best possible investigative plan.

The cause for using faulty methods may be poor judgment, failure to consider the range of available alternatives, or external constraints such as inadequate resources or insufficient time to complete the study. In any case, the report should indicate specific reasons that alternate methods were not feasible or were ruled out. When the report fails to make explicit the rationale for the procedures adopted, greater room for criticism remains. Thus, one of the first considerations: Does the report clearly indicate the reasoning behind methodological decisions?

Subjects

Is the population identified and described?

Does the report distinguish between the target and accessible populations?

Is the sampling unit consistent with that implied by the hypotheses?

Does the report indicate whether an entire population or a sample was studied?

Are the sampling selection procedures clearly described?

Is the sampling design likely to produce a representative sample?

If the sampling design is relatively weak (as in the case of nonprobability sampling), are potential sample biases identified?

Are the size and key characteristics of the sample described?
Does the report indicate the response rate (i.e., the percentage of contacted persons agreeing to participate in the study)?

Data Collection Methods: General

Are the data collection instruments clearly identified and described?
Is the rationale for the selection of the instruments discussed?
Are the data collection methods the most appropriate way to measure the critical variables?
If an instrument was developed specifically for the study, are the procedures for its development described?
If the instruments are new or adapted from earlier versions, have they been properly pretested?
Is evidence for the reliability of the instruments presented? (Reliability is discussed in chapter 3.) Are the reliability coefficients of an accepted magnitude? Is the type of reliability estimates obtained the most appropriate?
Is evidence for the validity of the instruments presented? Does the evidence indicate that the instruments are sufficiently valid for the use to which they are put? (Validity is explained in chapter 3).
Is the type of validity discussed (content, criterion-related, or construct) the most relevant for the instruments under consideration?
Do the instruments provide as objective a measure of the critical variables as possible?
Do the instruments use subjects' time efficiently?

Data Collection Methods: Specific Major Approaches

Methodological Instruments
Is the instrumentation system sufficiently described for the reader?
Are baseline data reported?
Was special training required for the use of the instruments and, if so, has it been reported?
Were special safety precautions for the instruments, if required, described?

Observational Approach
Are the behaviors or conditions to be observed clearly defined?
Are the definitions adequate for objective observation?
Are the phenomena under observation the same phenomena described in the problem statement?
Is the unit of behavior adopted appropriate for the problem being studied?
Is the degree of structure used in the observation consistent with the aims of the study?
Is the degree of concealment used consistent with the aims of the study?
Does the degree of concealment conform to ethical principles?
Are permanent recording devices used effectively?
Is the category system (if any) adequately described?
Is the category system comprehensive enough to rate adequately the phenomena under observation?
Is the degree of observer intervention appropriate?

Are the observers required to make an inordinate amount of inferences?
Are the observers required to code too many complex behaviors in too short a time?
Is the method of sampling behaviors discussed?
Is the sampling method the most appropriate?
Have the observers been sufficiently trained to use the observational methods?
Is interobserver reliability discussed and is it sufficiently high?
Are potential biases stemming from the observers or participants discussed?
Is the problem of subject reactivity and its implications discussed?

Interview Schedules
Is the interview schedule described or included in the report?
Do the questions adequately cover the complexities of the problem under investigation?
Are closed and open-ended questions used effectively and in correct proportions?
Do the questions assume a level of knowledge that some respondents may not possess?
Are the questions simply and clearly phrased?
Do the questions tend to bias responses in a certain direction?
Is the interview schedule of an appropriate length?
Are the directions for the interviewers clear?
Are the qualifications and training of the interviewers described?
Is the coding procedure for open-ended questions described?
Does the report describe the type and amount of probing that was pursued?
Does the report indicate where the interviews occurred?
Is there an indication of who was present during the interview other than the interviewer and respondent?
Is the length of the average interview mentioned?
Is the ordering of questions of the schedule appropriate?
Do the responses for closed questions adequately cover the alternatives?

Questionnaires
Is the questionnaire described or a copy included with the report?
Do the questions adequately cover the complexities of the problem under investigation?
Are open-ended and closed questions used effectively and in correct proportion?
Do the questions assume a level of knowledge or sophistication that some respondents may not possess?
Are the questions simply and clearly phrased?
Do the questions tend to bias responses in a certain direction?
Is the ordering of questions on the questionnaire appropriate?
Is the questionnaire of appropriate length?
Do the responses for closed questions adequately cover the alternatives?
Are the directions to the respondents clear?
Is the coding procedure for open-ended questions described?
Does the cover letter explain the purpose and importance of the study and describe the manner in which respondents were selected?

Was confidentiality or anonymity assured to respondents?
Are follow-up procedures described and, if so, were they suitable?

Scales
Is the rationale for selecting one scaling procedure over another explained?
Is the method for placing items on a scale judgmental or empirical (i.e., performed through factor analysis or item analysis)?
Are procedures for eliminating or minimizing response sets described?
Are negative and positive items balanced?
Is the scale unidimensional?
Are directions to the respondents clear?
If an existing scale was used, is its relevance to the objectives of the study clearly explained?

Research Design: General
Is the design of the study adequately described?
Is the general approach (i.e., experimental, quasi-experimental, or nonexperimental) the best approach for testing the research hypothesis?
Does the design control for history effects on the internal validity of the study?
Does the design control for maturation effects?
Does the design control for selection effects?
Does the design control for testing effects?
Does the design control for mortality effects?
What procedures are used to control for individual differences, and are these procedures the most effective ones possible?
Are threats to the external validity of the study given adequate consideration in the research design?
If a cross-sectional design is used, would a longitudinal design be more appropriate?
If a longitudinal design is used, are attrition problems and methods for reestablishing contact with subjects discussed?
Does the design account for all research hypotheses?

Research Design: Specific

Experimental Studies
Is the method for randomly assigning subjects to groups described?
Is randomization used whenever possible?
Is the precise design adequately described?
Is the rationale for the selection of the design specified?
Is the manipulation of the independent variable adequately described and fully implemented?

Quasi-Experimental and Pre-Experimental Studies
Is the method for the selection of comparison groups (if any) described?
Were adequate steps taken to ensure the equivalence of comparison groups?
Does the report indicate the degree to which comparison groups are equivalent?
If no comparison group is used, is a rationale provided for this lack?

If no comparison group is used, are methods used to facilitate the interpretability of the results? Are these methods appropriate and successful?
Is the independent variable adequately manipulated?

Nonexperimental Studies
Is the method for the selection of comparison groups (if any) described?
Were steps taken (such as matching) to produce roughly equivalent comparison groups and are those steps adequate?
Does the report indicate the degree to which the comparison groups used (if any) are equivalent?
Are the attributes or experiences that differentiate comparison groups (if any) clearly defined?
Are important uncontrolled extraneous variables described?

Research Procedures
Are the procedures used to execute the design described in sufficient detail to permit replication by another researcher?
Was a pilot study performed and are its execution, results, and effects discussed?
Are procedures for ensuring the constancy of conditions described?
Are procedures discussed for preventing the contamination of one treatment group by another?
Is the setting of the study (field versus laboratory) appropriate for the research question?
Did the study procedures place an unnecessary burden on subjects?
Were the rights of the subjects protected?

Evaluation of the Analysis and Results

The results of a study are affected not only by the methods of collecting the data but also by the procedures used to analyze them. The data analysis should be consistent with the objectives of the study, the research design, the measurement level of the data, and the assumptions underlying the use of a particular statistical test. Once these criteria are satisfied, it is desirable to use as powerful a procedure as possible. Beginning research workers whose statistical skills are weak may have some difficulty handling this part of the critique, but many of the following questions should prove adequate for routine appraisals.

Data Analysis Procedures
Are the data analyzed manually or by computer?
If the data are analyzed by computer, does the report identify the specific program or software package used?
Does the report describe the coding procedures used?
Is there an indication of how missing data were handled?

Descriptive Statistics
Are descriptive statistics presented?
Are the descriptive statistics appropriate for the data?

Are the descriptive statistics presented in a coherent fashion?
If only descriptive statistics are used, are they sufficient for the purposes of the research, or should inferential statistics be presented as well?

Inferential Statistics
Are tests of statistical significance used to test hypotheses?
Are parametric tests used when the assumptions for parametric tests are patently violated?
Are nonparametric tests used when a more powerful parametric test probably would have been appropriate?
Is specific information unnecessarily lost by converting specific measures into general measures (e.g., converting height in inches to the dichotomy "tall/short")?
Are the tests of significance appropriate for testing the research hypotheses?
Are the tests of significance congruent with the research design?
Does the report indicate the value of the computed statistics, the correct statistical procedures, and the level of significance?
Are all the hypotheses tested?

Statistical Findings
Are the results clearly presented?
Is the presentation of findings well organized?
Are tables and figures used effectively to highlight and streamline the results?
Are the tables and figures well organized, properly labeled, and easy to understand?
Are the important aspects of the tables and figures discussed in the text?
Are the findings of a primary nature given sufficient attention, or are secondary findings overemphasized?
Is there any evidence of bias in the reporting of the findings?

Evaluating the Discussion
The discussion section of a research report allows the researcher to make sense of the various statistical findings, to discuss the theoretical and practical implications of the findings, and to develop recommendations for new avenues of research. The discussion section is more subjective than other sections of the report. This subjectivity is not necessarily harmful, since great insights spring from personal experience, knowledge, and creative capacities—not from the data alone. But subjectivity can often block insights if investigators read into the data only what they want to see. In any event, of all the components of a report, the discussion section is usually the most vulnerable to criticism.

Interpretation of the Findings
Are all of the important statistical results discussed?
Is each result interpreted in terms of the original hypothesis to which it relates?
Is each result interpreted in light of findings from similar research studies?

Does the discussion include interpretations of negative or contradictory findings?

Are alternative explanations for the findings mentioned, and is the rationale for their rejection discussed?

Do the interpretations give due consideration to the limitations of the research methods?

Are the potential effects of uncontrolled extraneous variables on the results discussed?

Are the interpretations consistent with the results?

Are any unwarranted interpretations of causality made?

Is the language used in discussing the interpretations sufficiently tentative?

Are the interpretations organized in a meaningful fashion?

Is there distinct evidence of bias in the interpretations?

Does the interpretation integrate all the findings, or is each finding discussed separately?

Does the interpretation distinguish between practical and statistical significance?

Implications

Are implications of the study ignored, even though a basis for them is apparent?

Are the implications of the study discussed in terms of the retention, modification, or rejection of a theory/conceptual framework?

Are the implications of the findings described?

Are the discussed implications appropriate?

Are generalizations made that are not warranted on the basis of the sample used?

Is due consideration given to the study's limitations in discussing its implications?

Recommendations

Are recommendations made concerning how the study's methods could be improved?

Are recommendations for specific actions made on the basis of the implications?

Are recommendations made for future research investigations?

Are the recommendations thorough, consistent with the findings, and consistent with related research results?

Evaluation of Other Aspects of the Report

These questions are of a relatively peripheral nature. Weaknesses in the main body of the report are naturally more critical to the success of the study than weaknesses found in supplementary materials. Similarly, methodological and conceptual flaws are more serious than stylistic shortcomings or grammatical errors. Still, a critique of the overall quality of the final product should bear in mind the following questions:

The Title
Does the report have a title?
Is the title of reasonable length?
Does the title concisely convey the focus of the study?
Are important variables mentioned in the title?
Does the title suggest the population under investigation?

The Summary or Abstract
Does the report have a summary or abstract?
Is the abstract/summary of appropriate length?
Does the abstract/summary restate the research problem?
Does the abstract/summary restate important findings?
Is the abstract/summary too vague or too detailed?

Bibliography and Appendices
Is there a bibliographic entry for all cited references?
Is each bibliographic entry complete?
Are the entries composed according to the same bibliographic style, and is that style acceptable?
Are appendices used effectively to present lengthy or supplementary materials?
Are the appendices well organized and complete?

Stylistic Considerations
Are the overall structure and format of the report good?
Is the overall report overly detailed or insufficiently detailed?
Is the writing style pompous or pretentious?
Is the writing style too personal and subjective?
Is sexist language avoided?
Are sentences inordinately complex?
Are transitions smooth and is the report characterized by continuity of thought and expression?
Are sentences grammatically correct?
Are words spelled correctly?
Stylistically, was the report pleasant to read?

In judging the value of any study, a systematic assessment of each of its sections is essential. Evaluating research reports involves critical appraisal of both merits and limitations. Granted, many of the foregoing questions may have little or no relevance to a particular study. For every report, answering all the questions satisfactorily will not always be possible. This shortcoming is especially true for journal articles, in which the need for economy often forces a severe abridgement of methodological descriptions. All reports need not address every question. For instance, few reports (except perhaps theses) explicitly identify procedures for handling missing data. The questions here only suggest aspects of a study that often deserve consideration; investigators should not assume that questions that seem irrelevant to a particular study must be answered regardless.

Supplying answers to many questions may tax students' judgment as well as their knowledge. Determining whether the investigator used the data collection procedure most appropriate to the research problem necessarily involves a degree of subjectivity. Even experts disagree about the appropriateness of various strategies. Research workers can only strive to be as objective as possible and to indicate their reasoning for the judgments made.

Summary

A vital final step in any research project is reporting the results of the investigation. The report should contain four major sections: introduction, methodology, findings, and discussion. Ideally, the report should be so written that a knowledgeable reader could use it to replicate the project.

The introduction sets the stage for the readers of a report; it must adequately identify the problem and its importance so that readers can determine whether the solution was appropriate. The report must indicate the rationale for choosing the methodology used to solve the research problems. The analysis of the findings should be consistent with the objectives of the study, the research design, the measurement level of the data, and the underlying assumptions. The discussion section (the most subjective and creative portion of a report) allows the research worker to analyze the findings further, to discuss their implications, and to recommend further related research.

When the research findings confirm the original hypothesis, interpreting the results is easy. At times, however, the research does not support the hypothesis. Research workers should then reconsider the reasoning behind the hypothesis and reexamine the sample and the methods. Sometimes the only possible conclusion is that no apparent relationship existed between the variables. Yet even negative findings may add to professional knowledge and aid later research.

The research report should be as objective as possible. Any opinions should be clearly identified. The style should be clear and simple.

In social work, more than in most professions, research results are of interest to practitioners in the field. Therefore, all social workers should be aware that most studies contain some weak points; the reviewer should examine fairly both the merits and limitations of any research. The assessment questions listed in this chapter allow a comprehensive evaluation of most research reports. Not every question applies to every report. Still, if appropriate answers can be obtained for those questions that apply, then practitioners can rest assured that the document is a good research report, one that will enhance knowledge in the social work profession.

APPENDIX

Sample Case Study

The Social and Economic Impacts of Locating an Energy Center at Glasgow Air Force Base*

The following case study is taken from the files of one of the authors (MLA). It is an actual case study of a community in Montana. It examines the possible construction and operation of a coal gasification plant at Glasgow's abandoned Air Force base. This case study is part of a larger feasibility study that investigates the complete range of expected environmental impacts. The section presented here explores only the anticipated social and economic impacts of reactivating the base as an energy center.

Introduction

This section contains a study of the social and economic impacts that can be expected to result from the construction and operations of an energy center facility in northeastern Montana. The city of Glasgow, the Glasgow AFB, and Valley County, Montana, were selected as the primary areas of impact. Because of the physical isolation of the base and the great distance to other communities, it is anticipated that effects of population expansion will be

*Morton L. Arkava, "Socioeconomic Impacts." *Siting Energy Facilities at Glasgow Air Force Base*. Vol. 3. Washington, D.C.: Federal Energy Administration, FEA/G–75/421, 1975, pp. 57–101.

confined to these areas. Thus, this examination is limited to the geographic boundaries of Valley County.

The impact projections contained in this study are built around a specific plan, which calls for the construction of three energy center units by 1985 and also calls for a specific size of the construction work force. The estimated cost of the three units is projected at $1,350 million.

The impact projection methodology used in this study can be applied flexibly to different sets of assumptions, depending on the final mix of industrial facilities developed within each energy center. Full recognition is given to the possibility that the final energy center components may vary from those postulated in this study. Obviously, such factors as the size of the work force will vary according to the energy technology selected for use, as the costs of the final installations also will vary. This socioeconomic impact forecast was selected purely as a representative case for demonstration purposes.

An inventory is provided of facilities and services available in Valley County, the primary impact area. This inventory may be used with the recommended standards to determine the needs of the region according to the expected population changes resulting from energy center development.

General Social and Economic Background

Glasgow, the county seat of Valley County, Montana, owes its initial development to the westward extension of the Great Northern Railway. The community of Glasgow was begun as a railway camp in about 1887, although the town was not incorporated until 1902. In its early development, the economy and population of Valley County and Glasgow relied almost entirely on agriculture. During the past fifty years, Valley County has experienced periodic spurts of development characterized by convulsive population fluctuations. Glasgow's first population and economic boom occurred between 1910 and 1920, when the Milk River Irrigation Project was built. This project was funded with an initial $7 million federal appropriation and was one of the first of a series of projects that involved expenditures of large amounts of federal money within the region. During the same period, extensive homesteading in the area accounted for additional population growth. Homesteading was stimulated by the 1912 revisions of the homestead laws and the corresponding opening of vast tracts of land for homesteading in the region. Economic growth was also stimulated as a result of World War I, when the grain price increase provided a windfall to the area farmers. By 1920, the population of Valley County had grown to 11,542.

The second phase of development in the region began in 1933 with approval of an initial federal appropriation of $25 million for construction of the Fort Peck Dam on the Missouri River. At the peak of construction activity in 1936, more than 9,000 men were employed on the dam.[1] Large-scale construction continued at the site through 1938. Additional construction on powerplants and related structures continued during intermittent periods through the mid-1950s. A second large-scale powerplant project, costing $25 million, was initiated in 1957. During the Fort Peck Dam construction in the 1930s, the region experienced severe growth pains, housing shortages, school overcrowding,[2] and increases in the crime rate.[1]

During the boom period between 1930 and 1940, the population of Valley County increased from 11,181 to 15,181, and Glasgow grew from 2,216 to 3,799. In 1950, the population of Valley County declined to 11,353, while that of the city of Glasgow increased slightly to 3,821.

The 1950s saw the third period of development for the area with the construction of the Glasgow AFB about 15 miles north of Glasgow. Construction on the base began in early 1955 and continued through 1962. By 1960, the county population had increased to 17,080, while the city increased to 6,298—increases of 50 percent in the county and 68 percent in the city. The area again experienced problems associated with population increases as a result of the base construction and operation and the renewed construction of Fort Peck.[3]

With the closing of the Glasgow AFB in 1968, the area began another economic and population downswing.

The impact of the Glasgow AFB closure is especially apparent in the 1970 census. In 1970, the Valley County population had declined to 11,471, a 32.8 percent decline, while that of Glasgow had declined to 4,700, a 26.5 percent drop.

The economic impact of the Glasgow AFB closure is apparent from an examination of employment sources from 1967 through 1971. In 1967, more than 50 percent of the employed population in Valley County worked for the federal government. By 1970, the total had dropped to 6.5 percent. A slight increase to 6.9 percent was recorded for 1971. Thus, with the closure of the base, the major source of employment for Valley County was eliminated.

Clearly, the rate of future growth of Valley County is contingent on renewed industrial development. Without such development, it is likely that the population will settle at a level supported by existing local industry and agriculture.

Since the Glasgow AFB was closed in 1968, the facilities have been used by a small contingent of Air Force personnel and by a number of various businesses and government-sponsored projects. Valley County has begun recovery from the effects of the base closure. Since 1970, the population of the county has increased at a modest but steady rate. Estimates of the 1975 population for Valley County indicate that the population had grown to approximately 13,000 people. In addition, the Valley County area now enjoys one of the lowest unemployment rates in the State. Much of the increase in population can be attributed to the renewed activities at the base by various industries and to such government-sponsored projects as Mountain Plains and SAFEGUARD.

General Economic Conditions and Population Characteristics

An analysis of population trends in Valley County for the past forty years reveals the relationship between the two major government-funded projects and the corresponding growth of the region. An important feature often overlooked by those studying Valley County is the existence of a stable, permanent population of about 11,000 persons. The population of Valley County has returned to the 11,000 mark following the reduction of activities at the Fork Peck Dam and the Glasgow AFB. This analysis suggests the presence of two somewhat distinct populations, best described as permanent and transient. The significance of this finding is related to the recognition of a stable, permanent group of residents, whose economic survival is apparently not dependent on large-scale government-sponsored projects. This reaffirms the likelihood that the area remains more heavily dependent on agriculture and related agribusiness than is commonly believed.

Population Trends

An examination of general population trends in Montana and the United States provides a useful frame of reference from which to view the Glasgow area. These figures show that during the 1950s, Montana's population increased at a rate below that of the United States in general. The number of people in Montana increased from 591,000 in 1950 to 675,000 in 1960, or 14.2 percent, while the nation's population increased about 18.5 percent during the same period. Between 1960 and 1970, the population of Montana grew to 694,000, or about 2.8 percent, while United States population grew by 13.3 percent.

Thus, while Montana's population changed at a rate that varied from the rest of the nation, a closer look at population trends in Montana reveals dramatic differences in trends among different sections in the state. While population has generally increased throughout the state, the eastern portion of Montana, which is heavily dependent on agriculture, has experienced a general decrease in population. For example, Valley County declined by 32.8 percent during the decade 1960–70. The surrounding counties experienced population losses as follows: Phillips—10.6 percent, Daniels—17.9

percent, Roosevelt—11.6 percent, McCone—13.4, and Garfield—9.3 percent. During the same period, population in western Montana increased at a rate greater than the state average. For example, Missoula and Ravalli Counties grew by 30.5 percent and 16.8 percent, respectively.

Thus, the population decline for Valley County from 1960–70 was certainly due in part to the closure of Glasgow AFB in 1968; it was also part of a general population trend characteristic of eastern Montana. The dependence of the eastern Montana economy on agriculture is well documented. The Glasgow area is especially dependent on the production of field crops, particularly grain. According to the Montana Department of Inter-governmental Relations, the Glasgow–Glendive area derives approximately one-third of its total spendable income from agriculture. This region depends to a much greater extent on agriculture for economic stability than do other areas of the State.[4]

The general economic picture of Montana is less favorable than that of the entire United States. During the last decade, employment in Montana grew at a much slower rate than did employment in the nation as a whole. Between 1957 and 1970, Montana's employment grew by about 12 percent as compared to about 23 percent in the United States.[5]

Trends in per capita personal income (converted to 1958 dollars to allow for the effects of inflation) also parallel other economic indicators. During the period 1950–70, per capita income in Montana grew from $1,957 to $2,710, while nationally per capita income increased from $1,805 to $3,067. In other words, per capita income in Montana grew at a much slower rate than in the other United States. Furthermore, a detailed analysis of per capita income reveals that major swings in income were directly related to economic conditions in agriculture.[5]

The rural population decline, especially in eastern Montana, is largely because of technological changes in agriculture. Simply stated, the increasing mechanization of agriculture, especially in the heavy grain producing areas, has resulted in a decreasing need for farm labor. Adding to the attrition from increasing mechanization is a newly emerging restructuring of the agricultural production and processing system away from the traditional family farm and individual entrepreneurship into corporate structures that are difficult to compete with. The process leading to this trend is referred to as the "vertical integration of agriculture" and is thought also to share responsibility for the out-migration from rural areas.[6]

Welfare Costs

Although a number of different indices of economic conditions are available, one useful indicator is the extent of dependence of the population on welfare assistance. Statewide costs for Aid to Dependent Children increased by 106 percent between 1970–75, while corresponding costs in Valley County only increased by 66 percent; statewide Medical Assistance costs increased by 383 percent during the same period, while Valley County's costs increased by 314 percent. For General Assistance, a low-cost, locally funded program, statewide costs decreased by 8 percent during this period while Valley County's costs decreased by 31 percent.

Valley County has shared in the general statewide increase in welfare costs, but at a more modest rate than the rest of the state.

Population Projection

Impact Projection Methodology

The impact projection methodology used here can be easily adapted to a computer program for use with flexible modeling for estimating the impact of different projects at the Glasgow AFB site. The impact projection is in effect a study of the site rather than any particular industrial component. Adjustments can easily be made to accommodate different industrial components or to accommodate the project at hand with different coal gasification technologies. For example, the impacts of operating a Lurgi process coal gasification facility could be compared to another process, such as Koppers-Totzek, by providing a different work force estimate for each and using the remaining constants.

TABLE 1. Extra School Facilities 1974–75

Area	Enrollment	Capacity	Extra
Air Base			
West School	0	180	180
Junior High	0	300	300
North Star	458	660	202
Total			682
Glasgow			
Junior High	561	750	189
High School	487	600	113
East Side	259	360	101
Irle	321	360	39
South Side	202	630	428
Total			870
Total Extra Facilities			1552

TABLE 2. Population Projection for Valley County, 1975–85*

Year	County Population with 2 percent Increase from Previous Year's Base (Column A)†	Energy Center Population Change (By Year) (Column B)	No. of Families at Energy Center (Change by Year) (Column C)	Total Population (End of Year) (Column D)
1975				13,000
1976	13,260			13,260
1977	13,525	+ 875	+ 250	14,400
1978	14,688	+ 525	+ 150	15,213
1979	15,517	+ 700	+ 200	16,217
1980	16,541	+ 700	+ 200	17,241
1981	17,586	+ 440	+ 160	18,026
1982	18,385			18,385
1983	18,753	+ 440	+ 160	19,193
1984	19,576			19,576
1985	19,967	+ 440	+ 160	20,407

*Assumes a 2 percent annual increase in Valley County population
†Projection Method: Column A = Column D of previous year + 2 percent of Column D; Column D = Column A + Column B. Dependent projections are based upon following assumptions: 50 percent of construction personnel married; 80 percent of plant operation personnel married; 2.5 dependents per married energy park worker.

The impact projection provided in Table 1 was constructed by the following method:

Starting with a 1975 estimated population base, a population projection was calculated for each year through 1985 (Table 2). Population growth was based on the constants listed below:

1. The population base equals the sum of the 1975 population, plus the additional population resulting from the influx of energy plant construction, plus plant operation personnel projected in Table 3.
2. The succeeding year's population equals the sum of the previous year's population base plus the energy center population increase plus a 2 percent annual growth rate.
3. The impact on each service was estimated by identification of actual 1975 service levels and applying a recommended adequacy standard expressed in the form of a ratio per 1,000 of population. For example, the 1975 actual service level of doctors in Valley County equals eight; the recommended adequacy standard is one doctor per 1,000 of population. Thus, the projected need for doctors in 1976, based on a population of approximately 13,000, equals thirteen. This means that the area will be in need of five more doctors by 1976 in order to attain the recommended adequacy standard.
4. The remaining constants used for calculations are identified as assumptions for impact projections.

a. The population base for 1975 is approximately 13,000.
b. The population base starting with the year 1975 will increase at an average of 2 percent per year despite energy center development.
c. School age children will constitute the same percentage of the population base as present (approximately 27 percent).
d. The population impact projections are based on the manpower estimates and typical construction schedules in Tables 3 and 4, which project construction of three units by 1985.
e. An employment multiplier was not used in calculating the projected population impact of energy center construction.
f. The rate of use of services studied will either remain constant or not exceed recommended adequacy standards.

Population Estimation

The 1975 population estimate of 13,000 used as a starting point for the impact projections is at variance with other population estimates currently available. Three different sources provide population projections for Valley County. The United States Bureau of the Census projected a population of

TABLE 3. Typical Manpower Requirements

Year	Construction	Plant Operation	Total
1977	500	N.A.*	500
1978	800	N.A.	800
1979	1,200	N.A.	1,200
1980	1,600	N.A.	1,600
1981	1,600	200	1,800
1982	1,600	200	1,800
1983	1,600	400	2,000
1984	1,600	400	2,000

*N.A. = not applicable

TABLE 4. Typical Construction Schedule and Costs, Coal Gasification Plants and Ancillary Facilities, Proposed Glasgow Energy Center*

Construction Phases	Construction Started	Completed	Estimated Total Plant Cost/Unit
1	1977	1981	$ 400 million
2	1980	1983	$ 450 million
3	1982	1985	$ 500 million
		Total	$1,350 million

*Percentage of construction costs for salaries and wages = 15 percent. Total value of construction salaries and wages = $202 million.

13,000 for Valley County for 1973.[7] The same figure is provided in a 1973 Montana population estimate by Wallwork.[8]

A third population estimate of 14,500 for 1975 was provided in a Montana Health Department Study.[9] Each of these estimates is based on assumptions of continued population growth, in turn based on in-migration for Valley County. Current data available indicate that these estimates are high and that the 1975 population base for Valley County is approximately 13,000. The basis for this population estimate is derived from an examination of 1974–75 school enrollments and from comparisons with the 1970 census data on age groupings of Valley County and the State of Montana.

An examination of Valley County census data for the years 1930–1970 indicates there is a base population level that the county approximates in census years when there is no new massive spending program in the county. Using this data as a base, the Valley County trend for population, without massive spending programs, seems to be rising at a decreasing rate (1930–50, 1.52 percent; 1950–70, 1.03 percent). This population base, somewhat in excess of 11,000, exists regardless of spending programs in the county. The rate of increase declined 0.49 percent between 1950 and 1970, compared with 1930–1950. If the trend continues, a base population increase of 0.54 percent can be expected for Valley County by 1990, independent of new opportunities in the county. This would produce a county population of 11,533. However, since 1970, increasing use of the Glasgow Air Force Base by non-Air-Force personnel and other Federal programs (Mountain Plains, SAFEGUARD, etc.) tends to remove the population from its base level expectation. There is, in fact, a significant amount of activity resulting from the use of the base facility at this time.

School enrollment data for 1970 indicated total county enrollment of 3,070. This represented about 27 percent of the population. The population profile for Valley County indicates that this percentage can be applied to 1975 enrollment figures of 3,456 if consideration is made of decline in age cohorts and an assumption of population following 1970 Valley County and Montana trends is accepted. Using the school enrollment figure as a constant 27 percent of the total population, the 1975 population should be approximately 12,800. With the declining percentage of age cohorts in the school ages, a 1975 population of 13,000 can be approximated. This represents an annual increase of approximately 2.5 percent for the first five years in the 1970s.

To assume that the Valley population will continue to grow at this same rate seems unrealistic. Given the tentative nature of industrial development in the Valley County area and the historically documented tendency of the region to lose population when federal spending programs are cut back, a more conservative growth rate of 2 percent per year is assumed. Table 2 provides a population projection based on energy center development for Valley County through 1985.

217

Appendix

Projected Service Needs

Projections are provided for the service needs of the Valley County area resulting from energy center development. Selected services such as medical care, law enforcement, and school and housing needs were studied to determine the current 1975 level of each service. Table 5 provides a summary of those needs and the related projections. For each service area studied, adequacy standards are used to provide a constant standard against which to project needs. Differences between actual levels of service in 1975 and projected needs based on adequacy standards will be most apparent in 1976, the first year in which adequacy standards are applied.

Schools
A review of schools for Valley County reveals a total school enrollment of 3,456 students for 1974–75 and a total of 210 teachers.[10] This provides a county-wide ratio of one teacher per 16.5 students, a smaller average than the recommended standard of one teacher per 18.3 students. The majority of the school population (approximately 2,300) is enrolled in schools either in Glasgow or at the base. Both the town of Glasgow and the base school facilities are underutilized, as demonstrated in Table 1. Because the major impact of increased population is expected to bear most heavily on these two communities, the presence of nonutilized school facilities is most significant. Table 1 shows a surplus of school facilities to the extent of 1,552 unused spaces. Thus, the present school capacity equals 5,008. If the extra facilities in Glasgow and on the base are used as the population grows, then no new facilities will be required until the fall of 1983. Between 1983 and 1985, additional facilities for approximately 400 children will be required.

Health Care Personnel and Facilities
Valley County currently has eight resident physicians, a ratio of one physician per 1,625 persons. This ratio compares unfavorably with the state ratio of one physician per 893 persons and national average of one per 740 persons. A standard of one physician per 1,000 of population is recommended by the State Health Department.[9] Thus, the 1975 actual level of service is below recommended standards by five physicians. This deficiency is identified in Table 5 in the 1976 projected-needs column. Thus, the discrepancy between the 1975 level of service and the 1976 projected needs is primarily because of the application of an adequacy standard. Projected growth indicates the need for a total of twenty physicians by 1985. This projection is consistent with the projections made by the Montana State Health Department.[9]

Valley County currently has five resident dentists, a ratio of one dentist per 2,600 persons. This ratio compares favorably with the Montana State Health Department recommended adequacy standard of one per 2,500.[9] Based on the projections in Table 5, eight dentists will be needed by 1985.

Valley County has 15.5 registered nurses (RNs) and 18 licensed practical nurses (LPNs), a ratio of one RN per 838 of population and one LPN per 722 of population. The Montana State Health Department recommends an adequacy standard of one RN per 283 persons (3.5 RNs per 1,000).[9] No similar adequacy standard is recommended for LPNs; therefore, the present ratio of 1.4 LPNs per 1,000 of population is used to project needs. Table 5 shows a deficiency of about 44 RNs between present levels of service and recommended adequacy standards. It appears that the area suffers from a significant shortage of RNs. Projected needs for RNs indicate a need for a total of seventy by 1985. The shortage of RNs could possibly be alleviated by a program using more paramedical personnel, such as nurses' aides and LPNs or by a systematic recruitment program.

Valley County enjoys a surplus of hospital facilities. The Deaconess Hospital in Glasgow provides hospital care for the acutely ill. Constructed in the middle 1970s, the hospital has sixty-eight acute care beds and includes obstetrical services and general medical and surgical facilities. The hospital is used at less than 50 percent of capacity. In addition to the Deaconess Hospital, a fifty-bed hospital is available at Glasgow AFB. The base hospital is used as an outpatient infirmary and thus constitutes a reservoir of acute-care hospital beds. Thus, a total of 118 hospital beds is available. The full use of these facilities is contingent on the availability of health-care professionals to staff them.

In addition to the acute-care facilities already listed, a new sixty-bed nursing home is available, and a thirty-bed addition is under construction and scheduled for completion by June 1975. Thus, ninety nursing home beds will be available in June 1975.

The Montana State Health Department recommends an adequacy standard of four beds per 1,000 population for both acute care hospitals and nursing homes.[9] Thus, given the projected growth of the area, no new hospital needs will be required through 1985. However, the shortage of health-care personnel, especially doctors and nurses, may constitute a barrier to full use of these facilities.

Housing

The city of Glasgow and Glasgow AFB encompass the major impact area for the energy center development. Housing resources for Valley County as reported in the 1970 census indicate the availability of 5,289 housing units. Of those, 49 were vacant and for sale, and 1,207 were vacant and for rent in

219

TABLE 5. Impact Projection, Valley County Service Needs Through 1985, with Energy Center Development

	Actual			Projected							
	1975	1976	1977	1978	1979	1980	1981	1982	1983	1984	1985
Population Projection	13,000	13,260	13,525	14,688	15,517	16,541	17,583	18,385	18,753	19,576	19,167
Physicians Standard 1:1,000[a]	8	13	14	15	16	17	18	18	19	20	20
Nurses—RN Standard 3.5:1,000[b]	15.5	46	47	51	54	58	62	64	66	69	70
Nurses—LPN Standard 1.4:1,000[b]	18	18	19	20	22	23	25	26	26	27	28
Dentists Standard 1:2,500[c] (0.4:1,000)	5	5	5	6	6	7	7	7	7	8	8
Hospital Beds Standard 4:1,000[d]	118	53	54	58	62	66	70	73	75	78	80
Nursing Care Beds 4:1,000[d]	90	53	54	58	62	66	70	73	75	78	80
Law Officers 2:1,000[e]	18	26	27	29	31	33	35	36	37	39	40

220

School Population Projections[f]	3,456[g]	3,580	3,651	3,965	4,190	4,466	4,748	4,903	6,063	5,285	5,391
Housing Units 3.5 persons/ unit 290:1,000[h]	Surplus 556	74	150	482	719	1,011	1,310	1,538	1,644	1,879	1,990

[a] The ratio of one doctor per 1,000 population is based on standards recommended by the Montana State Department of Health. *Eastern Montana Areawide Health Plan*, 1st draft. Helena, Mont.: March 1975, p. 35. The increase in doctors between 1975 and 1976 is due to the difference between the actual 1975 level and the 1:1,000 standard used for projections in 1976.

[b] The ratio of one RN per 283 population (3.5 per 1,000) and 1.4 LPNs per 1,000 population is based on the recommendation of the Montana State Department of Health. *Ibid.*, p. 41. The differences between the actual 1975 level and the projected 1976 needs are due to the application of the above standards starting in 1976.

[c] The ratio of one dentist per 2,500 persons (0.4 per 1,000) is based on standards recommended by the Montana State Department of Health. *Ibid.* Part II.

[d] The ratio of 4 beds per 1,000 population for both hospital and nursing care is recommended by the Montana State Health Department. *Ibid.*, Part II.

[e] The recommended ratio of 2 law officers per 1,000 population is based on the recommendations found in Intermountain Planners and Werthberger Associates. *Powder River Basin Capital Facilities Study.* Cheyenne: Wyoming Department of Economic Planning, n.d. The increase in law officers between 1975 and 1976 is due to the application of the standard starting in 1976.

[f] The recommended ratio of 1 teacher per 18.2 students (54.5 per 1,000 students) is based on U.S. Office of Education Standards. Foster, Betty. GPO Publication, DHEW (OE) 73–11402. The calculation is based on the assumption that a stable 27 percent of the total population will attend public schools. It is further assumed that each additional teacher will equal an additional classroom. Thus, teachers and classrooms may be regarded as a unit for planning purposes. The 1975 level is at 16.5 students per teachers, counting administrators. This level has declined steadily since 1969, when the ratio was 19.7:1.

[g] Surplus of 1,552 unused student spaces; present school capacity is 5,608.

[h] Housing needs are based on the standard of 3.5 persons per unit (290 units: 1,000 population). This figure is based on the 1970 census data. For the baseline year of 1975, it is assumed that all of the present population is housed. Thus, housing needs for 1975 are reflected as the sum of the surplus units available.

1970. Present conditions in Glasgow indicate the ready availability of houses for sale in price ranges under $20,000 and over $35,000. Some rental housing is available in the town.

Glasgow AFB constitutes a vast reservoir of unused housing that could accommodate a growing population.

The full range of housing currently available at Glasgow AFB includes the following:

Permanent housing	1,227 units in 439 buildings
Semipermanent	200 units in 200 buildings
Trailer spaces	158 spaces

Also, there are the airmen's dormitories and bachelor officers' quarters. Of those permanent housing units, 273 are controlled by Mountain Plains (a private corporation presently leasing the facilities). The availability of these units for possible occupancy by energy center personnel is contingent on renewal of the Mountain Plains grant in 1975. Of the remaining 956 units, 556 units are vacant and available for occupancy, but several months of advance preparation are required to ready these units. Present rental costs for base housing range from $120 per month for a two-bedroom apartment to $160 per month for a four-bedroom unit (cost includes utilities and kitchen appliances).

The 200 semipermanent units are currently used by the Air Force and are not available for occupancy. The trailer spaces have not all been completed, according to the Base Housing Officer; only about thirty-five are available for use. Unused bachelor officers' quarters and airmen's dormitories also constitute an additional housing resource for single transient workers, especially those involved in the construction of the energy center. Thus, a definite surplus of 556 units is available if the Air Force further reduces on-site activity or if other present users, such as Mountain Plains, reduce activities. Based on the projection in Table 5, no new housing will be needed until 1979. If inexpensive and attractive housing can be provided for many of the single construction workers by use of bachelor officers' quarters, it may not be necessary to plan for additional housing until 1980. In addition, judicious planning is required to coordinate the remaining base housing with other industrial or military development at Glasgow AFB.

It is unlikely that all energy center personnel will settle at the base; many will settle in the Glasgow area and use other housing—either newly constructed or housing not listed in this inventory. Thus, it is likely that the housing needs projected in Table 5 will be met by a combination of base facilities and normal commercial sources.

Law Enforcement

Because Glasgow is the administrative center of Valley County, both city and county law enforcement agencies are available. The agencies and personnel available in Valley County consist of the county attorney and the assistant county attorney, the county sheriff with four deputies and twenty-four special deputies, the city police chief, and eight city police officers. Four State Highway Patrolmen are also stationed in Glasgow. In addition to the county and city police force, other law enforcement personnel include three FBI agents, the Tumpane Security Force from the base, security patrolmen who work for the Corps of Engineers at Fort Peck, and one customs agent at the Glasgow International Airport. Thus, regular city, county, and state law enforcement personnel total eighteen (not counting the twenty-four special deputies who work only in emergency situations). The present ratio of one police officer to approximately 722 persons is greater than the recommended standard of two per 1,000 of population.[11] However, if the base security force is counted, the balance places the ratio close to the recommended standard.

Table 5 shows a present deficiency of 8 law enforcement personnel when using the standard of 2 per 1,000 of population. Projections indicate a need for a total of 40 law enforcement officers by 1985. Depending on the occupancy of the Glasgow AFB, many of those new law enforcement officers are likely to be located at the base. The placement of city and county law enforcement personnel at the base may be regarded as a normal replacement for military security as the shift from military to civilian occupancy of the base progresses. Special planning between the local government and the industrial community occupying the base will be required to plan adequate police protection and to avoid duplication of services and personnel.

Recreation

Valley County is blessed with a variety of outdoor recreational facilities. The proximity to Fort Peck Lake and extensive public lands assures access for the general public.

The city of Glasgow provides facilities for tennis, swimming, baseball, basketball, and racquetball, and park space for other sports. An evaluation of existing parks was completed in 1966. This report indicated a deficiency of 78.3 acres of park lands for a population of 8,500, based on a national guideline of 1.5 acres per park and recreational land per 100 persons. The Glasgow population of 4,700 from United States Bureau of the Census would have reduced this requirement to 70.5 acres, or a deficiency in 1970 of 21.3 acres. The city is proceeding on a park expansion, construction, and improvement program that will soon meet these national guidelines. An additional consideration for the city of Glasgow is its location in the middle of open lands, which increases its recreational offerings tremendously. Within the city, new tennis courts and park areas are being constructed. The well-organized library, civic center, and museum present additional attractions.

Glasgow AFB, because of its design as a self-sufficient Air Force community, provides excellent public recreational facilities. The base has a gymnasium for indoor sports and excellent fields for football and baseball. There is a library/recreation center developed and maintained by the Air Force. The community also has a bowling alley, a movie theatre, and park areas for family recreation.

Recreational areas on the base are recently constructed, well maintained, and provide excellent opportunity for occupants of the area. In addition, the base location provides access to uncrowded scenic lands in all directions.

Eighteen miles southeast of Glasgow is Fort Peck Dam and Reservoir. This proximity provides ready access to camping, picnicking, boating, and water sport facilities. The Army Corps of Engineers maintains public recreational areas including Fort Peck Recreational Area, Big Muddy Sportsman Park, Downstream Recreation Area, Dredge Cuts Recreational Area, Pines Recreation Area, Bear Creek Fishing Camp, Rock Creek Recreational Area, Hell Creek Recreational Area, and Devils Creek Fishing Camp. These areas provide shelter buildings, toilets, picnic areas with tables, tent and trailer space (at most locations), and fireplaces.

Fishing at Fort Peck provides varied species of fish, including trout, coho, drum, pike, catfish, paddlefish, sauger, and white bass. The size of the lake (189 miles long with a maximum width of 16 miles) offers uncrowded fishing to suit the angler's preference.

The federal lands in Valley County provide miles of scenic roads and ample opportunity to "get away from it all." There is excellent hunting for big game, including deer, antelope, and elk. Waterfowl shooting is especially good because of the grain fields and extensive wetlands in the area.

The Charles M. Russell National Wildlife Range near Fort Peck provides opportunity for photographers, wildlife students, and birdwatchers to observe animals and birds in their natural environment. A guide book, provided by the U.S. Department of the Interior, is available to tourists for self-conducted tours of this area.

The Valley County area offers both residents and tourists an exceptional variety of recreational pursuits. Outdoor sports include boating, fishing, hunting, and camping. The area has parks and libraries, plus facilities for a number of organized team sports. Other entertainment and activities include summer theatre productions and wildlife sightseeing.

The area is unusually well endowed with outdoor recreational activities, and thus no special planning appears to be necessary to accommodate outdoor recreational needs. Community facilities in Glasgow appear to be limited, but this need is now being addressed by the city park expansion program. No new recreational facilities are required for the base until 1980, when the population will have outgrown existing housing resources. Assuming that the base recreational facilities will be fully used when all housing is full, additional ones will be required starting in 1980.

Economic Impact

Local Government

Two of the major sources of income of the county government are the trust and agency accounts and the *ad valorem* property tax. Trust and agency accounts are generally restricted in nature and are derived from state and federal sources. With the exception of revenue sharing funds, they are generally used for restricted programs, such as schools, welfare, special improvement districts, and the like.

The *ad valorem* property tax is based on the assessed value of real and personal property. The amount of tax collected thus is directly related to property values and the value of improvements and personal property.

Table 6 shows the county tax revenues for the ten-year period from 1965 through 1974. A brief review of tax revenues shows a steady increase over that period of approximately 6.3 percent per year. With the effects of inflation, this increase seems modest indeed. It appears, however, that the tax revenues have been somewhat independent of population trends.

The approximate $70 million in assessed valuation, which constitutes the county tax base (Table 7), does not include the value of the Glasgow AFB installation. Federal property is not taxable under the *ad valorem* property tax. Assuming that the energy center development will be a nongovernmental enterprise, once construction is under way the installation will assume taxable status. Thus, a property formerly not subject to *ad valorem* property taxes will revert to a taxable status and thereby increase the tax base of the county. To estimate the potential impact of the energy center development on local government finances, the estimated costs of the projected units provided in Table 4 is assumed to equal the taxable assessed valuation of the installations. Thus, the projected impact of energy center construction will in-

TABLE 6. Valley County Tax Revenues, 1965–74 [County portion only, excluding school district taxes]

Year	Receipts
1974	$922,447.04
1973	$980,598.72
1972	$797,949.59
1971	$766,746.21
1970	$708.553.02
1969	$661,037.90
1968	$640,802.36
1967	$547,915.51
1966	$543,806.53
1965	$538,950.21

Source: Valley County Treasurer's Office

225

TABLE 7. Valley County Tax Base, 1974

Asset	Assessed Valuation	Taxable Valuation (approximately 25 percent of assessed valuation)
Real Property	$27,730,266.00	$8,288,325.00
Personal Property	32,555,286.00	7,410,232.00
Railroad, Telephone, and Telegraph Property	7,774,533.00	2,439,289.00
Utilities	1,744,436.00	297,565.00
Royalties	1,742.00	1,742.00
Total	$69,806,263.00	$18,437,153.00

Source: Valley County Treasurer's Office

crease the taxable assessed valuation from approximately $70 million in 1974 to approximately $470 million in 1981, to $920 million in 1983, and to $1,420 million in 1985. This projection does not include a multiplier for increases in revenue from new housing units, automobile taxes, and other personal property accruing from the population influx.

In summary, the impact of constructing an energy center at the base will dramatically increase the tax base of the county by more than 2,000 percent over a ten-year period. This increase in the total assessed valuation will be accompanied by an increase in population of approximately 50 percent. The difference between the increase in population and increased tax base will allow either an expansion of municipal services and facilities or a reduction in the tax rate (mill levy) or both. Given the projected increase in the assessed valuation, local government should experience no financial difficulty in providing the additional services and facilities projected through 1985. It is extremely likely that a significant reduction in the tax rate will result from energy center development, since the assessed valuation will increase at a rate considerably greater than the population growth. Assuming the projected value of the energy center in Table 4 as the total of plant construction costs, this estimate of local government finances may be regarded as conservative because no tax multiplier is used.

General Economic Impacts

The concept of multipliers is used to estimate the potential economic benefit to a community when a new industry is added. Naturally, a direct measure of the economic benefits of a new industry can be established by calculating the estimated earnings of employees of the industry. However, the primary income earned by the addition of a new industry also generates other income and jobs. Additional income is derived on a secondary basis from the support

226

industries oriented toward serving the local population. Thus, a secondary source of income and jobs, usually referred to as derivative industry, is the basis for the income multiplier and employment multipliers. Although there are disagreements among economists about which method should be used to calculate income and employment multipliers, some general principles are well established. First, income multipliers are more reliable projection estimates than are employment multipliers because employment multipliers are based on less stable projection values such as future unemployment rates, wage levels, labor market conditions, and the like.[12] On the other hand, the income multiplier is based on spending patterns, such as the propensity to spend locally, which is a more stable predictor, especially in rural areas with great distances between communities.

A second principle of relevance to the income multiplier is that the smaller the community, the greater the likelihood of the second round of expenditures being made outside of the area, decreasing the impact of the multiplier on the small community.[13] Thus, income multipliers are only rough approximations used for planning. Projections based on these measures should be viewed with caution. The income multiplier suggested for use in estimating the potential impact of this project on the Glasgow area was selected from a ratio that was already calculated[14] for the purpose of making similar projections for the Colstrip Mining and Generation Project in eastern Montana. The Colstrip ratio was selected on the assumption that the ratio was correctly calculated and that the general geographic, economic, and employment characteristics of the Colstrip area in eastern Montana are similar to those in the Glasgow Air Force Base area. An income multiplier of 2.4 is suggested to calculate the projections based on Table 4 for the construction phase of the project. Thus, it is estimated that for each dollar of wages derived from new employment in the construction of the energy center, an additional $1.40 of income will be generated from wages in secondary support industry. Based on the values provided in Table 4, a total of $202 million in salaries and wages is projected for the construction work force between 1977 and 1985. This would yield a total of $484 million in salaries and wages when the income multiplier is used.

Because of the limitations of employment multipliers, no specific employment multiplier was used for this project. Instead, an annual growth rate of 2 percent was utilized. The arguments against use of an employment multiplier are briefly summarized.

1. The derivative or secondary jobs created in the service industries are only abstractly associated with energy center development. They are indistinguishable from other jobs in retail trade and services. They will in fact serve the entire population and not just the energy center workers.
2. Many of the secondary or support jobs are part-time and low-paying in comparison to jobs in energy development and construction. Thus, the

jobs are generally not competitive enough to attract new migrants. A great majority of the secondary jobs will tend to be filled by local residents and the dependents of the energy center work force and, thus, will not result in additional in-migration.

Possible Problems Resulting from Development

Several additional miscellaneous effects of energy center development should be anticipated. One such effect is the anticipated redistribution of population in Valley County. Glasgow constitutes the major population center of the county. Given the increase in industrial development at Glasgow AFB, the ready availability of low-cost rental units and all related facilities such as schools, recreation, and the like, an increasingly greater proportion of the population is likely to be concentrated at the base. This will eventually affect the political and social structure of the area. In a similar manner, the location of some new commercial enterprises may shift to the base area. For example, some heavy service industries may more advantageously be located closer to the energy center. The influx of large numbers of construction workers may also result in the opening of new restaurants and other services that will together serve as a nucleus for additional shifts to the base area.

Other anticipated effects of energy center development include the unwelcome possibilities of increased crime rates often associated with such development and increases in attendant social problems. For example, Wicks reported considerable increase in welfare recipients and child welfare services at the peak of construction on the Libby Dam Project in northwestern Montana.[15] He attributed this increase to an influx of job seekers who were attracted to the relatively high salaries paid to dam construction workers. A similar phenomenon may be anticipated in the Glasgow area.

Other more general economic and social effects are likely to result from energy center development. These include the possible increase in land and property values as a result of increased demand. This effect is not likely to occur on a large scale before 1980 because of the surplus of housing available. Land speculators could capitalize on this opportunity and even further inflate the price of real estate.

In addition, as the population grows and the influx of highly paid plant personnel occurs, private recreational facilities, such as summer homes at Fort Peck, will increase in cost and decrease in availability as a response to demand levels. Concurrently, as the demand for recreational facilities increases, public facilities also are likely to increase.

Although other less specific impacts may be felt as a result of energy center development, they must remain in the realm of conjecture. Data are lacking from which further extrapolations could be made.

Summary and Conclusions

The potential for energy center development for the Glasgow area is considerably enhanced by the projected social and economic impacts revealed by this study. The area has experienced several bust-and-boom cycles over the past forty years. Each cycle has been characterized by massive federal spending programs and great infusions of temporary workers. The population of Valley County and the Glasgow area has fluctuated by as much as 50 percent through these ups and downs. During the growth phases, the area has been faced with expanding facilities, such as hospitals, schools, and housing. During the population exodus stages, it has been left with extra, unused facilities.

The most recent exodus of population occurred in 1968 when the Glasgow AFB was closed and the county population declined drastically, from approximately 17,000 to approximately 11,500. Since 1968, the area has slowly regained population. Part of the new influx is related to a variety of enterprises conducted at the Glasgow Air Force Base. However, the scope of these enterprises has never approximated earlier developments. Furthermore, some of the projects, such as the Mountain Plains Educational Center, are government funded and have uncertain futures. A great many facilities on the base and in Glasgow are underused. The area enjoys an abundance of extra housing, extra hospital beds, extra school space, and the like. Furthermore, the people are eager to attract industry and regain lost population.

The estimated social and economic effects of energy plant construction appear to be primarily positive. Unused facilities would again be used, a more stable source of employment and income could be expected, and the prospects of growth would not be unwelcome. Indeed, the experience of the region with previous growth and excess housing and other facilities together increase the likelihood that many of the unpleasant and unwelcome byproducts of growth could be avoided. Many of the new boom towns in the West, such as Forsyth, Montana, and Gillette, Wyoming, have experienced distress with rapidly burgeoning trailer towns and massive increases in school enrollments. Most of these problems can be avoided in the Glasgow area, and many of the residents, because of previous experience, are in a position to avoid the disillusionment that often results from growth.

The benefits resulting from this development include a stable employment base, for a population formerly dependent on a dwindling agricultural economy, and a vastly increased tax base, which would insure the capability of the local units of government to expand services as the population grows. The potential tax windfall is so great that special planning may be necessary to derive maximum benefits from it.

A number of options for management of this resource exist. One option that merits further study is the possibility of creating a special tax district based on an expanded impact area. Special social problems of the region, such as poverty and unemployment among the Indians, may be addressed with these funds. Also, other problems of the region relating to energy needs and the problems of physical environment may be addressed. Special regional needs related to cold winters and home heating costs could be addressed by large-scale solar heating projects or the like. Clearly, the opportunities for planning are endless, given the new source of income. Every opportunity to plan creatively and broadly should be explored.

End Notes

1. Paladen, Vivian A. *From Buffalo Bones to Sonic Boom.* Glasgow, Mont.: Glasgow Jubilee Committee, July 1962.
2. "It was the construction of Fort Peck Dam which . . . caused early and unforeseeable inadequacy in the schools . . . enrollment in the grade school jumped from 560 to 999 . . . and in the high school from 380 to 546." *Ibid.*, p. 74.
3. "The influx of construction workers, military personnel, and additional people to carry on the increased merchandising activity soon had the schools overcrowded again. During the five-year period from 1957 to 1962 enrollment increased from 1,250 to 2,950." *Ibid.*, p. 78.
4. *Regional Economic Conditions in Montana.* Helena: Montana Department of Intergovernmental Relations, January 1975, pp. 9–10.
5. *Economic Report to the Governor.* Missoula, Mont.: Bureau of Business and Economic Research, University of Montana, December 1974, p. 9.
6. Social Welfare Research Institute. *Human Services in Rural America.* Research Monograph. Denver: University of Denver, May 1973, p. 4.
7. U.S. Bureau of Census. *Current Population Reports.* No. 19, p. 26.
8. Wallwork, Susan. "Montana County Population Estimates." *Montana Business Quarterly* 12. Spring 1974, p. 23.
9. *Eastern Montana Areawide Health Plan.* Helena: Montana Health Department. March 1975.
10. Valley County Superintendent of Public Instruction.
11. Police ratio recommended in: Intermountain Planners and Werthberger Associates. *Powder River Basin Capital Facilities Study.* Cheyenne: Wyoming Department of Economic Planning, n.d., p. 52.
12. Polzen, Paul E. "Urban Employment Models: Estimation and Interpretation." *Land Economics* 49, May 1973, pp. 226–233.
13. Graham, Robert E. "Personal Income in South Carolina." *Essays in Economics.* Bureau of Business and Economic Research, University of South Carolina, 1971, p. 158.
14. Westinghouse Environmental Systems, *Colstrip Generation and Transmission Project: Applicant Environmental Analysis.* November 1973, pp. 2–139.
15. Wicks, John. *Impact of Libby Dam Construction on the Economy of Lincoln County, Montana.* Missoula, Mont.: Bureau of Business and Economic Research, University of Montana, November 1969, p. 59.

Bibliography

A Manual of Style, 12th rev. ed. Chicago: University of Chicago Press, 1969.

Addams, Jane. *Twenty Years at Hull House*. New York: Macmillan, 1959. [Original publication, 1910].

American Psychological Association. *Psychological Abstracts*. Washington, D.C.: American Psychological Association, 1927–present.

American Psychological Association, *Publication Manual of the American Psychological Association*, rev. Washington: American Psychological Association, 1974.

Ary, D., Jacobs, L., and Razavieh, A. *Introduction to Research in Education*. New York: Holt, Rinehart & Winston, 1972, pp. 421–429.

Atherton, Charles R. "The Social Assignment of Social Work." *Social Service Review* 43:1969.

Auerbach, A. H., and Johnson, M. "Research on the Therapist's Level of Experience." In *Effective Psychotherapy*, edited by A. S. Gurman and A. M. Razin New York: Pergamon Press, 1977.

Babbie, E. *Survey Research Methods*. Belmont, Calif: Wadsworth Publishing Co., 1973.

Bach, Paul J. "A Cognitive/Behavior Treatment Program for Use with American Indian Alcohol Abusers." Master's thesis, University of Montana, 1979.

Baer, D. M., Wolf, M. M., and Resley, T. R. "Some Current Dimensions of Applied Behavior Analysis." *Journal of Applied Behavior Analysis* 1:1968.

Bailey, Kenneth D. *Methods of Social Research*. New York: Free Press, 1978.

Bales, R. F. *Interaction Process Analysis*. Cambridge, Mass.: Addison-Wesley, 1950.

Barnard, J. D., Christophersen, E. R., and Wolf, M. M. "Teaching Children Appropriate Shopping Behavior Through Parent Training in the Supermarket Setting." *Journal of Applied Behavior Analysis* 10:1977.

Bart, P., and Frankel, L. *The Student Sociologist's Handbook*. Cambridge, Mass.: Schenkman Publishing Co., Inc., 1971.

Bassett, J. E., and Blanchard, E. B. "The Effect of the Absence of Close Supervision on the Use of Response Cost in a Prison Token Economy." *Journal of Applied Behavior Analysis* 10:1977.

Berelson, B., and Steiner, G. A. *Human Behavior: An Inventory of Scientific Findings*. New York: Harcourt, Brace & World, 1964.

Bergin, A. E. "The Evaluation of Therapeutic Outcomes." In *Handbook of Psychotherapy and Behavior Change*, edited by A. E. Bergen and S. L. Garfield. New York: John Wiley and Sons, 1971.

Bergin, A. E., and Lambert, M. J. "The Evaluation of Therapeutic Outcomes." In *Handbook of Psychotherapy and Behavior Change*. 2d ed. Edited by S. L. Garfield and A. E. Bergin. New York: John Wiley and Sons, 1978.

Best, J. W. *Research in Education*. 2d ed. Englewood Cliffs, N.J.: Prentice-Hall, Inc., 1970.

Bickman, L. "Observational Methods." In *Research Methods in Social Research*, edited by C. Selltiz, L. S. Wrightsman, and S. W. Cook. New York: Holt, Rinehart & Winston, 1976.

Birchler, G. R., and Webb, F. L. J. "Discriminating Interaction Behaviors in Happy and Unhappy Marriages." *Journal of Consulting and Clinical Psychology* 45:1977.

Blenkner, M., Jahn, J., and Wasser, E. *Serving the Aging: An Experiment in Social Work and Public Health Nursing*. New York: Community Service Society of New York, 1964.

Bloom, Martin. *The Paradox of Helping*. New York: John Wiley and Sons, 1975.

Borgatta, Edgar F., Fanshel, David, and Meyer, Henry J. *Social Workers' Perceptions of Clients*. New York: Russell Sage Foundation, 1960.

Braithwaite, R. B. *Scientific Explanation*. Cambridge, England: Cambridge University Press, 1953.

Briar, Scott. "Family Services." In *Five Fields of Social Service*, edited by Henry S. Maas. New York: National Association of Social Workers, 1966.

_____. "Family Services and Casework." In *Research in the Social Services: A Five-Year Review*, edited by H. S. Maas. New York: National Association of Social Workers, 1971.

Briar, S., and Conte, J. "Families." In *Social Service Research*, edited by H. S. Maas. Washington, D.C.: National Association of Social Workers, 1978.

Brown, Gordon E. *The Multiproblem Dilemma*. Metuchen, N.J.: Scarecrow Press, 1968.

Burros, Oscar K. *Tests in Print*. Highland Park, N.J.: Gryphon Press, 1969.

_____, editor. *Mental Measurement Yearbook*. 7th ed., vols. 1 and 2. Highland Park, N.J.: Gryphon Press, 1972.

Cabot, Richard C. "Treatment in Social Casework in the Need of Criteria and of Tests of Its Success or Failure." *Proceedings of the National Conference of Social Work* 58: 1931.

Campbell, Donald T., and Stanley, Julian C. *Experimental and Quasi-Experimental Designs for Research*. Chicago: Rand McNally & Co., 1966.

Campbell, William G. *Form and Style in Thesis Writing*. 3d ed. Boston: Houghton Mifflin, 1969.

Carkhuff, R. R. *Helping and Human Relations*. 2 vols. New York: Holt, Rinehart & Winston, 1969).

Carr-Kaffashan, L. and Woolfolk, R. L. "Active and Placebo Effects in the Treatment of Moderate and Severe Insomnia." *Journal of Consulting and Clinical Psychology* 47: 1979.

Chein, I. "An Introduction to Sampling." In *Research Methods and Social Relations*. 3d ed., edited by C. Selltiz, L. S. Wrightsman, and S. W. Cook. New York: Holt, Rinehart & Winston, 1976, pp. 511–540.

Cochran, W. G. *Sampling Techniques*. 2d ed. New York: John Wiley and Sons, 1963.

Compton, Beulah R., and Galaway, Burt. *Social Work Processes*. Homewood, Ill.: Dorsey Press, 1975.

Coulton, Claudia, J. *Social Work Quality Assurance Programs: A Comparative Analysis.* Washington: National Association of Social Workers, 1979.

Current Contents/Social and Behavioral Sciences. Philadelphia: Institute for Scientific Information, 1969–present.

Efran, J. S., et al. "Should Fearful Individuals Be Instructed to Proceed Quickly or Cautiously." *Journal of Clinical Psychology* 33: 1977.

Fabry, Pamela A., and Reid, Dennis H. "Teaching Foster Grandparents to Train Severely Handicapped Persons," *Journal of Applied Behavior Analysis* 11: 1978.

Festinger, L., and Katz, D., editors. *Research Methods in the Behavioral Sciences.* New York: Holt, Rinehart & Winston, 1953.

Fischer, Joel. *Effective Casework Practice.* New York: McGraw-Hill, 1978.

Fischer, J. "Is Casework Effective? A Review." *Social Work* 18: 1973.

Fiske, D. W., "Methodological Issues in Research on the Psychotherapist." In *Effective Psychotherapy*, edited by A. S. Gurman and A. M. Razin. New York: Pergamon Press, 1977.

Fixsen, D. L., Phillips, E. L., and Wolf, M. M. "Achievement Place: The Reliability of Self-Reporting and Peer Reporting and Their Effects on Behavior." *Journal of Applied Behavior Analysis* 5: 1972.

Forcese, Dennis, and Richer, Stephen. *Social Research Methods.* Englewood Cliffs, N.J.: Prentice-Hall, Inc., 1973.

Frank, J. D. *Persuasion and Healing.* 2d ed. Baltimore: Johns Hopkins University Press, 1973.

Friedman, H. *Introduction to Statistics.* New York: Random House, 1972.

Gambrill, E. D., and Barth, R. P. "Single-Case Study Designs Revisited." *Social Work Research and Abstracts* 16: 1980.

Garfield, S. L. "Research on the Training of Professional Psychotherapists." In *Effective Psychotherapy*, edited by A. S. Gurman and A. M. Razin. New York: Pergamon Press, 1977.

Garlington, W. K., and Dericco, D. A. "The Effect of Modeling on Drinking Rate." *Journal of Applied Behavior Analysis* 10: 1977.

Geismar, Ludwig L. *Family and Community Functioning.* Metuchen, N.J.: The Scarecrow Press, 1971.

Geismar, Ludwig L., and Ayres, Beverly. *Measuring Family Functioning.* St. Paul: Greater St. Paul United Fund and Council, 1960.

Geismar, Ludwig L., and Krisberg, J. *The Forgotten Neighborhood: Site of an Early Skirmish in the War on Poverty.* Metuchen, N.J.: Scarecrow Press, 1967.

Germain, Carel. "Casework and Science: A Historical Encounter." In *Theories of Social Casework*, edited by R. W. Roberts and R. H. Nee. Chicago: University of Chicago Press, 1970.

Glass, G. V., and Stanley, J. C. *Statistical Methods in Education and Psychology.* Englewood Cliffs, N.J.: Prentice-Hall, Inc., 1970.

Gold, R. L. "Roles in Sociological Observation." In *Research Methods: Issues and Insights*, edited by B. J. Franklin and H. W. Osborne. Belmont, Calif., Wadsworth Publishing Co., 1971.

Goode, William J., and Hall, Paul K. *Methods in Social Research.* New York: McGraw-Hill Book Co., 1952.

Gould, Julius, and Kolb, William L., editors. *A Dictionary of the Social Sciences.* New York: Free Press of Glencoe, 1964.

Gruber, A. R. "The High Cost of Delivering Services." *Social Work* 18: 1973.

Guttman, H. A. "A Contraindication for Family Therapy." *Archives of General Psychiatry* 29: 1973.

Hall, J. *Information Services in Libraries.* ASLIB Proceedings. 24: 1972.

Hansen, Morris H., Hurwitz, William N., and Madow, William G. *Sample Survey Methods and Theory. I. Methods and Applications.* New York: Wiley, 1953.

Hardcastle, David A., and Katz, Arthur J. *Employment and Unemployment in Social Work: A Study of NASW Members.* Washington: National Association of Social Workers, 1979.

Hartley, D., Roback, H. B., and Abramowitz, S. I. "Deterioration Effects in Encounter Groups." *American Psychologist* 31: 1976.

Haynes, S. N. *Principles of Behavioral Assessment.* New York: Halstead Press, 1978.

Haynes, S. N., and Wilson, C. C. *Behavioral Assessment.* San Francisco: Jossey-Bass, 1979.

Hays, W. L. *Statistics for the Social Sciences.* 2d ed. New York: Holt, Rinehart & Winston, 1973.

Hersen, M., and Barlow, D. H. *Single Case Experimental Designs: Strategies for Studying Behavior Change.* New York: Pergamon Press, 1976.

Hesse, M. B. *The Structure of Scientific Inference.* Berkeley: University of California Press, 1974.

Hoel, P. G. *Elementary Statistics.* 4th ed. New York: John Wiley and Sons, 1976.

Hollis, F. "Explorations in the Development of a Typology of Casework Treatment." *Social Casework,* 48: 1967.

Horn, Robert E. *The Guide to Simulations/Games.* San Diego: Learning Resources Corp., 1979.

Horton, Robert L., and Duncan, David J. "A New Look at Telephone Interviewing Methodology." *Pacific Sociological Review* 21: 1978.

Howe, M. "Casework Self-Evaluation: A Single Subject Approach." *Social Service Review* 48: 1974.

Howe, M. W. "Using Clients' Observations in Research." *Social Work* 21: 1976.

Hudson, W. W. "Elementary Techniques for Assessing Single Client/Single Worker Interactions." *Social Service Review* 51: 1977, pp. 311–326.

Hudson, W. W., Acklen, J. D., and Bartosh, J. C. "Assessing Discord in Family Relationships," *Social Work Research and Abstracts* 16: fall 1980.

Hunt, J. McV., and Kogan, Leonard S. *Measuring Results in Social Casework: A Manual on Judging Movement.* New York: Family Service Association, 1952.

Hyman, Hurbert. *Survey Design and Analysis.* Glencoe, Ill.: The Free Press, 1955.

Index Medicus. Washington, D.C.: National Library of Medicine. (Must be used in conjunction with the annual *Medical Subject Headings* list)

International Bibliography of Sociology. (Published in *Current Sociology,* Chicago: Aldine Publishing Co., 1952–present)

Issac, S., and Michael, W. B. *Handbook in Research and Evaluation.* San Diego: Robert Knapp Publishers, 1974.

Jayaratne, S., and Levy, R. L. *Empirical Clinical Practice.* New York: Columbia University Press, 1979.

Johnson, S. M., and Bolstad, O. D. "Reactivity to Home Observations." *Jour-*

nal of Applied Behavior Analysis 8: 1975.

Junker, Buford. *Field Work: An Introduction to the Social Sciences.* Chicago: University of Chicago Press, 1960.

Kane, R. A. "Look to the Record." *Social Work* 19: 1974.

Kanfer, F. H., and Saslow, G. "Behavioral Diagnosis." In *Behavior Therapy: Appraisal and Status*, edited by C. M. Franks, New York: McGraw-Hill, 1969.

Kantorowitz, D. A., Walters, J., and Pezdek, K. "Positive Versus Negative Self-Monitoring in the Self-Control of Smoking." *Journal of Consulting and Clinical Psychology* 46: 1978.

Kaplan, Abraham. *The Conduct of Inquiry.* San Francisco: Chandler Pub. Co., 1964.

Kent, R. N., and Foster, S. L. "Direct Observational Procedures." In *Handbook of Behavioral Assessment*, edited by A. F. Ciminero, K. S. Calhoun, and H. E. Adams. New York: John Wiley and Sons, 1977.

Kent, R. N., et al. "Expectation Biases in Observational Evaluation of Therapeutic Change." *Journal of Consulting and Clinical Psychology* 42: 1974.

Kerlinger, Fred N. *Behavioral Research.* Chicago: Holt, Rinehart & Winston, 1979.

———. *Foundations of Behavioral Research.* 2d ed. New York: Holt, Rinehart & Winston, 1973.

Kiresuk, T. S., and Sherman, R. E. "Goal Attainment Scaling: A General Method for Evaluating Comprehensive Community Mental Health Programs." *Community Mental Health Journal* 4: 1968.

Klaus, D., Hersen, M., and Bellach, A. S. "Survey of Dating Habits of Male and Female Students: A Necessary Precursor to Measurement and Modification." *Journal of Clinical Psychology* 33: 1977.

Klonoff, H., and Cox, B. "A Problem Oriented System Approach to Analysis of Treatment Outcome." *American Journal of Psychiatry* 132: 1975.

Leitenberg, H. "The Use of Single Case Methodology in Psychotherapy Research." *Journal of Abnormal Psychology* 82: 1973.

Leitenberg, H., Burchard, J. D., Burchard, S. N., Fuller, E. J., and Lysought, T. "Using Positive Reinforcement to Suppress Behavior: Some Experimental Comparisons with Sibling Conflict." *Behavior Therapy* 8:1977.

Levy, C. S. *Social Work Ethics.* New York: Human Sciences Press, 1976.

Lieberman, M. A., Yalom, I. E., and Miles, M. B. *Encounter Groups: First Facts.* New York: Basic Books, 1973.

Locke, H. J., and Wallace, Karl M. "Short Mental-Adjustment and Prediction Tests: Their Reliability and Validity." *Marriage and Family Living* 21: 1959.

Lofland, John. *Analyzing Social Settings: A Guide to Qualitative Observation and Analysis.* Belmont, Calif.: Wadsworth Publishing Co., 1971.

London Bibliography of Social Sciences. London: London School of Economics, 1931–present.

Long, P. J., and Lazovek, A. P. "Experimental Desensitization of a Phobia." *Journal of Abnormal and Social Psychology* 66: 1963.

Macdonald, Mary E. "Reunion at Vocational High." *Social Service Review* 40: 1966.

Madge, John. *The Origins of Scientific Sociology.* New York: The Free Press, 1962.

Mahoney, M. J., Maura, W. G., and Wade, T. C. "The Relative Efficacy of Self-Reward, Self-Punishment and Self-Monitoring Techniques for Weight Loss."

Journal of Consulting and Clinical Psychology 40: 1973.

Markle, Allen, and Rinn, Roger. *Author's Guide to Journals in Psychology, Psychiatry and Social Work.* New York: Haworth Press, 1977.

McCall, G. J., and Simmons, J. L., editors. *Issues in Participant Observation: A Text and Reader.* Reading, Mass.: Addison-Wesley Pub. Co., 1969.

McKenzie, T. L., and Ruskall, B. S. "Effects of Self-Recording on Attendance and Performance in a Competitive Swimming Training Environment." *Journal of Applied Behavior Analysis* 7:1974.

Meezan, William, Katz, Sanford, and Russo, Eva Manoff. "Independent Adoptions." *Child Welfare* 57: 1978.

Meyer, Henry, Borgatta, Edgar F., and Jones, W. C. *Girls at Vocational High: An Experiment in Social Work Intervention.* New York: Russell Sage Foundation, 1965.

Miller, Rodney. "A Comparison of Brief Relaxation Therapies: Self-Report and Psychological Indices." Master's thesis, University of Montana, 1976.

Mowrer, O. H. "Apparatus for the Study of and Treatment of Enuresis." *American Journal of Psychology* 51: 1938.

Mungas, Dan M. "Pretesting and Therapist-Client Sex Matching Effects in Social Skills Training." Master's thesis, University of Montana, 1977.

Nay, W. R. "Analogue Measures." In *Handbook of Behavioral Assessment,* edited by A. F. Ciminero, K. S. Calhoun, and H. E. Adams. New York: John Wiley and Sons, 1977.

Nicholson, M. *A Dictionary of American-English Usage.* New York: Oxford University Press, 1957.

Nisbett, R. E., and Wilson, T. D. "Telling More than We Can Know: Verbal Reports on Mental Processes." *Psychological Review* 84: 1977.

Parloff, M. B., Waskow, I. E., and Wolfe, B. E. "Research on Therapist Variables in Relation to Process and Outcome." In *Handbook of Psychotherapy and Behavior Change,* 2d ed., edited by S. L. Garfield and A. E. Bergin. New York: John Wiley and Sons, 1978.

Patterson, G. R. "Naturalistic Observation in Clinical Assessment." *Journal of Applied Child Psychology* 5: 1977.

Patterson, G. R., et al. *A Social Learning Approach to Family Intervention.* vol. 1. Eugene, Ore.: Castalia Publishing Co., 1975.

Pilivian, I., and Gross, A. E. "The Effects of Separation of Services and Income Maintenance on AFDC Recipients." *Social Service Review* 51: 1977.

Powers, E., and Witmer, H. *An Experiment in the Prevention of Delinquency.* New York: Columbia University Press, 1951.

Psychological Abstracts. Washington, D.C.: American Psychological Association, 1927–present.

Rakos, R. F., and Schroeder, H. E. *Self-Directed Assertiveness Training.* Bama Audio Cassettes. New York: Guilford Publishing Company.

Reid, J. B. *A Social Learning Approach to Family Intervention.* Vol. 2. Eugene, Ore.: Castalia Publishing Co., 1978.

Reid, William J. "Client and Practitioner Variables Affecting Treatment." *Social Casework* 45: 1964.

———. "A Test of a Task-Centered Approach." *Social Work.* 20: 1975.

Reid, William J., and Epstein, Laura. *Task-Centered Casework.* New York: Columbia University Press, 1972.

Reid, William J., and Shyne, A. W. *Brief and Extended Casework.* New York:

Columbia University Press, 1969.

Richmond, Mary. *Social Diagnosis.* New York: Russell Sage Foundation, 1917.

Risley, T. R., and Hart, B. "Developing Correspondence Between Non-Verbal and Verbal Behavior of Preschool Children." *Journal of Applied Behavior Analysis* 1: 1968.

Roetheisberger, F. J., and Dickson, J. W. *Management and the Worker.* Cambridge, Mass.: Harvard University Press, 1939.

Rogers, C. R. "The Necessary and Sufficient Conditions of Therapeutic Personality Change." *Journal of Consulting Psychology* 21: 1957.

Rossi, Peter H., Freeman, Howard E., and Wright, Sonia R. *Evaluation: A Systematic Approach.* Beverly Hills: Sage Publications, 1979.

Rossi, R. B. "Helping a Mute Child." In *Task-Centered Practice,* edited by W. J. Reid and L. Epstein. New York: Columbia University Press, 1977.

Sattler, J. M. "The Effects of Therapist-Client Racial Similarity." In *Effective Psychotherapy,* edited by A. S. Gurman and A. M. Razin. New York: Pergamon Press, 1977.

Schmeckebier, L. F., and Eastin, R. B., editors. *Government Publications and Their Uses.* Washington, D.C.: Brookings Institute, 1969.

Selltiz, Claire, Wrightsman, L. S., and Cook, S. W. *Research Methods in Social Relations.* 3d ed. New York: Holt, Rinehart & Winston, 1976.

Siegel, S. *Nonparametric Statistics for the Behavioral Sciences.* New York: McGraw-Hill Book Co., 1956.

Social Science Citation Index. Philadelphia: Institute for Scientific Information, 1970–present.

Social Work Research and Abstracts (Washington, D.C.: National Association of Social Workers, published four times per year).

Sociological Abstracts. New York: Sociological Abstracts, 1952–present.

Spanier, G. B. "Measuring Dyadic Adjustment: New Scales for Assessing the Quality of Marriage and Similar Dyads." *Journal of Marriage and the Family* 38: 1976.

Statistical Abstracts of the U.S. Washington, D.C.: U.S. Bureau of the Census, published every ten years.

Steinglass, P. "The Home Observation Assessment Method (HOAM): Real Time Naturalistic Observation of Families in their Homes." *Family Process* 18: 1979.

Strauss, Anselm, Schatzman, Leonard, Bucher, Rue, Ehlich, Danuta, and Sabshin, Melvin. *Psychiatric Ideologies and Institutions.* New York: Free Press, 1964.

Strunk, W., Jr., and White, E. B. *The Elements of Style.* New York: Macmillan, 1959.

Strupp, H. H. "A Reformulation of the Dynamics of the Therapist's Contribution." In *Effective Psychotherapy,* edited by A. S. Gurman and A. M. Razin. New York: Pergamon Press, 1978.

Stuart, Richard B. *Trick or Treatment.* Champaign, Ill.: Research Press, 1970.

Stuart, R. B., and Stuart, F. *Marital Pre-Counseling Inventory.* Champaign, Ill.: Research Press, 1973.

Sundland, D. M. "Theoretical Orientations of Psychotherapists." In *Effective Psychotherapy,* edited by A. S. Gurman and A. M. Razin. New York: Pergamon Press, 1977.

Sze, W. C., Keller, R. S., and Keller, D. B. "A Comparative Study of Two Different Teaching and Curricular Arrangements in Human Behavior and Social Environment." *Journal of Education for Social Work* 15: 1979.

Teare, Robert J. "A Task Analysis for Public Welfare Practice and Educational Implications." In *The Pursuit of Competence in Social Work*, edited by Frank W. Clark and Morton L. Arkava. San Francisco: Jossey-Bass, 1979.

Thomas, E. J. "Research and Service in Single-Case Experimentation." *Social Work Research and Abstracts* 14: 1978.

Thomas, E. J., Abrams, K. S., and Johnson, J. B. "Self-Monitoring and Reciprocal Inhibition in the Modification of Multiple Tics of Gilles de la Tourette's Syndrome." *Journal of Behavior Therapy and Experimental Psychiatry* 2: 1971.

Thoresen, C. E., and Mahoney, M. H. *Behavioral Self-Control*. New York: Holt, Rinehart & Winston, 1974.

Tolson, E. R. "Alleviating Marital and Communication Problems." In *Task-Centered Practice*, edited by William J. Reid and Laura Epstein. New York: Columbia University Press, 1977.

Truax, C. B., and Carkhuff, R. R. *Toward Effective Counseling and Psychotherapy*. Chicago: Aldine, 1967.

Turabian, Kate L. *A Manual for Writers of Term Papers, Theses, and Dissertations*, 12th ed. Chicago: University of Chicago Press, 1979.

Turner, F. J. "A Comparison of Procedures in the Treatment of Clients with Two Different Value Orientations." *Social Casework* 45: May 1964.

Turner, John B., et al., editors. *Encyclopedia of Social Work*. 17th ed. New York: National Association of Social Workers, 1977.

United Community Service of the Greater Vancouver Area. *The Development Project Monographs, I, II, and III*. Vancouver, B.C., 1968–69.

U.S. Superintendent of Documents Catalog of Public Documents, 1893–1940. Washington, D.C.: U.S. Government Printing Office, n.d.

U.S. Superintendent of Documents Monthly Catalog of United States Government Publications, 1895–present. Washington, D.C.: U.S. Government Printing Office, published monthly.

Van Dalen, D. B., and Meyer, W. J. *Understanding Education Research*. New York: McGraw-Hill, 1966.

Wallace, David. "The Chemung County Evaluation of Casework Service to Dependent Multi-Problem Families: Another Problem Outcome." *Social Service Review* 41: 1967.

Ware, R. J., and Barr, J. E. "Effects of a Nine-Week Structured and Unstructured Group Experience on Measures of Self-Concept and Self-Actualization." *Small Group Behavior* 8: 1977.

Weed, L. I. "Medical Records that Guide and Teach." *New England Journal of Medicine* 278: 1968.

Werry, J. S., and Quay, II. C. "Observing the Classroom Behavior of Elementary School Children." *Exceptional Children* 35: 1969.

Winer, B. J. *Statistical Principles in Experimental Design*. 2d ed. New York: McGraw-Hill, 1979.

Wodarski, J., and Bagarozzi, D. A. *Behavioral Social Work*. New York: Human Services Press, 1979.

Wollersheim, J. P. "Effectiveness of Group Therapy Based upon Learning Principles in the Treatment of Overweight Women." *Journal of Abnormal Psychology* 76: 1977.

Wright, H. F. *Recording and Analyzing Child Behavior: with Ecological Data from an American Town*. New York: Harper & Row, 1967.

Index

AB design, 130–131, 138–139, 149
ABA design, 132–134
ABAB design, 133–136
ABACA reversal design, 145–147
Abstracts, 34–35
  evaluating, 206
Accidental sampling, 158–159
Acklen, J. D., 57
Addams, J., 192
Additivity, 164
Agreement, percentage of, 128
American Personnel and Guidance
    Association, 80
Analogue, 183
Analytic ideas, and observation, 178
Appendices, evaluating, 206
Applied research, 12–13
Area Development Project, 48
Ary, D., 115
Assertiveness training, 80–81
Atherton, C. R., 43
Audio equipment:
  and analogue, 183
  and observation, 181
  and prestructured treatment stimuli,
    79–81
  to reduce error, 21
Auerbach, A. H., 87
Authority, as knowledge source, 9

BAB design, 136–138
Baer, D. M., 138
Bagarozzi, D. A., 62
Bales, R., 180–181
Barlow, D. H., 120–121, 132–133
Barr, J. E., 106
Barth, R. P., 148–149
Bartosh, J. C., 57
Baselines, 120, 128–130
  definition, 121–122
  establishing, 122–124
  and graphing, 125–127
  multiple, 123
Basic research, 12
Bassett, J. E., 136–137

Behavior, dimensions of, 58
Behavioral Coding System, 56–57
Behavioral diary, 50
Behavioral Fear Questionnaire, 59
Behavior modification, 139, 142–143
Bergin, A. E., 60–61, 63–64
Between-group designs, 119–120
Bibliography, 36
  evaluating, 206
Bickman, L., 174
Biofeedback, 80
Blanchard, E. B., 136–137
Bloom, M., 62–63, 122
Briar, S., 45, 77–78, 84–86
Brown, G. E., 104
Burros, O., 22

Cabot, R. C., 19
Cambridge-Somerville Youth Study,
    77
Campbell, D. T., 104
Campbell, W., 197
Card catalog, 32–33
Carkhuff, R. R., 85
Carr-Kaffashan, L., 101
Case study, 177–188
  sample of, 209–230
Catalog:
  card, 32–33
  computer (COM), 33
Cattell Junior Personality Quiz, 47
Causal-comparative research, 114
Causality:
  and ABAB design, 135–136
  evaluating, 205
  and multiple baseline design, 139
  and nonequivalent control groups,
    112
  and retrospective research, 115
  and times series experiments, 111
  and variables, 120
Census, 167
Changing criterion design, 143–145
Chemung County Study, 47, 78
Cluster sampling, 159, 161

Coding, 28
Community Service Scale (CSS),
    21, 45–47, 49, 53–54
Comparison groups, 112–113
Compton, B. R., 61, 148
Computers:
    and coding, 28
    and data analysis, 27–28
    and library, 33, 35
    and subject assignment, 99
Concepts, scientific, 15–16
Conceptual framework, evaluating,
    198–199
Confidentiality, 5–6
Confounding effect, 100
Conte, J., 86
Content, of a measure, 49
Control, and scientific inquiry, 11
Control groups, 78, 95–99, 102,
    107–109
    and between-group designs, 120
    and factorial designs, 110
    hidden, 105
    matched pairs nonequivalent, 113
    nonequivalent, 111–113
    and times series experiments, 111
    posttest, 104, 105–106
    pretest, posttest, 103–105
Cost analysis, 65
Coulton, C. J., 189
Criterion validity. (See Validity,
    predictive)

Data:
    analysis of, 27–28, 195–196, 203
    collection of, 27, 181–182, 200–201
    evaluation of collection, 200–201
    individualized outcome, 62
    secondary sources of, 188–190
    standardized collection of, 181–182
Dating Frequency Questionnaire, 59
Definitions, operational, 16
Dependent variable:
    and BAB design, 136
    and baseline, 121
    and causality, 120
    and control groups, 103–104
    and retrospective research, 114
    See also Variables, dependent
Dericco, D. A., 145
Description, as research objective, 12
Descriptive research, 191
    See also Exploratory-descriptive
    study

Descriptive survey, 167
Design, structure of:
    AB, 130–131, 138–139, 149
    ABA, 132–134
    ABAB, 134–136
    ABACA, 145–147
    BAB, 136–138
Diary, private, and observation, 179
Dictionary of American-English
    Usage, 197
Disasters, natural, and research,
    114–115
Documents, 35
Double-blind experiment, 102
Duncan, D. J., 172
Duration, as a dimension of behavior,
    58
Dyadic Adjustment Scale, 55–56

Eating Patterns Questionnaire, 59
Education Resources Information
    Center (ERIC), 35
Effective Casework Practice, 148
Effectiveness, of program objectives,
    65
Efficiency, of program objectives, 65
Elements of Style, The, 197
Empirical Clinical Practice, 148
Empirical validity. See Validity,
    predictive
Empiricism, and scientific inquiry, 11
Epstein, L., 61–62, 84, 86, 148
Error:
    and data collection, 182
    recording, 21
    reducing, 21–22
    and sampling, 162
    sources of, 20–21, 54, 102
Ethics, 5–6, 101–102
    and ABA design, 133–134
    and ABAB design, 136
    and multiple baseline design, 138
    and no-treatment control group,
    120
    and therapist, 101–102
Evaluation, 53
    and observation, 181–183
    procedures, 61–62
    of research, 197–207
Evaluation research, 43–44, 192
Experience, as knowledge source, 9
Experiment condition. See Variable,
    independent
Experimental designs, 95–99, 190. (See

also names of individual
designs)
Experimental studies, evaluating,
202–203
Explanation, as research objective, 12
Exploration, as research objective,
11–12
Exploratory-descriptive study, 190–191
Exploratory study, 96
Ex post facto research, 114

Factorial designs, 106–111
Family functioning, measures of, 46,
53, 58
Fear Survey Schedule, 59
Field notes, 176–178
Findings:
evaluating, 204
interpreting, 28, 204
presenting, 28
Fischer, J., 63, 148
Fiske, D. W., 87
Fixed interval, 160
Form and Style in Thesis Writing, 197
Foster, S. L., 182
Frequency:
as a dimension of behavior, 58
and line graph, 125
Frequency counts, 50, 122–124, 128
Freud, S., 187–188

Galaway, B., 61, 148
Gambrill, E. D., 148–149
Garfield, S. L., 87
Garlington, W. K., 145
Geismar, L., 46, 112–113
Geismar Family Functioning Scale,
46, 53–55, 57
Germain, C., 83
Girls at Vocational High, 46–47,
76–77, 103–104
Glasser's Reality Therapy, 107
Goal Attainment Scaling, 61, 67
Goals, individualized, 61–62
Graphs:
and baseline information, 125–127
of research designs, 130–146
and treatment phase, 126–127
Gross, A. E., 108–111
Gruber, A. R., 65
Guttman, H. A., 63

Hartley, D., 63
Hawthorne effect, 96, 100

Haynes, S. N., 59, 182
Hersen, M., 120–121, 132–133
Historical research, 191–192
Hollis, F., 83–84
Home Observation Assessment Method
(HOAM), 57, 183
Homogeneity, 157
Horton, R. L., 172
Howe, M., 53, 63
Hudson, W. W., 57, 63
Hunt, J. M., 45
Hypothesis, 28
and data, 195–196
evaluating, 199, 204
stating, 26
Hypothesis testing, 196

Implications, evaluating, 205
Indexes, 34–35
Index of Family Relations, 57
Independent raters, 21
Independent variable:
and causality, 120
evaluating, 202
and factorial designs, 107–108
measuring, 162
and multiple schedule design, 145
and retrospective research, 114–115
See also Variables, independent
Individualized outcome, measures of,
60–63
Inductive reasoning, as knowledge
source, 9–10
Inference, and observation, 178
Interaction, 107
Interaction process categories, 180–181
Interlibrary loan, 36
Interpretation, of data, 195
Interval measurement, 164
Interval recording, 122–124, 128
Intervention phase, 127
Interview, 171–172
evaluating, 201
practices, 5
telephone, 172
structured, 167

Jacobs, L., 115
Jayaratne, S., 63, 148
Job Analysis Survey (JAS), 191
Johnson, M., 87
Journals, professional, 34–35
Junker, B., 175

Kane, R. A., 61
Kanfer, F. H., 59
Kantorowitz, D. A., 52
Keller, D. B., 113
Keller, R. S., 113
Kent, R. N., 182
Kiresuk, T. S., 67
Knowledge, sources of, 8–10
Kogan, L. S., 45
Krisberg, J., 112–113

Lambert, M. J., 63–64
Leitenberg, H., 145, 182
Levy, C. S., 6
Levy, R. L., 63, 148
Library:
    reference department, 36
    as source, 31
    use of, 32
Lieberman, M. A., 63
Line graph, 125–126. (*See also* Graphs)
Literature:
    search of, 25–26, 35–37
    types of, 32, 34–35
Locke, H. J., 55–56
Locke-Wallace Marital Adjustment Test, 55–56
Lofland, J., 176
Logical reasoning, as knowledge source, 9–10

Macdonald, M. E., 47, 77
McKenzie, T. L., 52
Mahoney, M. J., 49–50, 52
Manual for Writers of Term Papers, Theses, and Dissertations, A, 197
Manual of Style, A, 196
Marital Activities Inventory, 59
Marital adjustment, measures of, 55–56
Marital Pre-Counseling Inventory, 56, 59
Matched pair nonequivalent control group, 113
Matching assignment, 99
Maura, W. G., 52
Measurable objectives. *See* Objectives, measurable
Measurement:
    elements of, 162–164
    interval, 164
    levels of, 163–164

nominal, 163
ordinal, 163–164
posttest, 105
pretest, 105
problems, difficulty of, 13
ratio, 164
Measures:
    behavioral, 58–60
    cognitive, 58–60
    establishing, 42
    standardized, and reliability, 22
Mental Measurement Yearbook, 22
Miller, R., 81
Mowrer, O. H., 130–131
Multiple baseline design, 138–143
Multiple schedule design, 145–147
Multistaged sampling, 161
Mungas, D. M., 81

National Association of Social Workers (NASW), 189
National Conference on Social Work, 19
Natural disasters, and research, 114–115
Nature, as patterned, 10
Nay, W. R., 183
Negative outcomes, 63–64
New Haven Neighborhood Improvement Project, 48
Nicholson, M., 197
Nisbett, R. E., 58
Nominal measurement, 163
Nonequivalent control group, 111–113
Nonexperimental design, 96
Nonexperimental studies, evaluating, 203
Nonmeasurable objectives. *See* Objectives, nonmeasurable
Nonprobability sampling, 157–158
Nonreactive measures, 99
Normal curve, 122
Note-taking, 176–179

Objectives:
    measurable, 17–18
    nonmeasurable, 17–18
    program, 65
    writing of, 18
Objectivity, and scientific inquiry, 11
Observation, 174–175
    and notes, 176–179
    and reliability, 181
    roles of, 175–176

structured, 179–181
by two or more people, 127–129
Observers, use of to reduce error, 21
Operant conditioning, 133
Operationalism, 88–89
Ordinal measurement, 163–164
Outcome measures, 19, 42–43, 64–66, 78, 103
classification of, 49
historical development of, 44–49
selecting, 43–67
See also Variable, dependent
Outline, of report, 194–195

Paper-and-pencil tallies, 123
Parent-child interaction, measures of, 56
Parloff, M. B., 87–88
Patterson, G. R., 56–57, 182–183
Patterson Behavioral Coding System, 183
Percentage of agreement, 128
Periodicals, 34–35
Pezdek, K., 52
Pilot study, 169–170
Pilivian, I., 108–111
Placebo effect, 100–102
Population, choosing, 27
Post-test-only design, 104–106, 114
Posttest design, 96–97, 99, 104, 106
Practitioner manuals, 80–81
Pretest design, 99, 103–104
Probability sampling, 158–161
Problem:
evaluating, 198
identifying, 24, 198
Problem behavior, 121–122
See also Variable, dependent
Problem-Oriented Evaluation Procedure (PEP), 62–63
Problem Oriented Record (POR), 61
Program Objectives, 65–66
Program evaluation, 44, 64–67
Publication Manual of the American Psychological Association, 196–197
Pure research. See Research, basic
Purposive sampling, 159

Quality, as a dimension of behavior, 58
Quantification, 162–163
Quasi-experimental design, 111–115, 190

Quasi-experimental studies, evaluating, 202–203
Questionnaire, 167, 171
completing, 170
constructing, 168–170
evaluating, 201–202
Quota sampling, 158–159

Race, as a variable, 86–88
Random assignment, 97–99, 101, 104, 109
Random numbers, table of, 160
Random sampling:
evaluating, 202
types of, 159–160
Random selection, 112
Ratio measurement, 164
Razavien, A., 115
Reactivity, 50, 52, 181–182
Reactive changes, 97, 104
Reality, nature of, and scientific method, 10
Recommendations, evaluating, 205
Recording, 54, 174
in the field, 176–179
References, and reliability, 22
Reid, J. B., 182
Reid, W. J., 61–62, 78, 84, 86, 148
Relaxation training, 79–81, 101
See also Stress
Reliability:
and data collection, 127–129
evaluating, 200
of evaluation, 22
improving, 21–22
and interviews, 171
and observation, 181–183
and secondary data, 188
and self-monitoring, 52–53
sources of error in, 20
and variables, 19
Replication, 60, 89, 106, 115
and AB design, 149
as criterion, 89
and prestructured treatment, 82
problem of, 77–78
Reports, 194–195
evaluating, 203–207
writing, 196–197
Research:
applied, 12–13
basic, 12
evaluating methods of, 197–207
historical, 191–192

Research (continued)
  language of, 15–16
  need for, 4–5
  pure, 12
  purposes of, 3, 11
  retrospective, 114–115
  steps in, 6–7, 24–28
  types of, 12, 43–44, 191–192
Research design:
  evaluating, 202
  selecting, 26–27
  types of, 27, 95–99, 102–115
Resley, T. R., 138
Reverse approach to experimentation,
  115
Richmond, M., 60
Rogers, C. R., 85
Role-play, 183
Rossi, P. H., 192
Rossi, R. B., 85
Ruskall, B. S., 52

St. Paul Scale of Family Functioning,
  45–46, 47, 48
Sample, choosing, 27
Sampling:
  definition, 157
  and error, 162
  evaluating, 199–201
  size of, 161–162
  types of, 157–162
Saslow, G., 59
Sattler, J. M., 87
Scales, evaluating, 202
Scientific inquiry, 10–11
Scientific method, 3, 8, 10, 13
Self-help manuals, and prestructured
  treatment stimuli, 79–80
Self-reports, 49–52, 55–57, 62
  and behavioral data, 59–60
  and cognitive events, 58
  evaluating, 53
  reliability of, 52–53
  types of, 50, 52
Sex, as a variable, 86–88
Sheldrick, G., 276
Shyne, A. W., 78, 84
Simple random sampling, 159–161
Single-subject designs, 62–63,
  75–76, 90, 95–97
  advantages, 147–148
  disadvantages, 148–149
Social work, handicaps of, 41–44

Social Work Ethics, 6
Socioeconomic status, as a variable,
  86–88
Sociological Abstracts, 35
Solomon Four-Group Design, 105–107
Spanier, G. B., 55–56
Stanley, J. C., 76, 104
Statistics, 28, 203–204
Steinglass, P., 57, 183
Stimulus, 79
Stratified random sampling, 159–161
Stress:
  management of, 79–81
  measures of, 57
  and retrospective research,
    114–115
Structured observation, 179–181
Strunk, W., Jr., 197
Strupp, H. H., 85
Stuart, F., 56, 59
Stuart, R. B., 56, 59, 63–64
Studies:
  design of, 78
  evaluational, 46–47
Subject assignment, 97–99, 101
Summary, evaluating, 206
Survey methods, types of, 167
Survey Research Center (SRC), 169
Sze, W. C., 113

Task Achievement Scale, 61–62
Task-centered approach, 84–86
Task-Centered Casework, 84, 148
Task Implementation Sequence
  (TIS), 84–85
Teare, R., 190–191
Telephone interview, 172
Tests in Print, 22
Theory:
  in research, 25–26
  as a tool of science, 5
Therapeutic relationship, 85
Therapy, 85, 88
Thomas, E. J., 148
Thoresen, C. E., 49–50
Time-sampling, 122–124, 128
Time series design, 119
Time series experiments, 111
Tolson, E. R., 85
Tradition, as a knowledge source,
  9–10
Treatment:
  experimental, 78

methods of, 88–90
practices, 79
prestructured stimulus, 79–83
standardizing, 89
typologies, 83–86
withdrawal of, 132–133, 135, 138
Treatment condition. *See* Variable,
    independent
Treatment manuals, 81
Treatment phase:
    and line graph, 126–127
    of research design, 96
Trial and error, as knowledge source,
    9
Truax, C. B., 85
Turabian, K., 197
Turner, F. J., 84
Twenty Years at Hull House, 192
Typology, treatment, 83–86

Universe, choosing, 27

Validity:
    evaluating, 199
    and observation, 181
    predictive, 22–23
    and variables, 19
Validity coefficient, 23
Variables:
    and AB design, 131
    and causality, 120
    characteristics of, 18
    definition, 26, 89
    dependent, 19, 26, 27, 42, 75,
        88, 114
    and control groups, 103–104
    evaluating, 199–200, 202
    and factorial designs, 107–108
    independent, 19, 26, 114–115, 202
    definition, 89

and factorial designs, 107
manipulating, 76
measuring, 162
and line graph, 125
multiple, 107
and multiple baseline design, 138
outcome, and self-reports, 52–53
practitioner, 86–88
and retrospective research, 114–115
and secondary data, 189
sociological, 162
therapist, 86–88
See also Dependent variable;
    Independent variable
Video equipment:
    and analogues, 183
    and observation, 181
    and prestructured treatment
        stimuli, 79–80
    to reduce error, 21

Wade, T. C., 52
Wallace, K. M., 55–56
Walters, J., 52
Ware, R. J., 106–107
Waskow, I. E., 87–88
Weed, L. I., 61
White, E. B., 197
Wilson, C. C., 182
Wilson, T. D., 58
Withdrawal designs, 148
Within-subject designs. (*See* Single-
    subject designs)
Wodarski, J., 62
Wolf, M. M., 138
Wolfe, B. E., 87–88
Woolfolk, R. L., 101